Collaboration, Reputation, and Ethics
in American Academic Life

6/2/00
To John Lukacs
From an admirer
of your work and
your ethical standards

warm regards

Arthur

Collaboration, Reputation, and Ethics in American Academic Life

❖ ❖ ❖

Hans H. Gerth and
C. Wright Mills

Guy Oakes and Arthur J. Vidich

University of Illinois Press

Urbana and Chicago

Library of Congress Cataloging-in-Publication Data
Oakes, Guy.
Collaboration, reputation, and ethics in American academic life :
Hans H. Gerth and C. Wright Mills / Guy Oakes and Arthur J.
Vidich.
p.   cm.
Includes bibliographical references and index.
ISBN 0-252-02484-2 (cloth : alk. paper)
ISBN 0-252-06807-6 (pbk.)
1. Gerth, Hans Heinrich, 1908–1978   2. Mills, C. Wright (Charles
Wright), 1916–1962. 3. Sociologists—United States—Biography.
4. Sociology—United States—History. I. Vidich, Arthur J.
II. Title.
HM22.U6G486   1999
301'.092'273—dc21   98-58091
CIP

1   2   3   4   5   C   P   5   4   3   2   1

◆ ◆ ◆

Contents

❖　❖　❖

Acknowledgments

Permission to quote freely from the papers of Hans Gerth was given by Nobuko Gerth, who supplied most of the unpublished sources on which this book is based: letters exchanged between Gerth and C. Wright Mills, other items from Gerth's correspondence, and a large collection of his literary remains, including lecture notes, outlines for research, and unfinished drafts. Without her industry in organizing and collating Gerth's papers, her generosity in sharing the results of her work, and her willingness to mail us documents to which we would otherwise not have access, this book would not have been possible. Godehard Czernik duplicated Mills's letters to Gerth in Nobuko Gerth's possession and forwarded them to us. Gerth's letters to Joseph and Marilyn Bensman were provided by Marilyn Bensman.

Permission to examine the C. Wright Mills Papers, at the University of Texas at Austin, and to quote from Mills's correspondence was granted by Yaroslava Mills, executrix of the estate of C. Wright Mills. All quotations from Mills's letters have been examined by the Mills estate, and each quotation has been approved in writing. Some of the quoted letters appear in *C. Wright Mills: Letters and Autobiographical Writings,* ed. Kathryn Mills with Pamela Mills (Berkeley: University of California Press, 2000). Quotations from C. Wright Mills, *White Collar: The American Middle Class,* © 1951 by C. Wright Mills, are by permission of Oxford University Press, Inc.

Our thanks are due to the following: for suggestions and criticisms, Larry Carney, Jack Davis, Nobuko Gerth, Michael W. Hughey, Robert Jackall, Kathryn Mills, and Guenther Roth; for research assistance, Laima Serksnyte; for advice on archival sources, Ralph Elder, assistant director of the Barker Texas History Center at the University of Texas at Austin, and Ronald D. Patkis, head of archives and manuscripts, John J. Burns Library, Boston College.

Research on this book was supported by Franco Ferrarotti, Stanford M. Lyman, the Graduate Faculty of the New School for Social Research, and the Jack T. Kvernland Chair at Monmouth University.

Collaboration, Reputation, and Ethics in American Academic Life

❖ ❖ ❖

Introduction

Gerth and Mills: Madison, 1940

In 1940 C. Wright Mills, as he called himself by that time, was twenty-four, a brash and precocious Ph.D. candidate in sociology at the University of Wisconsin. In the spring of 1939 he had graduated from the University of Texas with both baccalaureate and master's degrees, leaving with a Phi Beta Kappa key and enthusiastic letters from his professors recommending him as the most gifted and promising student in the sociology department. As early as 1937 his plans for an academic career were firm and he had begun to develop the social skills and savoir faire important to academic success: socializing with his teachers and learning to discuss intellectual problems on their terms by employing the current disciplinary vocabularies.[1] In 1938 he was writing for publication in academic journals, submitting papers on pragmatism and the functions of philosophy to the *Philosophical Review* and the *Journal of Philosophy*. Although these submissions were not successful, he had better luck with two essays on the sociology of knowledge. "Language, Logic, and Culture" was published by the *American Sociological Review,* and the *American Journal of Sociology* accepted "Methodological Consequences of the Sociology of Knowledge."[2] These publications brought Mills to the attention of sociologists and philosophers working on social theory, pragmatism, and the sociology of knowledge.

Mills had entertained hopes for a fellowship from the University of Chicago, where he planned to earn a Ph.D. in three years. His undergraduate studies on William James, C. S. Peirce, John Dewey, and George Herbert

Mead formed the basis for the doctoral dissertation he had already envisioned: a sociological investigation of pragmatism. Chicago, the philosophical and institutional center of pragmatism after World War I, where
Mead had taught and Herbert Blumer, his student, was editor of the *American Journal of Sociology,* was the logical choice for the young Mills. Nonetheless, when he received a $300 fellowship from Wisconsin but no assis-
tance from Chicago, he decided in favor of Madison, where his candidacy
was supported by Howard Becker, the resident social theorist and one of
the readers impressed by "Language, Logic, and Culture." [3]

The original relationship between Hans Gerth and C. Wright Mills has
been characterized by Don Martindale, a contemporary of Mills at Madison and one of Gerth's doctoral students. During the academic year 1940–
41 Mills did not register for any of Gerth's courses, and his doctoral adviser
was not Gerth but Becker, from whom he later claimed to have learned
nothing. Nevertheless, Mills studied with Gerth, both by auditing his lectures and by gaining access to the long informal monologues for which
Gerth was famous. Martindale, recalling one of these lectures in a course
on social stratification, remembered it as a typically Gerthian performance,
the lecturer moving effortlessly from one idea to another, linking historical
and theoretical themes in an astonishing display of virtuosity comparable
to an intellectual trapeze act. Most of the students found this presentation
confusing.

> During the lecture the majority of students had experienced a mixture of be-
> wilderment and frustration. They sat with notebooks open and pens poised,
> realizing that something momentous was happening but unable to find a be-
> ginning or stopping place—some had been unable to take a single note. Dur-
> ing the lecture a powerfully built young man sitting near me, however, had
> no trouble. He watched the lecturer with bright, hard, appraising eyes and,
> though never missing a word or gesture, was taking quick careful notes. On
> the way out of class we found ourselves side by side. I observed, "That was
> the most extraordinary performance I have ever seen." "Gerth," he replied,
> "is the only man worth listening to in this department." [4]

Gerth arrived at Madison by a more circuitous route. In 1940 he was
thirty-two, an untenured and underpaid assistant professor at the University of Wisconsin subsisting on overloads and summer teaching. He
had left Germany in 1937, more than four years after the formation of a
National Socialist government in 1933 and late for a non-Jewish German
émigré in search of an academic position. As he often observed in com-

plaints that grew more bitter as the years passed, Gerth became a registered and fingerprinted enemy alien under town arrest, confined to Madison for the duration of World War II, permitted outside the city limits only on official authorization, and subject to wartime regulations that prohibited him from owning a radio, a camera, or a map.

Gerth claimed that his fascination with sociology began when he first read Max Weber's famous lectures "Politics as a Vocation" and "Science as a Vocation" as a high school student in his hometown of Kassel. He matriculated at Heidelberg in 1927 to study with Weber only to learn that the sociologist had been dead seven years. Karl Mannheim conducted a seminar on Weber, however, where Gerth met Hannah Arendt, Hans Jonas, Hans Speier, and Weber's widow, Marianne. He also worked as Mannheim's assistant, and when the author of the recently published *Ideology and Utopia* was called to a professorship at Frankfurt in 1930, Gerth followed, joining seminars conducted by Theodor Adorno, Erich Fromm, Max Horkheimer, Adolf Löwe, and Paul Tillich.

Although he had begun his studies in the intellectual excitement and glitter of the Weimar Republic, by the time he scheduled his oral examination for the doctorate in December 1933, the republic had collapsed. One consequence of the new Reich Ministry for Propaganda's strategies to incorporate the universities into the National Socialist state apparatus and achieve political control of academies of science and scholarly societies was an intellectual emigration. Several of Gerth's teachers at Frankfurt—including Mannheim, Tillich, and Löwe—were no longer in Germany. Gerth remained to complete his dissertation, expunging all references to persons, ideas, and books that the new regime might find offensive, including the names of his teachers and their publications. In 1934–37 he worked as a journalist in Berlin, first as a writer of feature articles and reviews on culture and politics for the *Berliner Tageblatt* and later as a correspondent for the Berlin bureaus of United Press and the *Chicago Daily News*. As a journalist he was bound by the protocols of Nazi political semantics that were introduced in 1933. Shortly after an interview with the Gestapo convinced him that he was about to be arrested for divulging secret censorship regulations imposed on the press, Gerth left Germany, making his way from Denmark to England and finally arriving in the United States in late 1937.[5] In 1977, the year before his death, he was asked whether he had been tempted to follow the path taken by his teachers and fellow students who had emigrated in 1933. He replied:

No, not then. Perhaps I still had those illusions too: "in four or six months the economy would collapse, etc." You could classify people according to those who thought the collapse was a matter of weeks, and to those who thought in terms of half a year. But why didn't I go? First, I had a beautiful fiancée. Second, one doesn't gladly leave one's fatherland, or motherland, if you prefer. One is bound to one's own language and would rather speak one's own language, which one can speak well, rather than a learned language, which one always speaks or writes badly. In addition, we heard through the press and in letters how hard things were for the refugees ... how hard it was to find any kind of job even as a secretary. So it was not exactly attractive to leave Germany if you didn't have to.[6]

Just as the moral theology of early cold war politics in the United States would later condemn "premature antifascism," the émigré groups of the 1930s decried a complementary deadly political sin: eleventh hour antifascism. When Gerth visited the New School for Social Research in New York, where the University in Exile had been founded as a haven for academic refugees from the Nazis, he learned that he had been denounced for remaining in Germany and working as a journalist during the Third Reich. His chief accuser seems to have been Günther Stern, Hannah Arendt's first husband. Stern, who had written for the *Berliner Tageblatt* under the name "Günther Anders," was an old friend of Gerth's from his student days. For Gerth, their first meeting after a lapse of some five years was a distinctly unpleasant surprise: at the New School Stern cut him dead with a stinging condemnation of the writing he had done for the *Berliner Tageblatt*.

During his tenure as a journalist, Gerth had behaved somewhat recklessly, engaging in a playful but dangerous experiment of pushing Nazi censorship rules to their limits. His method was to exploit ambiguities and vagueness in press regulations by writing an occasional article on an English diplomat or author or a German intellectual who was not a Nazi or by contributing a negative review of an anti-Marxist book or an anti-Semitic film. These pieces hinted that his sympathies did not lie with the New Order, marking him as an unreliable writer who warranted scrutiny by the Gestapo. Nonetheless, they did not succeed in establishing his antifascist credentials with the early émigrés, some of whom seem to have concluded that his profile as a journalist with a major Berlin newspaper during the years the Nazis were persecuting Jews, incarcerating and murdering social democrats and communists, and transforming a constitutional democracy into a model totalitarian state suggested that he had made a separate and dishonorable peace with the enemy, offering the sacrifice of intellect and ethics required by National Socialism.

Gerth's record in Germany provided evidence that this impression was not altogether mistaken. As he wrote Hans Speier in May 1938, his doctoral dissertation had finally been approved by professors who had survived the purges of 1933 and were "men of the Nazi university."[7] He had also been employed as a writer for nearly four years of Nazi rule, during which time articles under his name appeared in a newspaper that complied with the regulations of the Ministry for Propaganda. Perhaps it is not surprising that an obituary of Elizabeth Förster Nietzsche (1935), whose anti-Semitic credentials were impeccable, and pieces entitled "The Contemporary Idea of Race" (1935), "The Führer Takes His Ease Watching Old Art Films" (1935), and "Are the Japanese a Race?" (1936) led unsympathetic observers of the German scene in New York to conclude that he had made too many concessions. Gerth's Berlin persona thus discredited him with both the Gestapo and its victims. By failing to ingratiate himself with the new regime, he became persona non grata in Germany. At the same time, his reluctance to take a principled stand against National Socialism damned him in the eyes of some of the refugees of 1933. The result was a dilemma: threat of arrest by the Gestapo and denunciation by members of the early émigré community.

Speier, an original member of the University in Exile, explained Gerth's predicament to him in June 1938. One had to expect the first cohort of refugees from a dictatorial political system to condemn conduct that, viewed from within the system, was both unobjectionable and essential to survival. Actions that appeared heroic from the inside would be regarded as no more than minimally acceptable to those who had already escaped.[8] "Inside the whale," working within a repressive regime that seemed to have destroyed all effective opposition, Gerth believed he was living on the edge, writing as a political observer and recording his views in an underground coded language that would be understood by readers in the opposition. According to the early émigrés' sectarian ethic, this position was an accommodation and a surrender to evil. Thus did Gerth pay the costs and suffer the indignities of the social type he christened "the Aryan latecomer."[9]

Twenty years after Mills appeared at his lectures, Gerth was still in Madison, underpaid and financially pressed, intellectually isolated, and troubled by an American career that had fallen short of his hopes. Mills, on the other hand, had achieved a position that surpassed even his youthful dreams. A

leading figure in the American intellectual establishment, he was a professor at Columbia and the author of three books that were sociological
bestsellers, a description that today is virtually an oxymoron. In *White Collar, The Power Elite,* and *The Sociological Imagination,* he forged a style
and a mode of analysis that appealed to both academicians and a much
larger readership in the educated middle class. As an author he had won a
reputation for riding and shooting, as he liked to put it: writing with no
holds barred and speaking his mind without qualification or compromise.
A trenchant critic of the cold war, he was famous for his attacks on U.S.
national security policy. Even the clergy paid homage to the self-confessed
pagan and unbeliever for his fulminations against the militarization of
American society and his criticism of U.S. nuclear strategy and nuclear
weapons testing. A popular speaker at colloquia on public issues, he made
frequent appearances at symposia and lecture series in the United States
and Europe. Lauded by the nascent new left in England and the United
States, embraced by "Marxist humanists" in Eastern Europe, and anointed
as Fidel Castro's favorite sociologist, he was a member of a new international status group of postwar intellectual celebrities created by the com-
mercialization of airline travel, the popularity of scholarly and scientific
journalism, and the financial power of privately funded foundations. As a
consultant on public relations, the media, and middle-class consumption
habits, he was courted by large corporations. At the same time he was idol-
ized by the nascent New Left for his iconoclasm and rebellion against the
political and economic order of the Eisenhower years. Thus Mills became a
beneficiary of the largesse of the power elite as well as a hero of its enemies.

In 1940 Gerth and Mills began a thirteen-year collaboration, producing two books that now have classic status: *From Max Weber: Essays in
Sociology* (1946), the first English translation of Weber's specifically sociological writings, and *Character and Social Structure* (1953), the first sociology textbook based on Weberian premises. Some years ago an American
Weber scholar, consumed by enthusiasm for his subject, proclaimed that
whoever controlled the interpretation of Weber's work would control the
future of sociology. Even someone who has spent many years toiling over
Weber's writings would have to concede that this is excessive, but he had
a point. Weber defined a set of problems and framed a conceptual apparatus for handling them that set the agenda for subsequent inquiries into the
origins, trajectory, and significance of occidental modernity. To a remarkable degree the main issues of Weber's sociology are our issues as well, and
the most influential contributors to the debate on these questions gener-

ally find themselves obliged to come to terms with Weber. In this sense, important critics of Weber such as Michel Foucault and Jürgen Habermas remain neo-Weberians. These considerations do not entail that his writings occupy a canonical status in contemporary sociology. Nevertheless, Weber remains the dominant figure in social theory and the preeminent sociologist of the twentieth century.

In the United States Weber's reputation has depended overwhelmingly on translations. Before World War II access to his sociology was confined to the few with the requisite perseverance and competence in German to plow through the original texts of *Economy and Society* and the comparative studies in the sociology of religion. Before 1934 he was rarely mentioned in the American sociological literature, and none of his works had been reviewed in the *American Journal of Sociology*. The only English versions of his main works were Talcott Parsons's 1930 translation of *The Protestant Ethic and the Spirit of Capitalism,* which somewhat confusingly added as a prologue Weber's introduction to the first volume of his collected essays in the sociology of religion, and Frank Knight's 1927 translation of *General Economic History,* based on student transcriptions of lectures Weber delivered during his brief tenure at the University of Munich in 1919–20.[10] Thus in prewar American sociology, the elements of Weber's work for the most part remained terra incognita: his typological strategies; his comparative and historical studies of politics, the economy, religion, science, the military, ethics, art, and erotics; and the conceptual battery of Weberian sociological analysis later employed by social scientists of all persuasions—the concepts of class, status, status honor, church and sect, legitimacy, charisma, bureaucratization, rationalization, and routinization.

By the beginning of World War II, however, Weber's work had become an important research site on which a career in American sociology could be built. This development was due to a quite recent constellation of factors. The Nazi disfranchisement of German Jews and the political purge of the universities, the professions, and the civil service had led many German academicians influenced by Weber's work to immigrate to the United States. In 1934 *Social Research* was founded as the in-house journal of the University in Exile, and Emil Lederer, Albert Salomon, and Hans Speier began to publish articles that either analyzed Weberian sociology or outlined research programs based on its premises. Finally, in 1937, Talcott Parsons published his two-volume work *The Structure of Social Action,* a monumental study of European social theory that provided the first systematic discussion of Weber's sociology in English.[11] *From Max Weber* marked a sea change in American sociology by introducing key Weberian sociological texts to social scientists working in the English language. *Character and Social Structure* demonstrated how Weber's typologies, combined with his structural and historical analyses of institutional orders and cultural spheres, could be deployed to investigate the social bases of distinctive types of personality, character, and conduct.

The Ethics of Academic Career Management

In this study we chronicle the collaboration between Gerth and Mills and at the same time pursue a number of themes in the sociology of intellectual life. In doing so we follow two lines of inquiry and weave together two strands of material: a narrative and a set of analyses. We tell a story and construct arguments. Our strategy is to employ narrative in the service of the sociology of knowledge, which in turn provides a framework within which the narrative unfolds.

The partnership between Gerth and Mills was grounded in close collaborative relations and the many adjustments they entailed. It was also based on a personal bond that they both regarded, perhaps with some degree of self-deception, as friendship: an alliance between two intellectuals who regarded themselves, for rather different reasons, as outsiders confronting a hostile academic establishment. Gerth was a refugee without a reputation in the United States or even an American identity, desperate to achieve a position that would provide the economic underpinnings for an intellectual career. Mills was a graduate student from Texas, an outlander, as he later called himself, determined to make a career in the emerging middle-class university.

Early in the collaboration Gerth expressed doubts about their ability to work in tandem without quarreling. Mills responded with easy assurances and a metaphor: because he and Gerth were like two pieces of steel magnetized by common objectives, there would be no friction. This proved not to be the case. From the beginning relations were strained. The tensions were not due to the interplay of divergent intellectual styles and types of personality, which were differences that they both understood, in some instances saw as inconsequential, and in others regarded as beneficial to their work. The critical tensions lay deeper, in conflicts over intellectual ethics. The years of close collaboration in the face of fundamental differences, their struggle to work together "in spite of everything," as Gerth observed, and the devices they employed to use one another created a relationship of

Shakespearean complexity in which respect, trust, generosity, and perhaps even love did not exclude envy, resentment, deceit, and betrayal.

In the ensuing we consider several themes:

— the distribution of knowledge and power in collaboration and its importance in the social production of authorship, academic reputation, and intellectual authority;

— the dynamics of collaboration in the competition over credit for scientific and scholarly work and the validation of conflicting claims to precedence;

— the role of collaboration in forming and articulating opposing conceptions of intellectual ethics;

— the uses of collaboration for the purposes of self-promotion and marketing the products of intellectual work;

— the role of concealment, secrecy, and deception in the production of academic reputation and the uses of collaboration as an instrument of information management; and

— the importance of third parties, such as publishers, editors, department chairs, and prestigious colleagues, and their intervention in the collaboration as advocates, antagonists, mediators, or adjudicators.

These themes center on the desiderata that govern the project of academic career management, the values and priorities that are ascribed to this project, and its place in scientific and scholarly life. An ethic of academic career management is characterized by three parameters: cognitive standards, practical norms, and strategic controls. Cognitive standards specify possible forms of academic life and modes of managing the academic career. Practical norms differentiate acceptable or legitimate practices of academic career management from unacceptable or illegitimate practices. Strategic controls provide techniques for meeting or evading norms, maximizing the benefits of a real or apparent commitment to normative requirements and minimizing their costs, and concealing evasions and violations. An ethic of academic career management may be more or less systematic: at one extreme, a comprehensive, carefully designed, and internally consistent plan for the conduct of the academic life; at the other, a pastiche of inarticulate attitudes, shapeless ideas, and conflicting practices.

Within limits our study of the Gerth-Mills collaboration is an analysis of the ethics of academic career management. We examine how such an ethic operates in a specific historical setting, what consequences it produces, and what happens when an ethic confronts the state of affairs that Max Weber characterized as the ethical irrationality of the world: reality's resistance to moral imperatives and the irreconcilable conflicts between alternative ethics. Readers interested in speculations on the origins or genealogies of the ethics of academic career management, general hypotheses on the conditions for their causation or production, or even more abstract analyses of their forms, types, and functions will be disappointed by this book. We consider the collaboration as an artifact of intrinsic interest for the history of academic ethics, not as a case that supports some theoretical program. Our investigation represents a choice in favor of low levels of abstraction and modest generalizations. We present no ambitious theoretical designs or grand constructions. The result is an analysis built close to the ground it covers.

Because this essay is confined to a few issues in the sociology of intellectual ethics, it does not qualify as an intellectual biography; details of the careers of the protagonists are considered only insofar as they are relevant to the themes of our inquiry. Nor do we suppose that we have written the last word on the relationship between Gerth and Mills. Our study is based largely on primary sources, letters exchanged between Gerth and Mills during the years 1940–60. These same sources provide material for lines of investigation we do not pursue: the changing status and demands of the American academic career in the twentieth century; comparative studies of intellectual collaboration, competition for credit, and the production of reputation in science and scholarship; the role of truthfulness and deceit in scientific, scholarly, and academic institutions; an institutional history of American sociology that would focus on the sociology departments at Chicago, Columbia, Harvard, and the University of Wisconsin; the history of Weber's reception in the United States; and other inquiries that are beyond our competence, ken, or intellectual horizons.

The Gerth-Mills collaboration is an ideal site for an investigation of the ethics of academic career management. The dispute over *From Max Weber* was not confined to a disagreement on how credit for a book should be allocated. It also raised the more troubling and fundamental question of the norms that should govern academic collegiality. As Gerth and Mills recruited advocates to support their respective positions in the credit war, each claimed to represent a higher scholarly morality and launched blistering attacks against the ethics of the other. In this way ethical positions were used as weapons in the competition for credit. The collaboration magnified differences in normative commitments, exposed tacit oppositions that became explicit and inescapable, and refined nebulous disagreements to the point that they were interpreted as rigid and mutually inconsistent stands on matters of principle. The contractual maneuvers that ran parallel to the work on *Character and Social Structure* placed in relief the partners' respective positions on acceptable conduct for academic authors and the conditions under which the two men were willing to engage in concealment, trickery, and collusion to get what they wanted. By collaborating on tactics to confound and outsmart their editors and publishers, Gerth and Mills put into practice techniques of career management that neither had developed independently.

Our study is intended as a modest contribution to the history of academic ethics in our time. Moral philosophy is concerned with conceptions of how people ought to behave and with possible justifications for these conceptions. The standard repertoire of arguments in moral philosophy has little to say about the conditions for the production, distribution, and legitimation of these conceptions. This is our territory. We do not consider the views of philosophers or other moral thinkers on how intellectuals should conduct themselves, nor do we employ ethical theories or moral doctrines to render moral judgments. Our purpose is not to take sides, settle scores, or reach conclusions concerning who was right and who was not in the conflicts generated by the collaboration. The ensuing analysis entails no unambiguous moral consequences concerning the conduct of the protagonists, and our results are consistent with various moral judgments that can be taken on them. Our examination of the conditions under which *From Max Weber* and *Character and Social Structure* were produced also makes no judgments and entails no consequences about the scientific or scholarly value of these books. The supposition that there is an essential connection between the motives of intellectual workers and the quality of their work is a genetic fallacy that conflates questions of origins with questions of validity. A researcher acting on extra-intellectual interests may produce work of the highest order, and a thinker inspired by a disinterested commitment to the advancement of knowledge may achieve nothing of intellectual value.

We investigate the social dynamics of intellectual ethics in a specific setting: the American university roughly at midcentury. If this study can claim a relevance beyond the scope of the materials it investigates, it is because this period proved critical in forming academic norms, habits, and expectations that prevail today. We try to understand how certain American academicians live now by examining a story that exhibits quite clearly, and on occasion crassly, the circumstances under which this way of life was formed.

• 1 •

"Translated and Edited by Hans H. Gerth and C. Wright Mills": The Weber Project

The Beginnings of a Collaboration

The year before his death, Hans Gerth was asked why he devoted so much of his American career to translations of the work of Max Weber. His response was to tell a story about the first years of his life in the United States. As a German émigré and enemy alien during World War II, he replied, what else was he to do? Confined to the environs of Madison, uncertain about his job during the early years of the war, and worried that he might be interned in a detention camp until the cessation of hostilities, he was plagued by anxieties. "In the midst of all this," he explained, "translation was a way of passing the time, improving my English, and after the Weber material was published, it took on a momentum of its own."[1] On Gerth's retrospective view, the Weber translations began as a pastime, a therapy for handling the tedium of life in a university town in rural Wisconsin, and a way to strengthen his English. In its carelessness and nonchalance, this account obscures the circumstances that led to the first English translations of Max Weber's sociological writings.

In translating Weber for his courses at the University of Wisconsin, Gerth served as an emissary of the German sociological enlightenment, introducing his students to a new world of ideas that were developed with a philosophical and historical sophistication unmatched in the American literature. His early efforts were awkward and unidiomatic, however, marred by unmistakably and confusingly Germanic grammar and syntax. Sensitive to these weaknesses, he assigned favored graduate students the task of editing his drafts. In addition to Mills, Patricke Johns Heine and Ben Gillingham served as his student editors. After they had corrected his grammar and syntax and polished his style, Gerth would satisfy himself that the results conformed to the German original and then mimeograph the edited manuscript.

In 1940–43 Mills recast his relationship to Gerth and reoriented Gerth's work as a translator. The professor and his assistant became collaborators. The translations, which began as pedagogical exercises from which Gerth seemed to expect no reward, became a publishing venture. At the beginning of their collaboration, Mills worked out a division of labor. Gerth's job was to interpret and translate the German material. Mills's function was to edit, organize, and rewrite Gerth's drafts. He also assigned himself a variety of other tasks: targeting prospective publishers, submitting completed manuscripts for publication, managing relations with publishers, and promoting the finished product by circulating it among key academicians to ensure comprehensive distribution and maximum visibility.

This collaborative model, which was systematized and refined during the war years, was already in place before Gerth and Mills began to work together on Weber translations. Their first joint publication was "A Marx for the Managers," a critique of James Burnham's popular book *The Managerial Revolution: What Is Happening in the World* (1941). Burnham, a former Trotskyist and an editor (with Max Schachtman) of *New International*, argued that traditional social theory, with its bilevel stratification of modern capitalist societies into a working class and a propertied class, had failed to explain the major social change of the twentieth century: the emergence of a new political elite, a stratum of administrators and managers that represented the interests of neither class. The power of this group rested on two developments: contemporary capitalism's demand for specialists in managerial science and the contemporary state's dependence on specialists in administrative science. Employing the untranslated sociology of Max Weber, especially the discussions of political sociology and bureaucracy in *Economy and Society,* Gerth and Mills maintained that the functional indispensability of managerial and administrative expertise in the bureaucracies of the modern polity and economy did not automatically translate into political power for the group that exercised this expertise, nor did the experience of the twentieth century confirm the political dominance of bureaucrats. The evidence for their position was drawn largely from German sources, including detailed discussions of the economic and political stratification of Germany from the *Kaiserreich* through the National Socialist dictatorship, the war economy and political capitalism as determinants of German class structure, and the relationship between National Socialism and the prospects of the German middle classes.

Although the prepublication history of "A Marx for the Managers" is not altogether clear, Mills assumed responsibility for the essay's publication. In June 1941 he sent it to Cleanth Brooks at *The Southern Review,* a literary journal and therefore an unpromising venue for a sociological analysis. After Brooks's letter of rejection arrived, he tried *The Virginia Quarterly,* where it was also rejected. Finally, on September 11, he sent the paper to Charner Perry, the editor of *Ethics.* On October 31, four months after the manuscript was originally submitted, Mills, now in his first academic position at the University of Maryland, wrote Gerth that it had been accepted.[2] Mills also planned the distribution of the authors' fifty offprints, targeting recipients by drawing up three lists: a list of twenty who would receive copies from Gerth and Mills jointly; a second list of fifteen that would be made up by Gerth; and a third list of fifteen that Mills would compile. Although the plan for the circulation of the essay was Mills's, he left to Gerth the final decision on its implementation and agreed not to mail any offprints without the other man's approval. The purpose of this private distribution was to place the essay with academicians who served on the editorial boards of journals where the partners might place future essays.

The joint list included Burnham himself, Harold Lasswell, Sidney Hook, Robert K. Merton, Edward Shils, Louis Wirth, Hans Speier, Charles Beard, Talcott Parsons, and Dwight Macdonald.[3] Macdonald, the only nonacademician on the list, was a radical socialist, a critic of the U.S. entry into World War II, a member of the editorial board of *Partisan Review,* and the founder, editor, and publisher of *politics,* perhaps the most uncompromising of the little magazines on the Left published in New York during the war. Macdonald, who had been corresponding with Mills on political matters since the autumn of 1941, was impressed with "A Marx for the Managers" and its critique of Burnham's thesis that managers, administrators, engineers, and other specialists in knowledge formed a new political elite. In a letter to Mills, he expressed his disappointment that the piece had not been submitted to *Partisan Review,* where it would have appeared with his own review of Burnham's book. Mills took this remark to mean that Macdonald would be interested in other work he and Gerth might submit. He was right. Two years later he placed their first Weber translation with Macdonald in *politics.*[4]

In the autumn of 1943 Mills was planning the publication of "Class,

Status, Party," some nine pages Gerth had excerpted from *Economy and Society,* a passage in which Weber analyzes the concepts of class, status, and political parties. Mills discussed the possibility of publishing this essay with Macdonald and began the preliminary work of securing a license to print the excerpt by contacting the Office of the Alien Property Custodian in Washington, the wartime agency that controlled German copyrights. Although he had taken these measures independently, Mills assured Gerth that no decisions had been made on his behalf or without his knowledge. Indeed, Mills stressed that he had not even sent Macdonald the translation, nor would he would he do so without Gerth's consent. At that point it was not yet a polished work. Before showing it to Macdonald, Mills wanted to do further editing, following which Gerth would decide whether it was ready for publication.

Although Gerth and Mills had begun their joint work, they had not considered how credit for it should be allocated. It was Mills who first raised this issue, making a case for including his name on "Class, Status, Party" as cotranslator. At this juncture he still viewed the collaboration within the framework of the professor-assistant relationship. As Gerth's protégé he broached the question of credit with some hesitation, declaring himself prepared to accept Gerth's judgment on how his participation should be acknowledged. His proposal to Gerth is vague as to who actually did the translation. This resulted from Mills's use of the passive voice, which also clouded the question of credit: "Since it was one of the first things, indeed the first thing, that was translated, I believe that the decision on terms involved me enough to keep the translators as they are on the mimeograph: H. H. Gerth and C. Wright Mills. If, however, this is not agreeable to you and you want it to be your name alone, that is OK by me." [5]

On the one hand, Mills assured Gerth that if he preferred not to publish "Class, Status, Party" in *politics,* discussions with Macdonald would end. On the other hand, he believed that they should take advantage of the opportunity. Gerth agreed to name Mills as joint translator and editor, and on December 7, 1943, Mills forwarded the manuscript to Macdonald, confidently promising Gerth that even if it were rejected, he would clear the translation rights and arrange publication elsewhere. Although Macdonald took some six months to reach a decision, by early June 1944 publication was secure. Mills transacted all the necessary business with *politics,* reading the proof, making sure that Gerth checked his revisions against the German text, and meeting deadlines. In October 1944 "Class, Status, Party" was published in *politics.*

The Oxford Contract

Mills's success in placing "Class, Status, Party" encouraged him to set his sights higher. With the appearance of his own essay on intellectuals in the third issue of *politics,* he had begun to gain an independent reputation among New York intellectuals and publishers.[6] One of his readers was the head of Vanguard Press, who asked Mills to come to New York for a discussion of future projects, an invitation he interpreted as a proposal to expand the essay into a small book. Although he was not interested in this idea, he suggested to Gerth that they ask Vanguard to consider an alternative: a book of Weber translations. Mills envisioned a volume of roughly two hundred pages of translations, prefaced by a twenty-page biography of Weber and a twenty-page introduction sketching the main lines of his thought. A book would obviously require further translations from Gerth. Formidable editorial labors would also be needed to make Weber's recondite texts accessible to the American reader. These challenges notwithstanding, the project would be a relatively easy way to get a book into print quickly, or so Mills supposed, and a useful contribution to American social science. Finally, a book would be helpful to his career and even more important for Gerth, who needed a book because of his uncertain job situation at Madison.

Mills's division of labor for the project called for Gerth to translate the material into "rough English." He would edit Gerth's work, employing what he called a "systematic critique of style," and return the rewritten translations so that Gerth could check his revisions for consistency with the German. In addition, he would plan and organize the volume and place the finished manuscript with a publisher. In broaching the question of credit, he suggested that he receive "second author rights: Gerth & Mills." However, he recognized that his claim to credit, which would seem to name him as cotranslator and also as coauthor of the prefatory materials, might not be fully justified. Gerth might thus prefer to undertake the project independently or perhaps forget the idea entirely. If Gerth was interested in pursuing the former course, Mills would act on his behalf with Vanguard and withdraw.

> BUT: you may not be at all interested, and you may not think I should claim
> so much as full title page and book back credit. Indeed, I may be quite wrong
> about this. If you wish to do the job alone or under any other conditions you
> can think of, of course I will be happy to do what I can with the publisher
> when I see him, get him in touch with you, and wash my hands of a hellish

job! Well, let me know, my idea is not for either of us to spend much more time with it but to get it out carefully and fast. We can steal the whole market from Parsons *et al!*[7]

The book would focus on several clearly articulated themes in Weber's work. To interest a publisher, it would be necessary to "take some liberties" with Weber's texts and simplify his style generally. Mills's idea was to craft the book with a view to targeting a large market. Accordingly, the introduction should not impose excessive demands on the reader but rather make Weber's thought more accessible and attractive. It would serve as "a way to level down the translations" and make them more "inviting."[8] His preliminary outline included an introduction of forty pages and five thematically organized chapters of translations on politics, stratification, religion, comparative social structures, and bureaucracy. To verify the translations Gerth had completed, Mills listed the material he had received. This list indicates that by the spring of 1944, Gerth had completed drafts of the following: "Politics as a Vocation"; "The Protestant Sects and the Spirit of Capitalism"; "National Character and the Junkers," a section of Weber's essay "Franchise and Democracy in Germany"; fragments on Indian and Chinese religion from his comparative studies on the economic ethics of the world religions; the analysis of legitimacy and discipline from the chapter on the sociology of domination in *Economy and Society;* "Class, Status, Party," which would appear shortly in *politics;* and perhaps also "Religious Rejections of the World and Their Directions."

Mills's list ended with a comment: "The two intermediary essays from S*R I don't think would go."[9] "S*R" is an abbreviation for *Religionssoziologie,* that is, Weber's *Gesammelte Aufsätze zur Religionssoziologie,* the three-volume collection of his studies in the sociology of religion originally published in 1920–21. The reference to "the two intermediary essays" is less clear. It may refer to a single essay, the famous "Zwischenbetrachtung," or "Excursus: Religious Rejections of the World and Their Directions," one of Weber's seminal theoretical texts, which he inserted between the monograph on Confucianism and Taoism and the study on Hinduism and Buddhism in volume 1 of *Religionssoziologie.* Why Mills referred to "two intermediary essays" is not clear. Regardless of how he identified it, he seems to have found "Zwischenbetrachtung" too demanding for the readership of the Weber book as he then conceived it.

Although Mills was not able to interest Vanguard in a volume of Weber translations, this did not discourage him from pushing the project forward. His cultivation of connections in the New York scholarly and literary world had begun to bear fruit. In 1942 his enthusiastic appreciation of Franz Neumann's book *Behemoth: The Structure and Practice of National Socialism,* a study of the German National Socialist Party published by Oxford University Press, appeared in *Partisan Review.* Neumann, then at the Institute for Social Research, in Manhattan's Morningside Heights, put Mills in touch with H. T. Hatcher, his editor at Oxford, and agreed to write Hatcher in support of the Weber project. Following Neumann's efforts on his behalf, Mills corresponded with Hatcher and met with him in New York.[10] The prospect of publishing a book with Oxford University Press transformed Mills's commitment to the Weber project. As late as June 1, 1944, he made the gesture of declaring his willingness to leave the Weber book to Gerth.[11] Within a few weeks or perhaps even days, dropping out of the project and divesting himself of credit for the work were no longer options he was prepared to entertain. Oxford's interest convinced him that the American academic publishing market was ready for the sociology of Max Weber. He was confident that he and Gerth could capture this market with the book they had begun to design.

After meeting with Hatcher, Mills began to plan the organization and packaging of the book in more detail. He proposed to divide the translation into sections, each with subheadings identifying three themes, or "triads," such as "Prestige, Power, and Imperialism." In Mills's view, Weber's work could not be understood by reducing it to a system; it was necessary to locate and follow the thread of interconnected themes and theses that runs through his writings. By repeating specific triadic themes in several subheadings of the various sections of the translation, the book would make this thread clearly visible to the reader. Mills summed up his organizational ideas for Gerth in quite ambitious terms, stressing the respects in which this conception of Weber's writings departed from the version presented by Parsons in *The Structure of Social Action* and represented a more valid interpretation: "Then the volume as a whole 'exhausts' the combinations and permutations of Weber's main variables. This would give an architectonic shape to the whole and would knit our selections together without 'closing the system,' but rather to the contrary, this arrangement makes explicit the multi-perspectivism which is at least one thing we want to show up (as against Parsons etc. with their formalized SYSTEMS of every goddamned thing that anybody tries to do something with)."[12]

These various endeavors, which Mills made in Gerth's name and presumably on his behalf but without his permission or knowledge, led the younger man to add a note of reassurance: "I hope you don't feel badly about all these undiscussed initiatives I'm taking, but you have got to get on and stay on stuff like this and get it thru. Know that your interests are well protected in my hands."[13]

By the summer of 1944 Oxford had accepted Mills's proposal in principle, and he and Gerth were at work editing and translating. They also made the legal arrangements that would enable Gerth to visit Mills in Maryland at the end of August, the only occasion on which they would meet to work together on the Weber book. After completing his revisions of Gerth's earlier drafts of "The Protestant Sects and the Spirit of Capitalism," "Politics as a Vocation" (at this point entitled "Politics as a Profession"), and the material on power, prestige, and imperialism from *Economy and Society,* Mills began to edit the translations Gerth had recently completed: the discussion of charisma in *Economy and Society* and the "Zwischenbetrachtung," now slated for inclusion in the Oxford volume.[14] Mills was troubled, however, by the prospect of beginning a major project without a contract. Uncertain of Oxford's commitment to an informal agreement, he applied in his own name to the Alien Property Custodian for a license to publish all of Weber's work in the United States. Once these rights were granted, he observed to Gerth, "Parsons or anybody else will have to come to us for rights to print W in the U.S."[15] This would be a way of salvaging the Weber project even if Oxford decided against a contract. With the U.S. copyright to the Weber materials in his possession, Mills would be able to find another publisher. In fact, he had already developed precisely such a strategy, linking the Weber book to a contract for another projected book in the event that Oxford decided to withdraw.

In 1941 the textbook publisher D. C. Heath had signed Gerth and Mills to write an undergraduate text on social psychology. By the summer of 1944 the manuscript, for which they had been paid no advance, was long overdue and had not been drafted or even outlined. Mills began negotiations with another publisher, Prentice Hall, for the same unwritten text. His conversations with Prentice Hall editors in New York had convinced him that they would make concessions to acquire the book: not only a substantial advance, but also a contract for the Weber book. This was the arrangement he proposed to Gerth, a trade in which Prentice Hall would get the social psychology text and in turn give the two men a contract for their Weber project. Mills would escape from the Heath contract, perhaps by demanding an exorbitant advance. Free of their obligation to Heath, they could offer the social psychology text to Prentice Hall on the condition that they publish the Weber book as well. "I feel pretty sure I could swing that kind of deal," he confided to Gerth.[16]

At the same time Mills also wrote Neumann, pressing him to intercede with Hatcher. His plan was to send Oxford several pieces that had been edited, checked by Gerth, and revised once more: "The Social Psychology of the World Religions," "The Protestant Sects and the Spirit of Capitalism," "Politics as a Vocation" (still entitled "Politics as a Profession"), "Class, Status, Party," and "Structures of Power." On the basis of these materials, they could expect a commitment. He urged Gerth not to be discouraged, however, even if their plans with Oxford did not materialize. "I've got another deal brewing, just in case," he added, presumably referring to the Prentice Hall option.[17] Mills hoped to finish the Weber project during Gerth's visit of some three weeks, an estimate that turned out to be unduly optimistic. In preparing for an intensive period of joint work, he arranged his classes, his office space at College Park, and his domestic life so that he and Gerth would be able to concentrate fully on the Weber materials. His summer teaching schedule would enable them to spend entire days at the Library of Congress checking footnotes and references. In the light of what he called the "gamble" with Oxford, he also reserved time for a trip to New York: "We can browse around again with publishers and get some free lunches."[18]

On September 7 Mills's most pressing worry was put to rest. Hatcher sent Gerth and Mills a contract for their signatures, with the promise of a check for $250 as an advance against royalties. On October 11, after Gerth's return to Madison, Mills received a fully executed copy and the check. The uncertainties concerning the Weber project, it seemed, were finally resolved.[19]

The Shils Affair

In late October 1944 the prospects for the Oxford enterprise were darkened by the figure of Edward A. Shils. The University of Chicago sociologist, who had just returned from London, was preparing his own volume of Weber translations for the International Library of Sociology, published in England by Kegan Paul. The general editor of the series was Gerth's former professor Karl Mannheim. The American distributor for Kegan Paul was Oxford University Press.

Shils seems to have undertaken his project in some secrecy, without informing Weber scholars in the United States. Although Gerth was apparently taken by surprise,[20] as early as 1938 he had known that Shils was working on Weber translations. Mills recalled that while he was still a student at Madison, Gerth had drafts of several translations by Shils, including "Class, Status, Party," "Science as a Vocation," "Politics as a Vocation," and "Classes and Status Groups." All these materials were available to Gerth and Mills at the time they did their work on Weber. Nonetheless, they did not know that Shils was planning a Weber edition.

Shils was one of the links in the chain of connections that had enabled Gerth to establish himself as an academician in the United States. Some nine years after Gerth's death, Shils recalled that while Gerth was in London in late 1937 trying to arrange his passage to New York, Mannheim wrote to Shils asking him to act on Gerth's behalf and ease the difficulties the expatriate was likely to encounter during his first difficult months as a German émigré without friends or influence in the United States. Gerth and Shils met in the spring of 1938 in New York, where Shils was studying with the German Weber scholar Alexander von Schelting and translating Mannheim's book *Man and Society in an Age of Reconstruction.* Gerth needed an interim job and a publication in English that would enable him to compete for a permanent academic position. Shils claimed that he wrote Louis Wirth, a senior member of the sociology department at the University of Chicago, asking him to do what he could to assist Gerth. Gerth's interim position at the University of Illinois in 1938–39 seems to have been mediated by these connections.[21] Shils was also the midwife of Gerth's first American publication, a Weberian analysis of the organizational structure, social composition, and leadership of the Nazi Party. In the summer of 1938, after Shils had returned to Chicago and Gerth had relocated in Urbana, Gerth sent Shils an essay on this subject. Shils was impressed: it was the best analysis of the Nazi Party he had seen. After showing Gerth's manuscript to the editors of the *American Journal of Sociology* at Chicago, he spoke with both Wirth and Ernest Burgess to ensure that it would receive a sympathetic reading. He also submitted a written opinion to the editors, arguing that the strengths of the essay, which was too long for a conventional journal article, justified publication in two installments. When Wirth would not agree to serial publication, Shils made a case for dividing the manuscript into two separate articles: one on the structure of the Nazi Party and a second on the relationship between the party and the professions in Germany.

Although Shils maintained that Gerth's essay set a new substantive standard in the scholarly literature on the Nazi Party, he found the quality of

Gerth's writing execrable. The manuscript was badly organized, and Gerth had no sense of English syntax and no conception of how an English sentence should read. Pressing Gerth to work on his English, Shils sent him books to review for the *American Journal of Sociology,* both as a way to improve his English and as a means of making himself visible in the American sociological community.[22] The first part of Gerth's study, edited and revised by Shils, appeared in the *American Journal of Sociology* in 1940 under the title "The Nazi Party: Its Leadership and Composition." Thus Gerth, with Shils's backing, connections, and editorial efforts, had his first American publication.[23]

On his return to Chicago in October 1944, Shils saw the translation of "Class, Status, Party," recently published in *politics,* and also the notice at the end of the magazine that Oxford would bring out a volume of Weber translations by Gerth and Mills in the spring of 1945. In a letter to Gerth written shortly thereafter, Shils described his project, which would include several selections from *Economy and Society* as well as material from Weber's methodological and political writings. To avoid duplication in the two editions, he asked Gerth for an account of the pieces he intended to publish, and he also raised a more troubling question, a point he had meant to consider with Gerth before leaving for Europe in 1943. Shils had translated "Class, Status, Party" some years before Gerth began working on Weber translations. In the summer of 1938, when he was editing the Nazi Party article, he had given Gerth a copy. Now he claimed to see pronounced stylistic similarities between his translation and a mimeograph of Gerth's later translation of the same piece. Interested in Gerth's views on these similarities, he asked for an early reply. In this letter Gerth was no longer "Gertchen," the German diminutive of intimacy and affection that Shils had used in the 1938 correspondence, but "Gerth." Shils's signature, in full formal fashion, was now "Edward A. Shils."[24]

There is a handwritten draft of a response from Gerth to Shils's letter, with many corrections and passages struck out. Gerth was defensive concerning the correctness of his conduct in the matter of the translations and devoted much of his response to an issue Shils had not raised at all: an explanation of his decision to publish a book of Weber translations without consulting Shils. Although he regretted that the Oxford volume conflicted with Shils's plans, the responsibility for the unhappy coincidence lay with Shils. In 1938 Gerth had known that Shils was working with von Schelting on translations from *Economy and Society,* but he was under the impression that Shils was either collaborating with Talcott Parsons or perhaps working under Parsons's direction. In any case, Shils had done nothing to correct this impression. Moreover, Gerth had sent copies of his translations to Mannheim as early as the summer of 1943 and had also written Wirth about his work. Neither Parsons nor Wirth had informed him of Shils's plans. In Gerth's view, Shils's current difficulty was due to his clandestine manner of work and a lack of candor on the part of his mentors, Wirth and Mannheim. On this point, Gerth insisted, his own conduct was impeccable: "You cannot blame me for having been secretive"—a complaint Shils had not made.[25]

Gerth also maintained that had he been apprised of Shils's plans, he would not have signed the contract with Oxford. His entry into the market for Weber's work was largely fortuitous. Mills had arranged publication of "Class, Status, Party" and negotiated the contract with Oxford. Gerth had seen no reason to withhold his consent, nor had Shils given him any. In response to Shils's "inference" that there was a "very considerable stylistic and linguistic resemblance" between his translation of "Class, Status, Party" and Gerth's mimeograph, Gerth offered a series of denials. Shils was mistaken in thinking he had given Gerth a copy of his translation. Gerth had not seen Shils's translation, nor was he even aware of its existence. Had he been aware of Shils's suspicions, he would have permitted Shils to inspect his files, which contained the first rough draft of "Class, Status, Party." Since the collaboration between Gerth and Mills had begun with this draft, Shils should take up any questions about the English style with Mills.[26]

Shils answered Gerth in a temperate and politic fashion. The problems posed by the two editions were practical issues that could be resolved by compromise and goodwill on the part of the principals. Instead of pursuing the question of similarities between Gerth's draft of "Class, Status, Party" and his own, he outlined his edition and made suggestions for eliminating any overlap between the two projects. He had originally envisioned a one-volume collection to be entitled "Max Weber: Science, Politics, Power" and divided into three parts. Part 1, "Science and Ethics," would include "Science as a Vocation" and Weber's long essay on value neutrality in the social sciences, which he translated as "The Meaning of 'Ethical Neutrality' in Sociology and Economics." Part 2, "Politics," would include "Politics as a Vocation," Weber's 1895 Freiburg inaugural lecture on the national state and economic policy, and his lecture on socialism delivered to an audience of Austrian army officers during his brief tenure as a visiting professor at the University of Vienna in 1918. Part 3, "Power and Social Structure," would include selections from *Economy and Society* on political sociology and the sociology of religion. His most recent plan was to expand this edition into a two-volume work to provide a more coherent reading of *Economy and Society* as well as a more comprehensive picture of Weber's thought as a whole. Weber's 1904 essay " 'Objectivity' in Social Science and Social Policy" would be added to part 1; "Parliament and Government in a Reconstructed Germany," his proposals for the reconstruction of the German state contained in a long essay published in 1918 and based on newspaper articles written in 1917, would be added to part 2; "The Three Pure Types of Legitimate Domination," his analysis of rational, traditional, and charismatic domination first published in 1922, would be added to part 3.

Shils argued that the elimination of all redundancies between the two editions would diminish the likelihood of rancor between the translators. He had devoted several years to his edition and did not want the publication of Weber's writings in the United States to be associated with an unseemly competition for credit. There were, Shils suggested, several ways to handle the overlap. Some material could be moved from one edition to another. Presumably this meant that some of Gerth's translations would appear in Shils's book, in exchange for which Shils would shift some of his selections into the Oxford volume. Or Gerth and Shils could devise an equitable method of exchanging the rights to certain selections that both had already translated. These questions should be resolved quickly. The "other matter," as Shils vaguely characterized it—the allegation of similarities between the two versions of "Class, Status, Party"—could be postponed until he and Gerth met.[27]

These allegations and proposals left Gerth deeply troubled: worried that Shils might be able to prevent publication of the Oxford volume, distressed over the possible validity of Shils's implicit charge, and fearful about injury to his own reputation and the threat to his job. In a handwritten note to Mills, he indicated how seriously the overlap between the two projects damaged Shils's plans. Writing to Mills, he listed six items under the heading "common," apparently identifying translations scheduled for inclusion in both editions: "Science as a Vocation," "Politics as a Vocation," "Class, Status, Party," "Legitimacy," "Bureaucracy," and finally "Power Studies"—this last item seems to have included the sections "Power, Prestige, and the 'Great Powers,' " "The Nation," and "The Economic Foundations of Imperialism" from *Economy and Society.*"[28] He was also at a loss as to the best response. Although he saw no possibility of agreeing to any of the various compromises Shils had proposed, he was apprehensive about the consequences of a refusal, which might enrage Shils and lead him to hinder publication of their book. Nonetheless, Gerth believed that he and Mills had certain advantages. They were the aggrieved party, the victims of an intrigue by Shils. In addition, they could inform Hatcher of the matter and engage the power of Oxford University Press on their behalf.

Mills interpreted Shils's initiative as a genuine threat to the Oxford project. Shils had succeeded in playing on Gerth's sense of guilt and his inclination to blame himself for failing to consider his benefactor's interests in the competition to introduce Weber's sociology to an Anglo-American readership. Shils had also cleverly counted on Gerth's anxieties about his position at Madison and what might happen if he were charged with appropriating Shils's work. But exactly what did Shils want? In considering Shils's motives, Mills found it curious that although he had concealed his plans from Gerth, he blamed Gerth for the consequences. Shils saw his earlier efforts in support of Gerth not as an expression of friendship or generosity but as patronage. Gerth had incurred debts; now Shils was asking for repayment. He did not make the arch accusation that Gerth was guilty of a lapse of professional ethics in bringing out an edition of Weber's work in English. Nor did he charge Gerth with plagiarizing his translation of "Class, Status, Party." Mills nevertheless maintained that this charge was implicit in Shils's letter: "He accuses us of copying a draft he made." [29]

His analysis of the potential dangers of the situation created by Shils's allegation and Gerth's worries led Mills to intervene quickly and decisively. In a long review of the Shils problem written for Gerth, he employed a two-part strategy. First, he attempted to restore Gerth's wavering confidence. Shils's allegation was groundless, he maintained, both in ethics and in fact. Insofar as violations of professional ethics were at stake, Shils was the blameworthy party, not Gerth. Second, he took charge of the Shils matter, drafting a response for Gerth as well as another letter he would write under his own name. Both were intended to disarm Shils and neutralize the threat he represented. This plan was conceived, executed, and the results in the mail to Gerth just a few hours after Mills had received the news of Shils's letter.

To dispose of the premise that Gerth had employed Shils's translation of "Class, Status, Party," Mills argued that his own editorial work and stylistic changes guaranteed the authenticity of their translation. Further, when the partners originally translated "Class, Status, Party," Shils had said nothing about any resemblance between their version and his. Nor, for that matter, did he claim that the version published in *politics* had drawn on his work. In short, Shils's charge that Gerth's mimeographed translation borrowed from his was a fabrication. And even if this charge were valid, its implications for the version published in *politics* were not at all clear. If Shils had evidence that the *politics* text was derived from his mimeograph, he would have used it to contest the originality of their work. But he did not, raising instead a relatively innocuous and inconsequential objection about a putative similarity between two mimeographs. To Mills, this meant that Shils knew he had no evidence of plagiarism.

Mills also attempted to allay Gerth's worries that his version of "Science as a Vocation" might be seen as an paraphrase of Shils's translation. After all, Gerth had Shils's mimeograph at his disposal while he was working on his translation. Mills's reexamination of the two versions of Weber's lecture produced mixed results. A close reading of his edited manuscript of Gerth's draft revealed that certain of his own revisions were uncomfortably close to Shils's language. To forestall the charge that their translation was derived from Shils's, he would either restore Gerth's original language or devise a third rendition of the problematic passages. He also found that the style of Gerth's translation clearly differentiated it from Shils's. Gerth's reading was more literal and awkward and thus more aptly expressed the distinctiveness of Weber's prose. In particular, Gerth had succeeded in capturing the biblical tone of Weber's cadences in the final pages of the lecture. In an effort to persuade Gerth that his translation was superior to Shils's, Mills observed that there were many models of English style one could use in translating Weber; it would even be possible to translate Weber into the language of *The New Republic* or *The New Yorker*. Such a rendition, however, would violate the integrity of the German text and compromise the intellectual honesty of the translator. In translating Weber, Mills saw the value of an occasional infelicitous construction. "Maybe W didn't etch so much as block out in charcoal," he suggested. And in any case, "it looks better in English if one doesn't use too fine an acid."[30]

Mills contended that even if Shils decided to make a public charge of intellectual theft against Gerth, a possibility he found remote, Shils could not do so until their book was published. By that time any controversy over questionable similarities between unpublished translations would have no significance. And if he were foolish enough to raise accusations based on similarities between mimeographs after the book was published, Gerth and Mills had a conclusive answer. The only issue of weight was whether their book qualified as their own work. Shils would be unable to show that their published translations were derived from his manuscripts. Therefore, an accusation of plagiarism would appear ludicrous. It would also be self-defeating, damaging Shils's reputation, not that of Gerth and Mills. Mills saw the obvious advantage the partners enjoyed over Shils in any contest over priority. Whereas Shils could appeal only to his unpublished manuscripts, they would have a book on the market. Thus they had nothing to fear from Shils except accusations and slander, a risk all authors face.

In considering the ethics of the relationship between Gerth and Shils, Mills addressed Gerth's unacknowledged possession of Shils's mimeographs, arguing that any feelings of guilt on his part were misplaced. Gerth should not suppose that he had neglected his obligations or failed to measure up to his exacting standards of intellectual integrity. Shils was merely venting his resentment that anyone else had the temerity to enter the field of American Weber studies. His allusion to the work he had done on Gerth's Nazi Party article was intellectually dishonest, nothing more than an attempt to play on Gerth's moral sensibilities to his own advantage. Did Gerth actually expect Shils and Parsons to wire them congratulations on the news that they were publishing an edition of Weber's sociological writings? Gerth's response to Shils, Mills said, lacked fire and fortitude. His job at Madison depended on publication of the Weber book. The appropriate answer was not an apology but, at the very least, a display of indignation. Otherwise, what inference could be expected from the gatekeepers who controlled access to career paths in academic social science? Gerth's limp reply, his apparent contrition, and his failure to generate a minimally acceptable expression of anger might suggest that the charge implicit in Shils's letter was substantially justified. In short, Mills believed that Gerth's response was too soft and not commensurate with the competitive demands of academic life.

Mills was convinced that the Weber book required the sacrifice of Gerth's friendship with Shils. In examining the relations between Gerth and Shils, Mills showed no interest in Shils himself or his character. Mills hardly knew Shils and perhaps knew even less about his relationship with Gerth. He was concerned with the social psychology of the type of intellectual that Shils represented. Shils's intellectual identity, as Mills understood it, was determined by his institutional status, his occupational opportunities and limitations, and the prevailing market for intellectual labor and its products. These were the factors that explained his reaction to Gerth's Weber translations. In Mills's analysis of academic career chances, the conflicts of interest between Gerth and Shils over the publication of their respective Weber translations made the collapse of their personal relationship inevitable—unless, of course, Gerth agreed to withdraw from the field. Without such an act of self-abnegation on Gerth's part, Shils could not prevent publication of their book. Nevertheless, the feeling of rage engendered by his sense that he had been wronged would spur him to find ways to sabotage their Weber project and discredit Gerth.

"You must know," Mills explained to Gerth, "that nothing, nothing you can ever do will make him hate you less. You may as well realize that and get along in the world without his friendship"—"too bad," Mills concluded, "but inevitable." Gerth was torn by the conflict between the demands of friendship and the requirements of academic life. Mills urged him to persevere with the Weber book and resolve the conflict by subordinating his friendship to the imperatives of his career. He also maintained that it was Shils and not Gerth who had violated the ethics of friendship. Denying the validity of any possible accusation against Gerth, Mills reversed the moral positions of Gerth and Shils: Gerth became the victim of Shils's deceit, and Shils himself was blamed for any damage produced by the Oxford Weber project. If there was a guilty party in the incident, it was not Gerth but Shils, who would have to accept the consequences of his secretiveness. He could have informed Gerth of his plans or announced his intentions to the sociological profession at large, as Gerth and Mills had done, but neither Shils nor his colleagues had mentioned his translations in their correspondence with Gerth. In the end, Shils's "god damned secrecy and neurosis coldness" were responsible for his predicament.[31]

In explaining to Gerth the proper method for handling Shils, Mills made a number of practical suggestions. First, in view of the competition from Shils, they should finish their book as quickly as possible. There should be no further delays in Gerth's work on the introduction, the first two chapters of which Mills found in good order. Second, Gerth should check their translations against Shils's mimeographs to eliminate any parallels that might suggest unwarranted borrowings. Once the translations were typed, Mills would deliver them personally to Hatcher, at the same time discretely sounding him out to learn whether he had heard any rumors of Shils's allegation.

Third, Mills considered the possibility that Shils might write a follow-up letter to Gerth. How should he respond? Instead of leaving this question for Gerth to resolve, Mills took on the task of managing the Gerth-Shils relationship. Regardless of what Shils wrote and what he requested, the tone of Gerth's reply should be correct but also confident and firm, admitting nothing and generally shifting the blame for the problem onto Shils. After a conventional expression of regrets over the situation, Gerth should tell Shils to face the facts, which could not be altered. The problem, after all, had been caused largely by his secretive conduct. Gerth should also voice his irritation at the implication that either he or Mills had published Shils's work as their own. Here it would be useful to chastise Shils: his response to the translation of "Class, Status, Party" in *politics* was a great disappointment to Gerth, who would not have expected him to make such a vicious charge. If Shils, on reading the translations published by Gerth and Mills, actually believed they had acted unethically, he should say so, formally and publicly. Gerth, who knew he had done his own work, was confident of the outcome. "Shift the discussion always to published materials," Mills advised. Publication was the basis of academic reputation and the only possible foundation for a legitimate complaint on Shils's part.[32]

Fourth, Mills drafted his own reply to Shils and sent it to Gerth for his approval. Breathtaking in its self-confidence, insouciance, and disingenuousness, Mills's letter disarmed Shils, took apart his complaints piece by piece, and finally presented him with a lecture on intellectual ethics. Implying that he had only recently learned from Gerth that Shils was working on Weber translations, Mills generously forwarded an outline of their book, including a list of all the texts Gerth had translated. Deflating Shils's sense of the unique misery of his predicament, Mills observed he had heard that as many as four scholars were engaged in Weber translations and had the impression that Shils might be working on Weber's sociology of law, a part of *Economy and Society* not included in Gerth and Mills's book. After commiserating with Shils about the hard work of translation and the bad luck that their enterprises overlapped, he lightly chided Shils for the secrecy in which he had enveloped his project, observing that he had not seen any prepublication notices of Shils's edition. Mills contended that his interest in Weber was purely intellectual and pedagogical. In collaborating with Gerth, he hoped to improve his German, learn something of Weber's sociology, and produce otherwise unavailable texts for use in his courses at Maryland, in much the same way Gerth had done at Madison. Gerth and Mills had translated several hundred pages of Weber's work without any intention of publishing them and had been forthcoming in responding to requests for copies. The original proposal to publish their translations, he explained, was due to a third party, Dwight Macdonald, who was interested in "Class, Status, Party." In publishing this fragment in *politics,* they had done no more than comply with his request. Only then did the idea of compiling a book of Weber translations occur to Mills. When he happened to be in New York on other business, Mills "mentioned it to a fellow at Oxford," who informed him that Oxford University Press had been considering precisely such a possibility and immediately pounced on the idea. Thus the contract with Oxford, like the Weber project itself, was a largely fortuitous event.[33]

In response to the suggestion that a mimeographed version of their translation of "Class, Status, Party" resembled an earlier translation by Shils, Mills feigned surprise and took Shils to task for his recklessness in raising an irresponsible charge. Mills claimed he had never seen Shils's translation of this piece. Recounting the labors he and Gerth had devoted to their first venture into Weberiana, which passed through as many as five drafts, he explained the impression of parallels between the two translations as due to an allegedly "common apperceptive mass" that he, Gerth, and Shils all shared. His tone toughened when he finally addressed the implicit accusation of plagiarism. Mills objected to the suggestion that either he or Gerth would engage in a practice that both regarded as reprehensible. Moreover, he knew, and Shils should have known, that Gerth could not conceivably countenance such conduct.[34]

Finally, leaving no permutation of the Shils affair either to chance or to Gerth's judgment or improvisation, Mills gave his collaborator detailed instructions on what they should not do. They should betray no evidence of guilt and make no apologies. They had nothing to apologize for, much less to be ashamed of. They should keep closely in touch on any new turns the case might take. They should also impose a moratorium on the circulation of material slated for inclusion in their book, since further distribution of these texts would be interpreted as an admission of culpability.

The traditional liberal principle of science requires free and unobstructed communication and an unfettered distribution of information about the progress of research. Several considerations convinced Mills that he and Gerth could not afford to follow this principle. The competition that seemed to be intensifying among the small group of American Weber scholars, the dependence of academic success on demonstrations of scholarly originality or priority, and the necessity of proving their priority over Shils in the publication of Weber translations—these circumstances, together with Shils's penchant for concealment, required that they act instead on a principle of secrecy: circulate no prepublication drafts of work in progress.

Secrecy, Candor, and Friendship

During the Shils affair, Gerth's violation of Mills's principle of secrecy was a cause of tension between the partners. On learning that Gerth had shared several of their unpublished manuscripts with colleagues at Madison, Mills berated him and enunciated a rule he often invoked when he felt that Gerth had behaved irresponsibly. This rule articulates a Millsean principle of friendship: when disagreements between friends arise, especially over sensitive issues or fundamental questions, absolute frankness is necessary to expose conflicts and resolve them, for otherwise the basis of the friendship will be threatened. As Mills succinctly put it: "Unverbalized stuff affects future relations."[35] Mills's criticism of Gerth was not meant to diminish their friendship. On the contrary, his admonitions were grounded in the importance he ascribed to their relationship.

Acting on the principle that unsparing honesty is necessary to friendship, Mills asked Gerth not to share their work in progress with third parties. Specifically, he mentioned two of Gerth's colleagues in the Department of Sociology and Anthropology at Madison: Howard Becker and the anthropologist Scudder McKeel. Gerth had given Becker two pieces that, in Mills's view, no one should have seen. He found it especially galling that Gerth had shown their work to McKeel, who had been one of Mills's enemies on the faculty during his two years at Madison. Although McKeel's reputation has not survived, Mills rightly treated him as a formidable power and an important figure in the informal networks of social scientists who controlled access to research opportunities. McKeel had held a Social Science Research Council fellowship, a grant for which Mills entertained ambitions at the time, and participated in the influential seminars on personality and culture conducted by Abraham Kardiner and Ralph Linton at Columbia. Mills regarded the Social Science Research Council as a quasi-conspiratorial group of older men intriguing to restrict the distribution of research funds to their favorite candidates and damning to impecuniousness and insignificance anyone who had incurred their animosity. Because "the old SSRC men hang closely together and form an informal committee with cartel-like control of fellowships," any intervention by McKeel against Mills would doom his chances for funding.[36] Mills also suspected McKeel was the author of a letter then in circulation that charged him with claiming credit for work with Gerth that he did not deserve. The letter portrayed Gerth as brilliant but naive, an original scholar innocent in the ways of the world. Mills was represented as a brazen opportunist who had cleverly deceived Gerth to gain recognition for work he had not done. Mills reminded Gerth that he had vigorously defended his reputation against a similar attack. During Mills's first year at Maryland, Shils made a trip to Washington and took occasion to ridicule the unsystematic character of Gerth's thinking, maintaining that before he worked his editorial magic on it, Gerth's essay on the Nazi Party had been hopelessly disorganized. Vexed by Gerth's failure to silence McKeel, Mills recalled that he had been quick to come to Gerth's support and suggested that it was not too much to expect collaborators to defend one another against false and malicious accusations.

Mills found Gerth's conduct objectionable in two respects, both of which were germane to the elder man's incautious circulation of their manuscripts. First, Gerth lacked the moral courage to support Mills against McKeel's vicious interpretation of their work. Second, McKeel was able to take this initiative, which Mills regarded as a potentially fatal threat to his career, only because Gerth had not followed his principle of secrecy: no disclosure of work in progress. The obvious lesson was to say nothing about the Shils matter that could be understood as implicating them in a piece of intellectual fraud. Above all, Gerth should admit nothing, especially as regarded their retranslation of Shils's draft of "Classes and Status Groups," all mimeographs of which should be destroyed.

The "Kafka Minstrel Show": The End of the Shils Affair

Mills's elaborate prospectus for handling the Shils matter demonstrated that he had no confidence in Gerth's judgment. He understood that if Gerth were consumed by anxiety and irresolution, he would be dangerously unstable and a threat to their joint interests. Therefore, he not only tutored Gerth in the tactics that would be needed in a possible confrontation with Shils and his supporters but also did what he could to strengthen Gerth's determination so that the elder man would be ready if a battle were forced on them: "Come on, smoke a pipe, have a drink, get a good night's sleep and think how bad off we could all be. This is America, so smile, and be happy." [37] In his efforts to buoy Gerth's spirits, Mills stressed the importance of placing Shils's behavior in the proper moral perspective. "Who the hell does he think he is anyway?" Mills asked. Both Gerth and Mills had taken "enough shit off little people not to have to be fucked out of something that is ours by pseudo-monopolists." [38]

Mills's next move against Shils was to meet with Hatcher on November 18, deliver the entire set of translations, probe the editor for any knowledge of a contract between Shils and Kegan Paul, and leave New York with a firm commitment from Oxford to publish their book regardless of Shils's plans. How much did Hatcher really know about the Shils matter, and what were his intentions? Mills seemed prepared for the worst. His ultimate fear was that Hatcher would hold them to their contract but not publish the book, a device that would enable Oxford to distribute the Shils edition in the United States free of competition. In that case he hoped to gain a release from the Oxford contract so that he could negotiate another as quickly as possible. Much would depend on Hatcher, whose motivations Mills found difficult to decipher. His confidence in his powers of analysis, self-presentation, and salesmanship, however, convinced him that he would succeed. As he confided to Gerth, he would master the requisite idiom. To win Hatcher over, he would appeal to the traditions of academic publishing, Oxford's elevated ethical standards, and the editor's sense of fairness and propriety. By acting on the presumption that Oxford was committed to a genuine ethic of academic publishing and not merely a cynical corporate ideology, Mills expected to have his way. In handling Hatcher he would bring into play his full repertoire of techniques in microsocial impression management and dramaturgy: "the slowing up of speech process, the ponderous intent manner, the steady eye, the shining honest face, the stiff back, the slight smile." Ending with a word of advice, perhaps as much to himself as to Gerth, he urged that they concentrate on the book itself, channeling their worries into energy for work instead of indulging in "speculative anxiety." [39]

Mills took his own therapeutic suggestions to heart. In the week before the meeting with Hatcher, he returned to work on the book, even canceling his classes to devote more time to the manuscript. He edited Gerth's translation of Weber's analysis of the Chinese literati, wrote headings and subheadings for the chapters on bureaucracy, charisma, and India, reread all the translations once more to make stylistic changes, and prodded Gerth to send him the introduction so that he would have the strongest possible case for pressing Hatcher to make a firm commitment. By the morning of his trip to New York, the translations—edited, he admitted, somewhat unevenly—were complete and ready for the publisher. In spite of his detailed plans and stratagems, however, Mills remained apprehensive. Hatcher might already have an arrangement with Kegan Paul. Even worse, he might be the "end man in a Kafka Minstrel show." It was possible that Oxford had decided to distribute Shils's book without informing Hatcher.

It was also possible that Hatcher's superiors were unaware of his intention to publish the Gerth-Mills volume. In either case, Hatcher might unwittingly have made commitments to Gerth and Mills that Oxford would not endorse. In considering these possibilities, Mills gave free rein to his propensity for calculating every rationale that could motivate the conduct of his interlocutors. Above all, he needed to determine whether Oxford intended to delay, or perhaps even prevent, publication of their book until Kegan Paul brought out the Shils edition, in which case he would ask for a release so they could publish elsewhere without delay.[40]

In the end his fears proved groundless. Writing from Daniel Bell's office at *The New Leader* immediately after meeting with Hatcher, he reported to Gerth that all had gone well. After listening to Mills's account of the Shils problem, Hatcher assured him that Oxford would fulfill its agreement regardless of any contract Shils might have with Kegan Paul and even if Oxford were obligated to bring out both books in the United States because of its commitments as Kegan Paul's U.S. distributor. To resolve the contractual matter conclusively and simplify Oxford's accounting procedures, Hatcher dictated a memorandum for Mills's signature advising that all royalty checks for the Weber book "translated by Dr. Gerth and myself" be sent to Mills, who would then divide the money with Gerth. Regardless of the considerations responsible for the memorandum, it was a further step in the solidification of Mills's control over the Weber project, reinforcing his monopoly on the management of the partners' relations with Oxford and excluding Gerth from decisions concerning the transformation of the manuscript into a book that would provide the basis for prestige claims and career advancement. It also gave official legitimation to Mills's claim to credit for the translation. Once certified, this claim would prove difficult for Gerth to deny.[41]

A month later Mills closed the Shils matter, returning to Gerth all copies of the Gerth-Shils correspondence and retaining the option of deniability should the affair come to light. To cover his traces he would take the public position that his knowledge of Shils's mimeographs was limited to what Gerth had told him. He also congratulated Gerth on his part in handling Shils. The firm stand taken by Gerth in his letter to Shils was just what was needed, he asserted, hardly a surprising judgment, since Mills had proposed its main lines. The "conciliatory tone" of Shils's response and his failure to make explicit charges concerning the appropriation of specific translations convinced Mills that they had succeeded in silencing him, as was indeed the case. On the one hand, Mills regretted that their work overlapped and that Shils's interests had been damaged. On the other hand, his conscience was clear: "What the hell, he certainly acted slimy as did his colleague. So let them suffer a bit for their god damned secrecy and arrogant coldness."[42]

In a more cautious mood, Mills warned Gerth that they should not become intoxicated over their success in the Shils affair. Because the earliest completion of the manuscript was crucial, Gerth should finish the introduction so that Mills could send it to Hatcher as quickly as possible. Their entry into the field of Weber scholarship had not passed unnoticed. Mills reported that while in New York for his meeting with Hatcher, he had learned from contacts at Columbia that Robert K. Merton had been under the impression that Parsons was in control of the American Weber market and was upset over news of the Weber book. Mills assumed the aspect of the Cheshire cat. "I've got both hands crossed," he wrote Gerth.[43]

Mills had begun the collaboration with Gerth tentatively but confidently. Although he arranged publication of "Class, Status, Party" and pressed his claims to be named as cotranslator, he was willing to leave the decision on credit in Gerth's hands, adopting the behavior appropriate to an apprentice who defers to the authority and superior wisdom of his master. Gerth labored at rendering Weber's sociological texts into English, and Mills formed these materials into a book. As a result of their joint efforts, the sociological writings of the most important social theorist of the twentieth century were introduced to a large American readership. This achievement was perhaps somewhat incidental to Mills's principal objective, which was to get a Weber book into print as quickly as possible, minimizing the commitment of time and effort on his part and capturing the English-language Weber market before it was monopolized by Talcott Parsons, Inc. For Mills, the Weber project was primarily a venture in career advancement. Its success depended on whether he could control Gerth's participation in the collaboration and at the same time legitimate his own claim to credit.

The Shils affair demonstrated why it was important for Mills to monitor Gerth's performance with some care. Mills saw Shils's initiative as a threat to his plan to establish himself quickly by publishing a book in an important area of research. If Shils could produce plausible grounds that Gerth's translations were derived from his work, Gerth might weaken and concede the field to the man whose support had made a difference at the beginning of his American career. To defeat this contingency, Mills, whose skills as a crisis manager were formidable even at the age of twenty-eight, drafted letters of explanation and justification that would nullify Shils's threat and coached Gerth so that he would neither falter nor commit a serious misjudgment at a critical moment.

At the same time that he promoted the Weber book to Oxford, Mills advanced his claim to be named as cotranslator and coauthor. During the planning phase, when the book was nothing more than a collection of Gerth's drafts and his marketing ideas, Mills proceeded gingerly, even conceding that his argument for joint credit might not be warranted, in which case Gerth would be free to pursue the project independently. When Oxford became interested, he made no further concessions on credit. Indeed, as Oxford's commitment solidified, he grew bolder in pressing his position on the distribution of credit. Mills no longer understood the issue of precedence as a question of intellectual ethics: to what extent would he be justified in taking credit for the book? Now it was a tactical problem in the pragmatics of career planning: how much credit could he extract from Gerth, and what measures would be required for this purpose? As a result, the Weber book became a battleground on which Mills played a zero-sum game with Gerth. Any credit that Gerth succeeded in claiming would be lost by Mills. Mills would make sure that this did not happen by planning his moves in the credit game so that any net losses in priority after the Oxford contract was signed would be suffered by Gerth. If he succeeded, publication of the book would establish his reputation as an expert on Max Weber's sociology and confirm his status as a theoretician whose work was grounded in the most advanced European social theories.

• 2 •

The Precedence Dispute:
November 1944–June 1946

The Origins of the Controversy

In 1944 Gerth was thirty-six, a refugee working on probationary contracts and uneasy about his prospects for the following year. At twenty-eight Mills was a promising and ambitious sociologist determined to work his way out of the University of Maryland, which he saw as a swamp of mediocrity and pettifogging bureaucracy, but without the credentials he needed for a more prestigious position. The Weber book was an effort by Gerth and Mills to establish their careers. The two brought strikingly different strengths to this enterprise: on Gerth's side, impressive erudition, comprehensive knowledge of Weber's work, and a firm grasp of Weberian sociology; on Mills's part, editorial and organizational skills, energy and discipline, and a facility for moving easily between the worlds of academia and publishing. Although these asymmetrical contributions were important to the success of the collaboration, they were also the source of a protracted and bitter dispute over the attribution of credit.

On November 15, 1944, Mills received Gerth's rough draft of the introduction. When he began his revisions the following evening, he noticed a credit notation penciled on the manuscript in a handwriting he did not recognize: "By Hans Gerth (Edited by C. Wright Mills)." Mills had understood that he was the junior partner in a project for which he would be able to claim full credit. Because the notation violated his understanding, he rejected it, writing Gerth and reminding him that this understanding had been explicitly stated and reconfirmed in their correspondence. The two would share credit for the entire work: "It was to be Gerth and Mills throughout with no qualifications whatsoever."[1] Although they had begun to work together when Mills was still a graduate student, several years had passed, and Mills had embarked on his own career. Did Gerth still regard Mills as his student editor? He had given no explanation for the notation, nor had he even mentioned it. As a result, Mills was bewildered about Gerth's position on their roles in the project and how credit would be allocated. Did Gerth write the new credit line? Had he changed his mind about the distribution of credit? Had Mills misunderstood Gerth's feelings on this matter, or had Gerth perhaps failed to make them clear?

Although Mills was in no position to answer these questions, he was ready with a solution to the difficulty they posed: what to do if Gerth was unwilling to accept his understanding of the terms governing the collaboration. If he could not claim equal credit for the project as a whole, he would abandon it to Gerth. Should Gerth attempt to diminish his credit, he would simply withdraw, and Gerth could take all the credit. In the margin of the letter in which he responded to Gerth's draft of the introduction, he underscored the gravity of the issue by adding a handwritten note saying that he had made this resolution "honestly and with all intentions of fulfilling it." Mills represented his position as a moral stand: he would not compromise, nor would he engage in a petty debate about who deserved how much credit for which parts of the project. Finally, he had made his position clear and unequivocal, unlike Gerth, who had not stated frankly what he wanted but insinuated his demands in a cryptic fashion. In any case, Mills claimed, he had grown tired of working on Weber and was beginning to feel unappreciated. Gerth's last letter had suggested that when Mills traveled to New York to meet with Hatcher, he would do no more than "peek at the manuscript on the train," a remark Mills regarded as a gratuitous insult intended to denigrate the value of his contribution. Mills's position seemed to be that collaboration with Gerth, a delicate undertaking under the best of conditions, had become more difficult because of these irritating and inscrutable maneuvers. Perhaps he would be better off if he simply withdrew.[2]

Was this resolution a sincere offer on Mills's part or a move designed to force Gerth's hand, a way of compelling him to confirm Mills's understanding of their original agreement? In his letter on the credit line for the introduction, Mills documented his labors on the book, noting that it had already consumed a substantial part of two years of research.[3] He wanted to publish his way out of the University of Maryland, and the Weber book was a means to that end. Moreover, could he reasonably expect Gerth to accept his extravagant proposition? It did not seem likely, and for several reasons. Mills believed that Gerth's moral standards would not allow him to take credit for work he had not done. His declaration of principle reduced the question of credit to an absolute alternative that admitted no qualifications: either they would divide the credit equally, or Mills would accept none. Because the latter option was patently unfair and intellectually dishonest, Gerth would not consider it. As a result, his formula would force Gerth into the former option, which rested on Mills's understanding of the terms of their collaboration. He also knew that it would be professionally embarrassing for Gerth to publish the book under his name alone. By the end of 1944 the fact that they were working together on Weber translations could not be conveniently denied. Colleagues at Wisconsin, Maryland, Columbia, and Chicago and editors in the little political and literary magazines in New York and in academic publishing houses knew about the collaboration. Under these conditions it was not clear how Gerth could make a plausible case for exclusive credit if Mills withdrew.

Finally, Mills had good grounds to be confident that Gerth could not complete the book without his help. He had conducted all the negotiations with Oxford, for whom Gerth was no more than a name. Gerth—diffident, often contemptuous of Americans, and at the same time uneasy in his dealings with them—had no experience working with American publishers. The publication of his first American article had been managed through the good offices of Shils. Mills had handled "A Marx for the Managers" and "Class, Status, Power." Gerth's written English was awkward. He was not equal to the editorial tasks Mills had assumed, nor could he write a substantial introduction in idiomatic English. In sum, Mills had excellent reasons to suppose that Gerth would not and could not accept his proposal to abandon the project.

And of course he did not accept it. During January 1945 Mills continued to transact business with Oxford, pressed on with his editorial work on the manuscript, and prodded Gerth to complete the introduction. In early February he was revising the biographical material on Weber that Gerth had written. They had originally conceived the introduction as a two-part essay, the first on Weber's life and the second on his thought. Mills detached Gerth's extended discussion of Weber's politics from the biographical section and reorganized the introduction into three chapters: biography, politics, and thought.[4] At that point two incidents occurred, one following swiftly on the other, that sharpened the disagreement over credit.

At the beginning of February, Oxford mailed a catalog announcing its spring list, including a half-page notice on the publication of *From Max Weber* in August. The notice transposed the names of the partners as they appeared in their contract with Oxford, appearing to give Mills priority over Gerth. Mills immediately notified Hatcher of the error and asked him to correct it in all subsequent publicity and in the book as well. In an observation that inspired a furious response from Gerth, he made light of the mistake, suggesting that it was perhaps not so surprising since he had managed the partners' affairs with the publisher. On the same day that he received the catalog, Mills sent Gerth a copy of his letter to Hatcher, expressed his regret for the mixup in the strongest terms, emphasized that he was not responsible for it, and finally apologized, declaring his willingness to take any further steps Gerth might find appropriate, although he saw no need for additional measures.[5]

Two days later Mills received from Dwight Macdonald the galley proofs of Meyer Schapiro's critique of "Class, Status, Party," which was scheduled for publication in the forthcoming issue of *politics*. No copy of the proofs was sent to Gerth. Schapiro, a professor of art history at Columbia and a member of the editorial board of *Partisan Review,* was a New York intellectual of impeccable credentials. In his article Schapiro also transposed the order of their names: "Gerth and Mills" again became "Mills and Gerth." This was the occasion for another apology to Gerth, in which Mills voiced his incomprehension and dismay and assured Gerth of his innocence. In a postcard to Macdonald Mills noted the error and asked him to correct it before the article was published.[6] Although Mills found the repetition of the mistake unfortunate, he emphasized that he was doing all he could to rectify it as quickly as possible. As if he had not done enough to atone for errors not of his own making, Mills reiterated his commitment to his conception of their agreement and ended with a personal confession of his intellectual debt to Gerth. "Finally, Gerth, let me say flatly to you, in view of the recurrence of the mix up in the order of our names, that I am most sincerely in full and intimate agreement that you are the senior author in all that we have done with Max Weber, that I am not only content, internally and externally, with being the junior author of the book, but am most grateful to have had the chance to learn what I have of Max Weber while acting as the junior partner with you."[7]

Gerth seems to have reacted to these mishaps with an explosion of outrage. Although Gerth's response has not survived, a letter from Mills to Gerth written nine days after Mills's confession summarizes Mills's view of the charges Gerth raised against him: Mills was held responsible for the transposition of names in the Oxford catalog, blamed for misrepresenting their roles to Hatcher, and chastised for the explanation he had given Hatcher of the order of their names in the contract with Oxford. As Gerth apparently read Mills's explanation, his name was listed first not as a matter of precedence, reflecting his position as the senior scholar and translator and his more substantial contribution to the book, but only because the letter *g* precedes the letter *m* in the alphabet. Finally, Mills's account suggests that Gerth threatened to write Hatcher and expose Mills as an impostor who could not read Weber's German well enough to translate it. After relieving himself of these charges and accusing Mills of "outright immodesty" and "incredible conceit," it seems that he then declared that the matter was closed.[8] This conclusion could not have been more wrong.

These incidents marked the beginning of an increasingly acrimonious quarrel that continued for two months and quickly involved not only the two principals but also their editor at Oxford and the sociology departments at Wisconsin and Columbia, where Mills was now working under Paul Lazarsfeld at the Bureau of Applied Social Research. Accusations were not confined to the roles of the partners in the Weber project. At its most vicious the dispute approached the level of unconditional moral warfare in which each antagonist mounted a full-scale assault on the integrity of the other. The dispute over scholarly precedence became an argument about the moral worth of Gerth and Mills as human beings. Moreover, the threat to appeal to Hatcher shifted their disagreement into a more public arena in which third parties in the publishing industry and academia were called on to take positions on the charges and countercharges raised by the principals. As a result, questions concerning their personal morality and scientific ethics were adjudicated by others.

Moral Claims and Public Adjudications

Had Gerth called Mills a liar? Mills thought so. In addition, he found it unconscionable that Gerth would impugn his character and blandly conclude that there was nothing further to say. Mills responded in a mood of icy fury, undertaking to refute point by point what he understood as Gerth's accusations. More important for their relationship, he counterattacked, charging Gerth with bad faith and character assassination. In this way Mills would alter the balance of moral power, depriving Gerth of the higher ground he presumed to occupy. By showing that the blame for the dispute lay with Gerth, Mills would confound and embarrass him and at the same time convict him of hypocrisy: measured against the standards to which he feigned commitment, it was Gerth, not Mills, who would be found wanting.

Mills also put Gerth on notice that he could not expect to escape the consequences of his accusations. The first consequence was a letter of February 16 from Mills to Hatcher outlining the background of Gerth's position and engaging Hatcher as a moral broker who would intervene on his behalf and isolate Gerth. The letter to Hatcher is a consummate piece of Millsean rhetoric that demonstrates his flair for clear organization and a crisp formulation of issues. Mills confined himself to three concisely stated points. First, he reaffirmed his position that Gerth was the senior translator. In appraising his own competence in German, he conceded that it was not equal to the challenges posed by Weber's writings. Accordingly, he would not have considered attempting an independent translation of Weber. This was an equivocal self-evaluation, suggesting that although he could not have produced his own edition of Weber, he was capable of collaborating on a translation. He simply needed a co-worker with a better command of German. Mills sustained this ambiguity, leaving open the question of whether he actually did or was competent to do Weber translations, by adding that his responsibilities were confined to the "English side of the translation": rewriting English sentences that "block out" a bit of German text and making choices among alternative English translations of German expressions. It seems that translating Weber had two aspects, a German side and an English side. Did the English side, Mills's self-described job, require a comparison of the "blocked-out" English sentences with the corresponding German texts? Making decisions between alternative translations of an original text seems to presuppose an ability to read the text and make an informed choice. Or was it his task to rewrite a draft of a translation already written in English? In other words, was his function purely editorial, confined to reworking Gerth's English into a style acceptable for publication? If Mills's English side of the project was exclusively editorial, working only with Gerth's English drafts of Weber's German, did this constitute translation? Did he qualify as a translator of the Weber materials in any sense, even though he was not the senior translator?

Ignoring these questions, Mills moved to his second and third points. He had not misrepresented Gerth's role in the book. Gerth's name preceded Mills's in the contract not because the letter *g* precedes *m* in the alphabet but because Gerth was the senior translator. Any impression to the contrary should be corrected. Finally, he stressed that he was writing Hatcher on his own initiative and apologized for involving him in the minutiae of a dispute between two of his authors, but Gerth's charges were so serious that he could not let them pass. They could be answered conclusively only by a third party who was in a position to confirm that they were groundless. That third party was Hatcher, the only person with independent knowledge of the way Mills had represented the roles and responsibilities of the authors to Oxford. In a postscript Mills asked Hatcher to notify Gerth of his receipt of this letter, thereby forcing Gerth to confront Hatcher's knowledge of his position.[9]

Mills sent Gerth a copy of the Hatcher letter together with a note blaming him for an incident that had now become an embarrassment. In Mills's view, the transposition of names was a trivial error that Gerth had magnified into a calculated act of treachery. Although Mills recognized that his appeal to Hatcher exposed them to ridicule, he felt that Gerth's accusations had left him no alternative. Indeed, if Gerth was not satisfied with this letter, Mills suggested he write Hatcher on his own account and send a copy to Mills, who promised to write Hatcher once more should he find anything of merit in Gerth's response. The conflict would be adjudicated by a diplomatic exchange of letters, with Hatcher acting as arbiter. Mills taunted Gerth by saying that he lacked the inner resources to admit that his accusations were without foundation. Offended, angry, and insisting that he would not descend to the level of Gerth's charges, Mills finally dissolved their friendship. In the past he had opened himself to Gerth, revealing his most personal reflections and intimate feelings. In a stinging valedictory laced with irony at his own expense, Mills assured Gerth that he would be spared these confessions in the future.[10]

Gerth's response was uncharacteristically swift and decisive. Instead of waiting for Hatcher's confirmation, Gerth wrote their editor on his own behalf and apologized not for his conduct but for Mills's indiscretion. To the original injury Mills had inflicted on Gerth in misrepresenting their relationship to Oxford, the younger man now added the insult of publicizing a private matter by tactlessly drawing Hatcher into the dispute. Gerth was deeply suspicious of Mills's motives and convinced that his own rights to priority in the Weber project were in jeopardy. The reversal of names in the Oxford catalog and Mills's explanation of this confusion only strengthened his suspicions. As he explained the matter to Hatcher, much more delicately than he had put it to Mills, he "could not escape the conclusion that Dr. Mills had failed to represent my interests adequately."[11]

On the same day he wrote Hatcher, Gerth sent a scathing reply to Mills, denying that he had accused Mills of lying and refusing to admit that he had attacked Mills's character. Mills's three-point letter to Hatcher left Gerth unrepentant. Repeating his distaste over Mills's lack of propriety in revealing the details of their private quarrel to "a gentleman unknown to me," Gerth remained unpersuaded that Mills had disposed of his original charges. His letter to Hatcher merely cleared up retrospectively matters that should have been stated unequivocally when he began to negotiate with Oxford: Gerth's position as the translator, Mills's inability to translate Weber, and his subordinate role as editor of Gerth's English drafts. Further, Mills had supplied this clarification only because the reversal of the order of their names in the Oxford catalog compelled him to do so. An ex post facto admission by Mills, forced on him by an unexpected contingency, did not convince Gerth of his innocence.

After congratulating Mills on the bad taste displayed in his letter to Hatcher and the gratuitous insults and insinuations in which he indulged himself, Gerth ridiculed his pseudomoralism: "It's a pity Mills, that our glorious rows finally have come to the unglorious end. Unable to follow to the glorious heights of your moral elevation, I look forward to seeing you vanish in the snow white peaks of your moral Olympus."[12] "And now to business," he continued, without hesitation or explanation, noting that he had received Mills's revisions of the introduction and planned to begin work on them. During the precedence dispute Gerth and Mills began to detach their personal relationship from their joint research, compartmentalizing their differences to finish the book. Both seemed willing to wage the war for credit with all the weapons at their disposal because neither believed that the collapse of their friendship would jeopardize their work on Weber. Even at its most vicious, the dispute never threatened the completion of the Weber project. In the end their career interests prevailed, outweighing their principles and wounded sensitivities and effecting the compromises that were necessary to sustain the collaboration.

Meanwhile Gerth acted to protect his claims to priority. In his first draft of the conclusion to the preface of the book, he defined the responsibilities of the partners in the following terms: "Whatever merit the stylization and arrangement of the joint work may have are to the credit of Charles Wright Mills. The senior author assumes primary responsibility for the content of the prefatory essay, for the selection, and adequate rendering of meanings of the translations."[13]

It would have been difficult to frame the marginal character of Mills's contribution in more damning terms without excluding him altogether. Gerth, now promoted from senior translator to senior author, assumed credit for selecting, from the thousands of pages of Weber's writings, the material that would provide the best introduction to his sociological thought and also for translating this material into English. He also took the chief credit for the introduction. What was left for Mills? He was banned to the periphery of the project as a mere wordsmith and Gerth's copyeditor. The conditional language of Gerth's first sentence, the grammar of which confirmed his need for an editor, suggested that Mills might deserve no credit at all, unless some merit could be found in the "stylization and arrangement" of the material. Gerth's statement of the division of labor seemed to deny that the book was a joint work. Mills's contribution, if it can be said that he made one, was not intrinsic to the project. An analogy or a comparable venture in collaboration that clarifies Gerth's definition of their roles does not spring immediately to mind. It is not as if Gerth had composed the score of a work and Mills orchestrated it. Nor did Gerth write a work that Mills revised. Gerth, it seems, had designed and built a house and chose the furnishings, leaving to Mills the task of clearing away the debris of construction and arranging the furniture.

In view of the dismal relations between the partners by the late winter of 1945, Mills's response was remarkably restrained. Did Gerth actually suppose that Mills would accept his draft of the preface? Although the implications of Gerth's conditional syntax were not lost on Mills, he did not press the issue. Personal relations had deteriorated to the point that further discussion of the priority issue was futile. Reconciliation of their differences was possible only on the basis of mutual trust: a foundation of understandings that would support the assurance that each could depend on the veracity, decency, and goodwill of the other. Because this foundation had been undermined, the moral basis of their friendship was irreparably damaged. Mills concluded that it would be pointless to engage in further exchanges of personal abuse. Gerth was revolted by Mills's conduct, and Mills returned the compliment. Gerth saw no reason to revise his remarks or alter his behavior, nor did Mills. Since their personal differences had become irreconcilable, Mills would not attempt to end the quarrel about credit on the basis of trust. That was no longer possible. In the future he would attempt to get his way by means of power. Once the

Oxford contract was signed, he possessed all the advantages in this contest. The former graduate assistant no longer recognized the professor's authority, and the friends had become competitors and antagonists. Because Mills understood that a modicum of civility and goodwill was necessary to complete the book, he voiced his muted dissatisfaction with Gerth's draft of the conclusion to the preface and deferred further discussion of the apparently intractable problem of allocating credit.[14]

Meanwhile Hatcher, who had been laid up for weeks with the flu, resurfaced in early March 1945 and responded to the correspondence he had received from the partners in February. Affable and optimistic, he attempted to mollify Gerth by suggesting that any misunderstanding could be cleared up with a demonstration of generosity. Although he did not say from whom generosity should be expected, Hatcher reconfirmed Mills's three-point declaration of February 16 without any qualifications. Neither in correspondence nor in conversation with Hatcher had Mills misrepresented Gerth's status. Even in their initial discussions, he had made it clear that Gerth would be principally responsible for the translation and should be named as the senior figure in the book. This did not mean, however, that Gerth could claim the chief credit for the project as a whole. The reversal of their names in the spring catalog was due not to deceitful machinations on Mills's part but to an unhappy but innocent mistake caused by wartime understaffing and the pressures of a hectic schedule. Hatcher, practicing the diplomacy of a sage editor, blamed himself for the mixup, or rather dismissed it as a collective and corporate error. In any case, the mistake, which would be corrected in Oxford's fall catalog, was innocuous and could hardly be taken seriously. In conclusion he advised Gerth to place this insignificant incident in the larger picture of the Weber project. For the first time the American reader would have a satisfactory rendition of Weber and his work, an achievement for which Gerth and Mills deserved equal credit.[15]

Thus Gerth was granted his desire to be recognized as senior translator. But what had he won? Although Hatcher was silent on the question of Mills's main contribution, his endorsement of Mills's formula for the distribution of credit—Gerth was given precedence, but both partners would receive credit for the work as a whole—implied that Mills's labors, regardless of how they should be understood, were not inferior to Gerth's. It followed that the generosity required to rectify the misunderstanding was demanded of Gerth, who should graciously concede that Mills's work on the book, although different in kind from his, deserved equal recognition.

This was exactly the result Gerth had hoped to avoid. In his angry letter to Mills and also in his draft of the conclusion to the preface, he had rejected an equal distribution of credit in favor of an alternative principle. Since he never offered an explicit statement of this principle, the question of its precise terms cannot be resolved with any confidence, but it is clear that he placed Mills's contribution in a subordinate position and reserved the substantial credit for himself. Such an outcome was not to be. This was the resolution of the dispute that Hatcher, speaking for Oxford on Mills's behalf, definitively rejected, albeit in suave and honeyed terms. No principle that distinguished inferior and superior contributions could be reconciled with Hatcher's concept of equal distribution. Thus Hatcher not only embraced the position Gerth had exerted himself so arduously to defeat; he did so as a result of Gerth's own efforts, which proved to be disastrously self-defeating.

On March 10 Gerth drafted a letter of apology to Hatcher saying that he had done Mills a regrettable injustice. By way of explanation, he added that even though Oxford had been notified of the error in the spring catalog, he had received no response from his publisher. Moreover, the same error had appeared in *politics*. Gerth seems to have regarded these considerations as sufficient to account for his conduct, which he classified under the heading of "misapprehensions." [16] On the same day he prepared a copy of this letter to Mills, declaring himself satisfied that Mills was not, after all, to be blamed for the several confusions over the order of their names. His apology was less than unqualified, however, and he was not yet ready to lay down the weapons of moral warfare. Although he was happy to learn that, in this particular case, his misapprehensions about Mills's dishonesty turned out to be just that, he made it clear that he absolved Mills of responsibility only as an ethical pragmatist, one who judges morality by reference to the actual consequences of conduct and independent of intentions. In other words, Gerth left open the more basic issue of Mills's use of the Weber book to gain prestige for himself at Gerth's expense. Was Mills's strategy to extract as much credit as he could, regardless of the impact on Gerth's interests? Was this the real purpose behind his control of the partners' relations with Oxford, even though the instance under dispute did not conform to this intention? Although he may not have deceived Hatcher about Gerth's role in the Weber book, did he have a grand design to build his career on Gerth's work? Gerth's pseudo-absolution of Mills on pragmatic grounds indicated his suspicions about the answers to these questions.[17]

In misinterpreting editorial and printing errors and translating them into questions of honor and moral principle, Gerth appeared petty and foolish. His threat to involve Hatcher backfired badly. In the sphere of microsocial tactics, he was no match for Mills, who forced him to perform a ceremony of self-degradation. Moreover, his humiliation was suffered at the hands of Hatcher, that "gentleman" he did not know but whose authoritative voice he was compelled to obey. For reasons of self-protection, Gerth felt obliged to share Hatcher's letter and his own apologies to Hatcher and Mills with Thomas McCormick, chair of the Department of Sociology and Anthropology at the University of Wisconsin, thereby announcing the facts about his conduct to the faculty at Madison and creating a further source of embarrassment. It is difficult to imagine how this incident could have been more costly for Gerth. "I had to excuse myself," he complained, "to a man at Oxford press, whom I don't know, for what seems a moral affair." [18]

Although there is no evidence that Mills responded to Gerth's somewhat hollow apology, he soon discovered that he had new grounds for complaint. In February 1945, when the explosion over priority occurred, he was under consideration for a faculty appointment at Columbia. During the quarrel with Gerth, another critical letter from Madison arrived at Columbia, this one characterizing Mills's role in the Weber project in quite unflattering terms. He blamed Gerth not for writing the letter but for mobilizing his old adversaries at Madison and supplying them with fraudulent information to use against him. Gerth was not impressed. If poisonous letters damaging to Mills had been sent from Wisconsin to New York, Gerth replied, Mills should recall his abrasive conduct during his years at Madison and the enmity it had inspired. If their quarrel had become public, Mills had only himself to blame. After all, he had submitted the matter to a third party for judgment. Although Gerth cheerfully wished Mills the best of luck in his job prospects, he refused to hold himself accountable for any difficulties their dispute might create at Columbia. "Take it or leave it," he concluded." [19]

Casuistries and Threats

In February, when Gerth's fury was at its peak, Mills was willing to defer the question of attribution of credit, but he could not be expected to allow Gerth's draft of the final paragraph of the preface to stand. In April this draft became the occasion for further friction. Initially confined to the right of each to claim equal credit for the introduction, it quickly became a more general disagreement over their roles in the book as a whole.

On April 9, 1945, the day he delivered the Weber manuscript, sans preface, to Oxford, Mills wrote Gerth concerning reading proof for the book, which he would take in hand. His main purpose, however, was to take up the sensitive question of Gerth's claim to sole credit for the introduction. In addressing this issue he reconstructed the history of its composition, stressing his own part in writing the first draft. In the absence of an alternative version of this history, and Gerth had offered none, he seemed to think that his account should settle the question.

The critical episode in Mills's story was Gerth's visit to Maryland in late August 1944. He described their work on the introduction as a dialogue:

> As I recall, the bulk of these three chapters [constituting the introduction] were composed with heavy reliance upon Max Weber (as is properly acknowledged in the footnotes) in Washington last fall. Various passages were read aloud by yourself and we had extended discussions concerning them, often bordering on arguments, as to their appropriateness, their relevance, their meaning for the character, structure and politics of the man, and so on. Out of these discussions were typed excerpts by myself, which I then had Miss Toda [Mills's typist] type again. After you had left, I stuck these together, wrote transitions, cut out and finally formulated the drafts which I then mailed to you and which are the main body of what is finally to be printed.[20]

Thus in his reconstruction, Mills wrote the original draft of the introduction on the basis of conversations in which both authors were full participants. In the light of this interpretation, it is hardly surprising that he refused to accept Gerth's claim to exclusive credit.

> In view of this, I am not ready to have you flatly state that the content of the introduction is your responsibility, without any reference whatsoever to my thought and writing. Indeed, I am frankly surprised that you should have talked yourself into such a belief. It is my own feeling that "by Gerth and Mills" is quite accurate and adequate recognition of the respective parts which we have played in that work [the introduction], indeed in the work as a whole. That is the formula to which we originally agreed, as you may see from consulting previous letters; and it is a formula from which I have never deviated in any way whatsoever.[21]

In this manner Mills attempted to convince Gerth, as he had convinced Hatcher (and perhaps himself as well), that he deserved credit not only for the English side of the project but for the introduction and the translation as well: in other words, for the entire book.

Mills also chided Gerth mercilessly for his naïveté in complaining that his senior colleagues at Madison had failed to consider his work on Weber in their decisions on his salary increases and promotion. The Madisonites, Gerth supposed, believed that Mills had succeeded in making him a "sucker": by inflating his own priority claims, Mills had deprived Gerth of credit that was rightfully his. Mills found this lament laughable, above all because it demonstrated Gerth's ignorance of the reward structure in American social science and the subordinate place it reserved for translating and editing in the hierarchy of scientific values. "Quite apart from our respective shares of the great glory," he observed, translating or editing was not work on which claims to scientific prestige could be built, regardless of how well it was done and the intellectual demands it imposed. To disabuse Gerth of his illusions concerning the recognition he could expect as a Weber scholar and translator, Mills suggested that he examine the announcement of a forthcoming complete four-volume translation of *Economy and Society* into Spanish, in which the translators were not even identified, or the new Oxford edition of Alfred von Martin's *Sociology of the Renaissance,* which also failed to mention the translator. In a summary of searing clarity and unsparing frankness, he grasped the unhappy truth of Gerth's career as a scholar, translator, and editor: "The relative lack of recognition which you will continue to get from all save a very small circle who knows what is involved, is not due to my getting any of 'your share' but due to the simple fact that neither of us will get much." [22]

In his response to Mills, Gerth continued the struggle over credit for the introduction and the project generally but gave ground on crucial points. He explained his decision to reserve the introduction for himself as an effort to insulate Mills from controversies in which he would not be qualified to participate. Just as there was a Marx philology, a tradition of scholarship on the interpretation and analysis of Marx's writings, so there was a substantial German secondary literature on Weber. "My comment about 'content' [of the introduction] and my responsibility for it was due to the fact that I felt you might not feel too sure about 'what Max Weber really meant' as you know his work but second hand. I wrote it thus in order to give you the chance to keep somewhat out of the fray if it should become sharp." [23] That is, because Mills knew Weber only on the basis of what he had learned from Gerth, he might not feel confident in being held accountable for interpretations of Weber's views. In taking credit for the introduction, Gerth had given Mills the opportunity to remain behind the lines and out of danger if heavy battles among real Weber scholars developed over these interpretations.

On the composition of the introduction, however, Gerth was adamant. In the field of Weber studies, he had no intellectual debts to Mills. Indeed, he seems to have found preposterous the suggestion that Mills might have any independent insights into Weber's work. "In spite of whatever 'arguments' we may have had at your home, I fail to see what possible 'thoughts' on Max Weber, German politics, or methodological problems of Weber's work I owe to you. In your 'private' letter of February 7, you stated 'I am most grateful to have had the chance to learn what I have of Max Weber while acting as the junior author in collaboration with you.' I owe no knowledge of Max Weber and no thoughts about Max Weber to you."[24] As Gerth saw the matter, Weber's life was a closed book for Mills. He did not own and had not read Marianne Weber's biography, and Gerth was obliged to bring along his own copy to Maryland. In view of his primitive background in Weberiana, what contribution could Mills make to the difficult task of selecting from the immense Weberian corpus the key texts to include in an English edition of his sociological writings? Although Hatcher had pleaded with Gerth to be generous, Mills had pressed his capacity for magnanimity beyond its limits.

These considerations notwithstanding, Gerth was willing to acknowledge certain debts to Mills. Shifting the discussion from the more specific, immediate, and inflammatory issue of credit for the Weber book to the less contentious question of what Mills had done for him generally, Gerth noted several important contributions Mills had made to the collaboration. As a quick study and a nimble and imaginative pupil, he had posed challenges that proved useful to Gerth in framing his ideas in English. He had also served as Gerth's "good mentor," singular praise in this troubled phase of their relationship. For Gerth, good mentoring meant "prompting me, reminding me, scheduling tasks, and intellectually stimulating me no end." Finally and unsurprisingly, Gerth found Mills most helpful in improving his English. These concessions hardly conform to the language and apparent intent of Gerth's draft of the preface. He even recalled that in a previous letter he had assessed Mills's work on the Weber book as no less significant than his own: "of equal importance and relevance to what I have contributed." This was why he had raised no objections to Mills's terms: both their names would appear on the title page, and all work would be signed by both partners. Was Gerth confused or merely being evasive? In his lapses of self-control, he was capable of striking distortions of fact that led him to draw erroneous inferences and form mistaken judgments. On occasion the result was irrationally self-destructive conduct that sometimes found its way into his correspondence. He was not generally a careless writer, however. In this case it seems most reasonable to suppose that although he recognized Mills had made certain contributions to his thinking, they did not extend to his work on Weber.

While typing this letter, Gerth was interrupted by news of President Roosevelt's death. The death of FDR, "just five yards before the goal" of the Allied military victory in Europe, turned his mind from what now seemed a contemptible quarrel over credit for a job of translating and editing to more somber reflections on the conduct of American foreign policy, the future of world politics, and the tragedy of political leadership at the highest level. At least for the moment, he was able to put his dispute with Mills in a more sensible perspective: "Listen, what a world and what quibbling worries *we* 'fight over'—."[25]

Mills's answer to Gerth included no reflections on FDR, the fate of great leaders, or *Weltpolitik*. Passing over in silence Gerth's more conciliatory gestures and the generous tone of some of his remarks, he responded instead to Gerth's reading of the history of the Weber project, which he could understand only as an expression of Gerth's arrogance. Although he had been liberal in acknowledging what he had learned from Gerth, this admission did not exclude the possibility that Gerth had also profited from their dialogues. Mills was crushed by Gerth's claim that their exchanges had taught him nothing about Weber. Nonetheless, he believed it finally gave him a true picture of the value Gerth placed on their relationship and his genuine estimate of the merits of their respective efforts, an assessment that contradicted his repeated affirmations of the equal status of their labors. For the first time Mills saw himself from Gerth's perspective: as a mere sounding board, occasionally useful when the encyclopedic thinker needed help in clarifying his ideas.

Gerth's letter of April 12, 1945, opened Mills's eyes to a joyless truth. The precedence dispute disclosed a more profound disagreement, exposing two radically opposed visions of their partnership and personal relations. In Mills's view, their differences could not be resolved at a distance, an idea to which he ascribed considerable importance. The critical distance was not the mileage between Madison and Maryland or New York but the manner in which Gerth had distanced himself from Mills. Mills saw distancing as a destructive mode of intellectuality for which Gerth had an unfortunate propensity. Creating distance between himself and reality by a process of abstraction and fictionalization, he produced a distorted picture of reality. The abstract conception of Mills and his conduct that Gerth had constructed was hopelessly remote from the man himself. The actual Mills, whom Gerth had erased from his life, was replaced by an imaginary person —deceitful, manipulative, and malevolent. Exaggerating his misconceptions, Gerth drove them to extremes, producing an even greater distance between his idea of Mills and the real man. As a result, his perceptions were desperately at odds with the facts, as demonstrated by his suspicions that Mills had deceived him and lied to Hatcher about their roles in the Weber project. His fabrications were also morally pernicious, for neither collaboration nor friendship was possible in a relationship transacted, in this special Millsean sense, at a distance. Mills believed that Gerth's excesses could have been checked had the partners followed his own principle of complete frankness and the candid discussion of differences. Gerth's preference for indirection, however, and his habit of secretly harboring imagined affronts until they overwhelmed him made this impossible.

On Mills's interpretation, Gerth's indulgence in fictionalized abstractions was a manifestation of his arrogance. Because he believed he had made Mills, Gerth dismissed as unthinkable the possibility that Mills might be capable of developing an independent analysis of Weber's work and arriving at his own conclusions in social theory. The sociologist called "C. Wright Mills" was a product of Gerth's lectures and monologues. This conceit explained his contempt for Mills's understanding of German social science and philosophy and his unwillingness to acknowledge Mills's contributions to the Weber project. This was too much for Mills, who concluded that further discussion of Gerth's draft of the preface would prove futile. Instead of proposing revisions, he sent Gerth an alternative draft backed up by an ultimatum. Mills's draft was based on a simple premise: since both their names would appear on the title page, they were both responsible for the book as a whole. Although his version of the critical sentences on credit distinguished the primary responsibilities of each author, it represented the book as their "mutual work." This meant that the actual execution of the project and the division of labor on which it was based, the paramount considerations in Gerth's draft, were immaterial. The order of their names on the title page would give Gerth the priority on which he insisted. Gerth's status as the senior partner in the project was stressed by designating him senior translator, a title that was not without its uses for Mills since it implied that there was also a junior translator: Mills. The distinction between junior and senior translators suggested that Mills, like Gerth, had read the original texts of Weber's writings and collaborated on their rendition in English.

If Mills's draft of the preface did not satisfy Gerth, what alternatives remained? Mills saw only one: a reconsideration of the format of the title page and the entire question of priority for the book. This would require new negotiations with Oxford, deliberations on which Gerth could expect no assistance from him. If Gerth remained unhappy with any new agreement he might reach with Oxford, Mills would withdraw the book from Oxford's autumn list and refuse to allow its publication rather than publicize a "cheap squabble" over who should receive credit for what.

Mills's ultimatum, which reduced Gerth's options to the choice between an endorsement of his draft and a renegotiation of the contract, placed Gerth in a decidedly disadvantageous position. Mills had handled all their business with Oxford. New discussions occasioned by a conflict of interest between the partners would require Gerth to confront Hatcher for the first time: the gentleman whom he did not know, the editor with whom Mills had established a working relationship and who had settled the February dispute by supporting Mills and humiliating Gerth. This prospect posed a challenge Gerth could not be expected to accept. It was even less likely that he would be willing to pay the price Mills threatened to exact should he move the credit dispute from the author-publisher relationship into a more public realm. Unlike Mills, Gerth had devoted virtually all his research efforts of the previous four years to the Weber project and had produced no independent publications during this period. Moreover, it would not be unreasonable for Gerth to see Mills, a recent recipient of a Guggenheim Fellowship, as a rising star in sociology, eclipsing the powerless and largely unknown émigré. Mills's job at the Bureau of Applied Social Research, although not secure, seemed much safer than his fragile year-to-year contract at Madison. He apparently believed that if the Weber book were not published in 1945, any hope for a renewal of his appointment would be dashed. The book was the "one straw" to which he was clinging. Without it, he might not survive in academia.[26]

Gerth capitulated on April 17. The book was published as the "mutual work" of the partners for which they were "jointly responsible," the principle on which Mills had insisted from the beginning.[27] Here the precedence dispute rested, at least for the present. On June 21, 1946, *From Max Weber: Essays in Sociology* finally appeared. The title page concealed a long and bitter struggle: "translated, edited, and with an introduction by H. H. Gerth and C. Wright Mills."[28] Although a limited cease-fire was declared in the spring of 1945, the dispute over credit continued for years. Thereafter, the relations between Gerth and Mills resembled the Thirty Years' War: a permanent state of hostility suspended by interludes of uneasy peace and punctuated by incidents of virtually uncontrolled destructiveness. Even the death of both principals did not end it. The advocates and adversaries of Gerth and Mills survived them and perpetuated their quarrels, not only as a way of representing the putative claims of the deceased antagonists and settling old scores, but also as a means of fighting new battles. Especially after the death of Mills, his status as a hero of the New Left transformed the dispute. For the political romantics of the 1960s, its implications for a judgment on Mills transcended questions of fact and intellectual ethics, assuming a larger historical significance due to Mills's standing as a prophet of "the movement." For the New Left, the dispute became a struggle for the legitimation of a new academic politics and social science.[29]

• 3 •

Credit, Contracts, and the Ethics of Publishing: *Character and Social Structure*

The Origins of *Character and Social Structure*

In 1941, during his second year at the University of Wisconsin, Mills sent a memorandum to Howard Becker from Gerth and himself on the subject of "sociological psychology." At least from the standpoint of Mills's curriculum vitae, Becker was his most important professor. In two years at Madison he had taken a course with Becker each semester, including four during his first year. Becker was also Mills's dissertation supervisor, Gerth's senior colleague, and the editor of D. C. Heath's series of textbooks in sociology and social psychology. In 1935 Becker had been a lecturer in sociology at Harvard, following which the Harvard sociology department recommended him for an assistant professorship and a three-year contract. Although his reputation had perhaps diminished since the mid-1930s, when Talcott Parsons regarded him as a competitor in the enterprise of importing German sociology into the United States, he remained a powerful figure.[1] In the memorandum Gerth and Mills proposed to write a "socially and historically relevant" textbook in psychology. They did not envision an abstract account of the mechanisms of personality development, then the fodder of conventional social psychology texts. Instead their book would construct typologies of personalities and careers and tie specific personality and career types to the institutional and historical conditions for their formation and selection. This memorandum was the genesis of *Character and Social Structure*.[2] Like the story of the Weber book, the twelve-year compositional history of *Character and Social Structure* was marked by disputes over credit as well as difficulties with publishers and colleagues.

Two years later, when Mills was teaching at the University of Maryland and he and Gerth had a contract for the book with Heath, he mailed Becker a preliminary table of contents and a preface. At the same time he sent Gerth a memo outlining in some detail a division of labor for the first draft. At this point the book was conceived as a thirty-four-chapter *magnum opus monstratum*. Before leaving Madison Mills had organized Gerth's files of lecture notes so that they corresponded to the book's thirty-four chapters, arranging the notes in separate chapter folders and filing the entire apparatus in a cabinet in Gerth's office. He assigned sixteen chapters to Gerth and eighteen to himself, distributing the drafting so that Gerth would be able to write chapters for which he had lecture notes. The plan required each partner to write his assigned chapters and send them to the other for revisions, so that the entire draft would be worked over by both. Even at this stage Mills was concerned about Gerth's ability to adhere to a schedule and meet deadlines. If Gerth had difficulties with a particular chapter, Mills suggested, he could send an outline with notes and a bibliography, and Mills would attempt to draft the chapter on the basis of these materials.[3]

Although *Character and Social Structure* had been promised to Heath, Gerth and Mills had been paid no advance. By the summer of 1944 Mills was attempting to sell the unwritten work to Prentice Hall, an effort that gained the support of Herbert Blumer, who served as an advisory editor for the Prentice Hall series in sociology. Over lunch with Prentice Hall editors, Mills was offered an advance of $500 without even an outline of a manuscript. At the beginning of the project, when Gerth had expressed doubts about their ability to find a publisher, Mills had maintained there would be no difficulties. The Prentice Hall offer confirmed his confidence and convinced him that they should not have given the book to Heath without demanding a generous advance. Because of what he had begun to call their "tentative contract" with Heath, he could not encourage Prentice Hall, at least not yet — and, of course, $500 would hardly be sufficient. The larger the advance, Mills instructed Gerth, the more the publisher would spend promoting the book. If he were writing the book independently, he would simply dissolve the contract with Heath, or so he claimed. Because of Gerth's insecure appointment at Madison and Becker's power to decide his future, however, they could not afford to leave Heath and embarrass Becker. "Or can we?" Mills asked, making an initial probe and introducing the idea of breaking the contract. In posing what seemed to be a rhetorical question and reinterpreting their contract with Heath as a tentative agreement, he began Gerth's education in American academic publishing. His first lesson was to teach Gerth to regard a contract as a commercial opportunity rather than a solemn promise. If Gerth, under Mills's tutelage, came to understand a contract as nothing more than a shifting relationship of power, he could be persuaded to treat the agreement with Heath as an instrument of convenience rather than a firm commitment. In that event, he might be willing to abandon Heath to pursue more lucrative offers from other publishers.[4]

By July 1944 Becker was pressing Gerth for drafts of chapters to show Heath. Mills resisted, suggesting instead they follow a rule that would give them substantially more autonomy than Becker was disposed to allow: no manuscripts would be submitted until they were both satisfied the material was ready for publication. In addition, he asked, why accede to Becker's demands when an advance was available from another publisher? Mills's position amounted to a repudiation of Becker's editorial authority. He had been on unhappy terms with Becker since December 1940, when Becker presented a paper on George Lundberg's conception of sociological method at the Christmas meetings of the American Sociological Society. Mills was convinced that this paper constituted an unauthorized use of an essay he had written on Lundberg. "I don't have to 'prove myself' to that son of a bitch with ms. nor do you," he wrote Gerth. If Becker rejected their terms, this would create opportunities rather than difficulties. Mills believed there was an abundant supply of publishers eager to acquire their book and pay handsome advances: editors who "talk with money rather than constant requests for mansc."[5]

Although Mills was willing to leave the final decision on Becker's request to Gerth, he devised a strategy that would enable them to withdraw from the Heath contract and accept the Prentice Hall offer. This was the trade of the social psychology text for the Weber book, which was motivated by Mills's fears that Oxford might embrace Shils and Mannheim, leaving the partners without a publisher for their translations. In view of Prentice Hall's enthusiasm for *Character and Social Structure,* the key to this plan was the cancellation of the Heath contract. Mills would ask Heath for an advance of $500, claiming that another house was prepared to meet that demand. Heath would refuse to pay, and he and Gerth would be free to move to Prentice Hall. In a singular misjudgment, he assured Gerth that Prentice Hall would assist the partners in gaining a release from Heath and that Becker could be counted on to pose no obstacles. As a result, Gerth should feel free to inform his department chair that he would shortly have contracts for two books: "You can tell Mac [McCormick] the deal about the trade: translations for text." Because of his animus against Becker and regardless of financial considerations, Mills found this solution a more appealing way to dispose of *Character and Social Structure:* "Personally, of course, I abhor the very idea of having that dirty son of a bitch's name on any book that bears my own."[6]

The Cleveland Protocol

With the question of the Heath contract still unresolved and the quarrels over credit for the Weber book only recently behind them, Gerth and Mills met in March 1946 at a conference of the American Sociological Society in Cleveland to consider how they might resume work on *Character and Social Structure* in spite of the bitter dispute of the previous year. More than 300 pages had been written, most of the material apparently drafted by Mills on the basis of Gerth's notes. Under what conditions would further collaboration be possible? After this meeting Mills was under the impression that they had arrived at a modus vivendi for future work. On March 13 he wrote Gerth a long letter summarizing their conversations and outlining an agreement. This was the Cleveland protocol, the substance of which Mills reduced to four main points.

1. *The contract.* The collaboration would continue, but not on the basis of the contract with Heath. Although the task of terminating the agreement would be left to Gerth, Mills did not waste an opportunity to advise Gerth on tactics. Canceling a contract, he maintained, was a simple matter, a generalization that the contractual history of *Character and Social Structure* would not confirm. Gerth could write Heath and state his preferences. Since the partners had received no advance, they could not be held to the agreement. Once the old contract was dissolved, Mills would negotiate another, perhaps with Oxford if Gerth was willing, with a $500 to $600 advance. He also had hopes for a more generous offer from Knopf. The choice of a publisher could be made later. The first move was Gerth's.

2. *Credit.* Unlike the Weber book, *Character and Social Structure* would make no distinctions of priority. There would be no senior author or principal investigator, and credit would be divided equally. To avoid disagreements over precedence, Mills drafted a short statement on joint and

equal responsibility, which he suggested they place at the beginning of the preface:

> This book is in every sense a collaboration. The order of our names is merely alphabetical. The work as a whole was thoroughly discussed between the two authors over a period of several years. Each of us then took common drafts of notes made during these discussions and assumed responsibility for first drafts of about half the chapters. We have exchanged criticisms and have re-written one another's material to such extent that we are equally and jointly responsible for the entirety of the book as it is now presented.[7]

3. *A division of labor.* The manuscript would comprise not more than 600 pages divided into twenty-five or twenty-six chapters, reduced from the thirty-four originally proposed to Becker. Mills had already drafted roughly 300 pages, based on what he called "common notes." Gerth's task was to write 250 to 300 pages from "the notes we have made" and other manuscripts he might have and send them to Mills, who would edit Gerth's drafts and revise his own 300 pages.

4. *A schedule.* The manuscript would be completed by June 1947 and published by early 1948.

Although Mills trusted that his summary accurately reflected their talks in Cleveland, he invited Gerth's emendations so that their joint commit-ment to an agreement governing the division of labor and the distribution of credit would be unequivocal.

The Cleveland protocol obscured certain facts about the project's his-tory that would undermine a case for equal allocation of credit. In particu-lar, Mills's statement on joint credit concealed an important ambiguity. Because the partners would engage in mutual criticism and each would rewrite the other's material, he inferred that both had an equal claim to credit for the entire manuscript. This inference is difficult to sustain in view of the provenance of the "notes" used to write the original drafts. They were drawn from the voluminous and detailed lecture notes Gerth used in his courses at Madison and the mimeographed outlines and analy-ses he distributed to his graduate students. These were the materials in Gerth's office that Mills had collected in folders with headings correspond-ing to the planned chapters of *Character and Social Structure.* Gerth shared his files fully with Mills during the work on the book, and much of this material is now housed with the Mills Papers, at the University of Texas. Mills characterized these notes as a product of discussions between the partners. In fact, they were the basis of these discussions.

Mills's claim to credit for the Weber book rested on ambiguities concerning what constituted translation and how the introduction was written. Now he wanted Gerth to accept a principle of equal credit for equal work, a rule that would not have served his interests in the earlier book. His circumstances in this project were different, and his case for equal credit reflected these differences. First he redescribed Gerth's original analyses and lecture notes as common property for which neither partner could claim priority. Then he stipulated that they both contribute roughly the same amount of first-draft manuscript. This division of labor seemed to justify, and perhaps even require, the principle of equal credit for equal work.

Mills regarded the Cleveland protocol as a contract, a formalization of terms to which both authors would subscribe, and he expected Gerth to add his amendments and endorse the agreement. Because they had both opposing and common interests, collaboration, at least at this point, consisted in agreeing to a document that enumerated their rights and responsibilities. The rhetoric of his earlier conception of collaboration—two authors dealing frankly and honestly with one another—was still in place, but it was reinterpreted in a quasi-legal and commercial fashion. Now Mills was a negotiator attempting to sell Gerth on a certain distribution of responsibility and credit. If he was successful, Gerth would accept his proposition, effectively signing the contract and buying his proposal.

In view of Mills's appeals to the intimacy of their relationship and his repeated declarations that their partnership was based on friendship and affection,[8] the formalistic and implicitly adversarial style of the Cleveland protocol seems peculiar. Friendship is grounded not in contracts, negotiations, and the maximization of self-interest but in trust, sensitivity, and a readiness to sacrifice personal interests for the sake of the friend and the friendship. The Cleveland protocol hardly qualifies as an expression of these virtues. Mills's somewhat relaxed conception of contracts, expressed in his reflections on how the partners might escape their commitment to Heath, is also striking. He regarded a contract not as a promise he was obligated to honor but as an opportunity he might pursue or ignore, depending on current contingencies and their bearing on his interests. This position hardly served his purpose in convincing Gerth to accept the Cleveland protocol. What confidence could Gerth place in a contract with Mills? If Mills understood the Cleveland protocol as nothing more than an instrument of convenience, it is not clear why Gerth should have agreed to it.

"A Difference Which Makes No Difference"

In fact, Mills's efforts in pressing Gerth to endorse the Cleveland protocol were not successful. On March 25 Mills wrote that he had not yet received Gerth's answer to "our agreement."[9] When Gerth finally answered, almost two months after Mills's original proposal, his reply did not take the form dictated by Mills's request: either a ratification of the agreement or negotiations that would end in a ratification. Gerth's response was evasive and, on some points, opaque. He suggested that they forget their respective proposals, apparently also forgetting he had made none, and leave matters as they stood. But exactly how did the collaboration stand? What agreement had been made? On these questions, which Mills regarded as crucial to the future of their joint work, Gerth was silent. He seemed to assume that the collaboration had been suspended, or perhaps that his response suspended it. In either case, work on *Character and Social Structure* had reached a dead end. "Hence," Gerth concluded, "let's forget about my proposals and about your proposals and leave things as they are or where originally agreed upon. If you should be interested at some time in the future to resume interest and work let me know."[10]

Mills was confused by Gerth's reply and his resistance to a clarification of their relations. It was Gerth, he recalled, who had resurrected *Character and Social Structure* in Cleveland by raising the question of what to do with the material they had assembled for the project. Mills claimed he had done no more than summarize the results of their discussion on this matter. If so, why was Gerth reluctant to commit himself? As Mills saw things, he had begun from the premise of the "common notes," to which neither partner had a privileged claim. On this assumption he had written half the book and Gerth had done nothing. Or was there some aspect of their joint and several responsibilities he had failed to grasp? He was especially befuddled by Gerth's insistence that matters be left as they stood. "Where is that?" he asked. Because of these uncertainties, he reiterated his position that an explicit agreement on the terms of the collaboration was needed. If Gerth was dissatisfied with Mills's proposal, he should revise it or suggest an alternative. Their quarrels over the Weber book had convinced Mills that some formal statement on the distribution of responsibilities and credit was indispensable.[11]

In spite of Mills's persistence, Gerth remained obstinate. He would not agree to Mills's terms, nor would he enter negotiations on the grounds Mills had chosen. Instead he avoided both conflict and commitment by means of passive resistance and obfuscation. On August 27 he answered Mills's most recent appeal in a manner that seemed willfully obtuse. In reconstructing the six-month history of their dance around this issue, he maintained that in Cleveland he had agreed to what he thought Mills wanted, but only so as to win Mills's consent to resume the collaboration and return to work on *Character and Social Structure,* confirming Mills's assertion that the initiative to revive the project in spite of the quarrels over the Weber book was Gerth's. Nevertheless, he found that Mills's résumé of their conversations departed so radically from what had actually been said and was so obviously inconsistent with their mutual interests that he had decided to "forget it." He summed up his position thus: "Forget the Cleveland talk and your proposals and we are where we were." He still said nothing, however, about where this was. Were they working together, or was Mills on his own? And if they were collaborating, how should they proceed? Gerth did not take up these questions. Instead he adopted the surprising position that the Cleveland protocol was unnecessary because they already had an agreement, which was implicit in some of Mills's "old letters." He could cobble together excerpts from these letters and send them to Mills. But to what end? Presumably Mills had his own copies of this correspondence. "So why carry coal to Newcastle?" he asked, as if announcing a truth whose self-evidence was transparent.[12]

Gerth's August 27 reply to Mills's plea for clarification of their situation is a baffling document. Did he and Mills have an agreement or did they not? On the one hand, his rejection of the Cleveland protocol seemed to say that they did not. On the other hand, he also seemed to say that an agreement had been made, at least by implication, in Mills's "old letters," which presumably did not include the Cleveland protocol letter of March 13. He did not identify these letters, however, or the agreement they allegedly contained. For the rest, he declared there was nothing to fight about. He would not accept Mills's "new agreement," nor would he offer an alternative. He offered the following explanation for this position: "For the new agreement which you want to have—well, I just don't like your 'conditions' and I have none to make to you as a difference which makes no difference is no difference." As if this were not sufficient to leave Mills bewildered, Gerth added that he would shortly send drafts for *Character and Social Structure,* indicating his readiness to forge ahead with the project, on what terms he did not say.[13]

Here the question of responsibility and credit for *Character and Social Structure* would remain, at least for the time. This, in any case, was the conclusion Mills reached. Unable to understand Gerth's view of the project's status and confused by his sibylline reasoning, Mills made the inevitable inference that Gerth was not interested in clearing up these matters. Gerth had decided to suspend discussion on the issues Mills regarded as of paramount importance but still proceed with the book, even though the terms under which work would be done remained undefined. In view of the labors Mills had already invested in *Character and Social Structure,* he was not prepared to jeopardize the project by repeating the threat that had worked so well in the battle over credit for the Weber book: it would be published on his terms or not at all. Instead he conceded this round to Gerth. The partnership and work on a first draft would continue, leaving the outstanding problems of a division of labor and the allocation of credit unresolved.[14]

Selling *Character and Social Structure:* Contractual Confusions and Legal Borderlines

Over the next two years no work was done on *Character and Social Structure.* Mills wrote *The New Men of Power,* his study of labor leaders in industrial unions, and continued his investigation of white-collar workers. He remained in touch with Gerth on both projects, seeking editorial advice and criticism. Gerth responded with a multitude of ideas and suggestions, as if he were sustaining the teacher-assistant relationship. Mills also did his obligatory bread-and-butter survey research at the Bureau of Applied Social Research under Paul Lazarsfeld.[15] Gerth edited a manuscript by Karl Mannheim after his death, compiled a comprehensive bibliography on Max Weber, and tried to interest Mills in further collaboration on Weber. Mills's brief career in Weber studies was over, however.[16] He had his own books to write and was doing so independently. It is not clear that the same could be said for Gerth. Perhaps for these reasons—his difficulties in publishing independently and his inability to win Mills for another Weber project—he made another attempt to revive *Character and Social Structure* in November 1948.

Mills was receptive. *The New Men of Power* had just been published, his work on *White Collar,* he thought, should be completed by the following summer, and he was reducing his obligations at the bureau. Plunging back into the project, he began to set priorities and organize tasks. The contractual matter should be settled first. He asked whether Gerth could arrange cancellation of their agreement with Heath. If so, Mills would have no difficulty negotiating a more advantageous contract with Harcourt Brace, his publisher for *The New Men of Power,* or perhaps with Oxford. He envisioned an advance of $1,000; Prentice Hall's earlier offer of $500 was no longer on his agenda. He also promised to bring his files on the project to the University of Chicago, where he had accepted a visiting appointment in the undergraduate college for the winter quarter of 1949. While he was in Chicago, they would be able to discuss further plans for the book in detail. Questions of responsibility and credit could be deferred until a satisfactory contract had been negotiated.[17]

On January 13, 1949, shortly before his departure for Chicago, Mills had lunch with James M. Reid, the trade editor for textbooks in the social sciences at Harcourt Brace. The two discussed *Character and Social Structure,* as Reid put it, "up and down, sidewise, and forward." The same afternoon Reid sent a résumé of this discussion to his editorial advisers in social psychology: Ernest R. Hilgard, a psychologist at Stanford, and Robert K. Merton, Mills's colleague at Columbia. Mills had given Reid a preface, now two years old, that sketched the main lines of the book "he" proposed to do, a table of contents, and chapter outlines. Reid's summary described *Character and Social Structure* as Mills's project: Mills was the architect of the enterprise and the principal author of the manuscript to be. Gerth was mentioned only as a possible contributor, someone Mills was considering as a coauthor. From his conversation with Mills, Reid inferred that although Gerth might be a brilliant thinker, his role in the book would be "peripheral." Mills was "the real producer," and little work could be expected from Gerth until Mills wrote a first draft.[18]

Reid's summary misconstrued the relations between the partners, Gerth's role in the project, and the intellectual provenance of the book. Who was responsible for these misconceptions? There seem to be two possibilities, which are not mutually exclusive: Mills misrepresented the project to Reid, or Reid misunderstood Mills. Consistent with his obligations as editor, Reid took the latter possibility into account, writing Mills the following day to return the preface and the table of contents and enclosing a copy of his letter to Hilgard and Merton, with the request that Mills correct any inaccuracies.[19] No response from Mills has been found in either the Nobuko Gerth Collection or the Mills Papers, nor do these collections include any record that Mills sent Gerth copies of either Reid's résumé or his request for corrections.

Reid's conception of *Character and Social Structure* was based on his perspective as a marketer of college textbooks. He hoped the book would make the next major move in social psychology by synthesizing the most advanced thinking in both sociology and psychology. If Mills succeeded in producing a book designed for introductory and intermediate-level college courses, he might be able to compete with the more successful social psychology texts of the time and perhaps dominate the market. Although Reid found Mills's ideas to be "forward looking" and perhaps even "revolutionary," they lacked the marketing orientation needed to produce a best-seller. Most important, Mills's outline did not follow the standard format of texts in social psychology published by Harcourt Brace's competitors, such as Krech and Crutchfield's *Theories and Principles of Social Psychology* (McGraw-Hill), Newcomb and Hartley's *Readings in Social Psychology* or Otto Klineberg's *Social Psychology* (Holt), and Sherif's *Outline of Social Psychology* (Harper). To repair this deficiency, Reid suggested an additional collaborator, a psychologist.

Would Mills—and, Reid added, Gerth as well—make the adjustments needed to transform the outline into a commercially successful textbook? In Mills Reid believed he had found his man. Mills was flexible. He saw the importance of writing the book with a psychologist—the right psychologist, of course; Mills "did not respond favorably" to Reid's suggestion of Jerome Bruner, then a junior professor at Harvard. He also needed the money and wanted a best-seller. Reid was excited by the possibilities the book presented and asked his advisers Hilgard and Merton to think carefully about how to make the final product sell. Mills would expect a decision, and probably a substantial advance, by the beginning of March.[20] Nonetheless, Reid's enthusiasm was not based solely on the prospects for *Character and Social Structure* in the textbook market. In the covering letter that accompanied his résumé, he assured Mills that although Harcourt Brace hoped the manuscript would target this larger market and be written with a psychologist, he promised to publish the book as it was currently conceived: as a collaboration between Gerth and Mills intended for a more limited readership. In his view, the book was "an exciting project and an important one" for both of the authors and the publisher. Although he would rely on Mills to keep him informed about Gerth's views, he offered to travel to Madison to ensure Gerth's participation and the acquisition of the book by Harcourt Brace.[21]

Mills made sure that no contacts between Reid and Gerth would be necessary. He would handle relations with Harcourt Brace in much the same way he had dealt with Oxford. In drafting a formal proposal to Reid ("my guy at Harcourt Brace") for Gerth's approval, he attempted to set out, as he put it, "all the selling elements I can think of!"[22] His promotional strategy was designed to secure both a contract and a release from teaching obligations for himself and Gerth at Harcourt Brace's expense. Although he rejected the idea of recruiting a psychologist as a third coauthor, he emphasized that the book would cover the same range of topics discussed in major social psychology texts, albeit from a different standpoint. Thus he and Gerth would still be able to compete in the market for social psychology textbooks that Reid hoped to enter. Mills also promised a book conceived on a level appropriate to undergraduate courses and written in language unmarred by inflated and mind-numbing technical jargon. Even though the book would attack the problems of social psychology from a new perspective, it would not pose undue difficulties for the reader.

Although the partners had not decided on a schedule, Mills suggested a timetable that would produce a manuscript by the end of 1950. Gerth and Mills would draft chapters during the academic year 1949–50 and work together the following summer. By taking leaves of absence during the autumn semester of 1950 and continuing to work together at Mills's cabin in Ontario, they would finish the manuscript by the end of the calendar year. But how could leaves of absence for both authors be arranged? "This is where you come in," Mills advised Reid. To complete the manuscript according to Mills's plan, he and Gerth needed to work together for five or six months, an arrangement that would require one-semester leaves of absence without pay. An advance from Harcourt Brace was needed to cover their living expenses. Would Reid finance these leaves? Anticipating resistance, Mills cajoled, persuaded, and politely threatened. Playing hard to get, he maintained that *Character and Social Structure* was not the only item on his agenda. There were various pieces of research he might take up in the autumn of 1949, each, he vaguely suggested, involving "research funds." If he devoted his time to research instead of writing a book for Harcourt Brace, he would not need to teach in the autumn. As he put it: "There is money for research; is there money for writing this book?" In the draft of this proposal sent to Gerth, he maintained that "one (or preferably both)" partners would need leaves to complete the manuscript in 1950. In the final draft to Reid, his position on the importance of dual leaves of absence was stated more unequivocally: "In order for us to do such a book under optimum conditions, we have to be together for a stretch of time, at least five or six months. In order to be together, we have to take leaves without pay."[23]

Reid would "greatly aid" Mills in arriving at a decision by informing him of the maximum advance Harcourt Brace was prepared to offer. He followed this polite request with a warning: if Harcourt Brace proved unwilling to meet his demands, he would take the book elsewhere. Mills took a position, threatened to exit if his terms were not met, and then took the edge off the threat with a witticism. Conceding that the project entailed obvious risks for Reid, he then asked, "But what fun would you ever have if you didn't have to gamble now and then?" [24]

In the expectation that Harcourt Brace would offer an acceptable advance, Mills asked Gerth for a progress report on the cancellation of the Heath agreement and advised him to proceed with discretion. Since Mills was preparing to sign a contract with another publisher for a book already under contract to Heath, it was important "not to be too explicit with Becker about what's up." [25] By late February there were apparently "big confabs between the boys" at Harcourt Brace. What did this mean? The answer was clear to Mills and worth spelling out to Gerth in uppercase letters: "GET ON THE HEATH DEAL AND GET IT FIXED UP AS SOON AS YOU CAN." [26] In 1944 cancellation of the contract with Heath had been barely conceivable. Because of the risks it would have entailed for Gerth at Madison, Mills raised it only as a tentative question. Some five years later a rhetorical possibility had become a necessity. Now Mills was intent on realizing his new plans for *Character and Social Structure* regardless of the difficulties they might pose for Gerth.

Mills's sales pitch to Reid, with its suggestion that he would find life more interesting if he took some risks on Mills's behalf, seemed to work. On March 8 Reid informed Mills that Harcourt Brace would meet most of his terms. Most important, Reid's offer included a $2,000 advance, the largest sum Harcourt Brace had offered on a textbook contract. Mills had broken a historic barrier in a venerable publishing house, where advances had been paid less as an economic incentive than as a mark of good faith and a demonstration of the publisher's commitment to a book. In the rapidly expanding textbook market of the post–World War II university, competition among publishers for successful texts and authors passed an important threshold. Under the G.I. Bill of Rights, which provided servicemen with scholarships to further their education, a veteran qualified for as many months of higher education as he had served in the armed forces; twelve months of service was the equivalent of three semesters. Scholarships covered tuition and included a monthly living subsidy and a book allowance. After the war returning servicemen dramatically increased the size of student bodies and created a demand for large lecture courses. Textbook vouchers and the new demographics of the student population

changed academic publishing by increasing the demand for undergraduate textbooks. These new conditions also changed the traditionally genteel
relations among publishers and authors, which presupposed a modest and
stable demand for texts. The postwar market provided the basis for a more
commercial relationship, encouraging authors to bargain for advantages
and concessions.

Would the Harcourt Brace advance satisfy Mills's financial requirements
and meet his request to support two leaves of absence? Reid, realizing that
it probably would not, addressed some of the objections he expected Mills
to raise. Gerth and Mills should be satisfied with four months of work
together in the summer of 1950. Completion of the manuscript by the end
of 1950 was not a major consideration. If the authors needed an additional
seven or eight months, they should work through the academic year 1950–
51 and submit the manuscript in the summer of 1951. This would enable
Harcourt Brace to publish the book by January 1952, the beginning of
the spring semester. The compressed timetable in Mills's plan would entail needless expense and a sacrifice in quality. Merton and Reid believed
Character and Social Structure would become the leading text in social psychology, but only if the work was done properly.

Shortly after he received Reid's offer, Mills sent Gerth his assessment:
"There is a lot of bullshit in this letter but there is one important item: they
are prepared to give a total of $2,000 advance." Mills was not impressed.
What did the advance really mean? Gerth would be relieved from a single
summer session at Madison, and Mills, who claimed he needed to earn an
extra $2,000 each year above his Columbia salary to stay afloat financially,
would be secure for six months. Since Oxford had advanced Mills $2,000
for *White Collar,* a book that was expected to sell no more than four or
five thousand copies, he had set his hopes higher. If Gerth agreed, he was
ready to reopen negotiations with Reid during a mid-March trip to New
York. In the interest of bargaining, he suggested that Gerth defer a reply
to Reid. In New York he would try to negotiate a larger advance, an extra
$500 to $750 for typing expenses, and royalties graduated from 10 percent
to 15 percent based on sales volume, an increase over the flat 10 percent
Harcourt Brace had offered. He realized that his bargaining position was
weak, however. Merton, who was familiar with his finances, knew that the
advance, although not princely, was more than he could afford to refuse.[27]

Because of the imminence of a deal with Harcourt Brace, Mills was
concerned about the Heath contract: "They *could* cause us trouble," he
warned, "if some bright guy there gets wind of [a] deal with Harcourt."[28]

On March 15 he wired Gerth from New York that he and Reid had agreed to an advance of $3,000 with royalties of 18 percent based on the net wholesale receipts of sales. Now an immediate termination of the agreement with Heath was critical. Otherwise, Gerth and Mills might find themselves committed to two contracts, an encumbrance that could damage their reputations.[29]

On April 4 Reid mailed Mills three copies of the contract, which he signed and sent on to Gerth with a note and a copy of a letter he had written Reid. The contract listed Mills's name before Gerth's. In the letter Mills repeated a point he had made in previous correspondence with Reid and had emphasized in their recent meeting in New York: since he and Gerth had not yet settled the question of precedence, Harcourt Brace should make no assumptions about the order of their names on the title page of the book. In Mills's view, priority should be decided on the basis of the work done by the authors after the contract was signed, a criterion for the allocation of credit at odds with his earlier insistence in the Cleveland protocol that he receive credit for the 300 pages he claimed to have written before March 1946, a draft that predated the Harcourt Brace contract by three years. He closed his letter to Reid by noting that the contract would be signed shortly, thereby promising Gerth's agreement.[30]

Would Gerth sign? Mills's note to Gerth urged him to take this course, even though it was, at least for the interim, illegal, or as Mills put it, "somewhat so": "The Heath contract says we got to give it to them and this contract says the ms is owed to nobody but Harcourt. But it's a thing we've just got to gamble on, I suppose."[31] Mills, who had playfully invited Reid to gamble on *Character and Social Structure,* was ready to risk a more serious gamble of his own and implicate Gerth as well, urging Gerth to sign a contract he believed to be fraudulent and even suggesting that Gerth draw his half of the advance immediately to make a payment on a house. The interpersonal, intercollegial, and legal dimensions of the negotiations over *Character and Social Structure* had become quite complex and included the personal economic pressures faced by both authors. In addition, Mills, the self-confident manager of human relations, was in the uncomfortable position of depending on Gerth to void their agreement with Heath. In his advice to Gerth, he repeatedly stressed the importance of maintaining absolute secrecy about the Harcourt Brace arrangement until Heath had issued a formal release. Although Becker seems to have been his main worry, Mills was of two minds about the damage Becker could inflict. In spite of Becker's malice, it was unlikely he could do any actual harm; after all, Mills knew how to "pressure Heath til they yell like mad." He doubted that Becker understood this, however. Thus if Becker discovered the Harcourt Brace contract, the partners might be dangerously exposed.[32]

By mid-March Gerth had a clearer picture of the problems Becker posed for a nullification of the Heath agreement. Before Christmas 1948 Becker had taken the initiative on the Heath matter and offered to intervene on Gerth's behalf by proposing a cancellation of the contract to John Walden, Heath's editor for textbooks in the social sciences. Months passed, and this letter had not been written. When Becker finally summoned Gerth to his office and questioned him about the status of the project, Gerth asked him to write the letter he had originally suggested. Although Becker complied, Gerth noticed that, as he put it in his creative English diction, Becker was "somewhat discomfortable" and "frictitious." What was responsible for Becker's fractious tone? Why did he seem "discomfortable"? The answers to these questions lay in Becker's own contractual history with Heath, which was disclosed to Gerth by Don Martindale, by that point a member of the sociology faculty at the University of Minnesota. Becker's relationship with Heath was more complex than Gerth and Mills had realized and posed problems they had not anticipated.

At about the same time that Gerth and Mills published *From Max Weber,* Becker and Martindale brought out a two-volume photomechanically reproduced textbook on sociology. Although Becker and Martindale had each written one volume, they both received credit for the text as a whole. Gerth described the book as a chatty and engaging popularization of Weber "with much poetry." In his view Becker had not been altogether forthright about the sources of the book's ideas, which was why he did not publish it after *From Max Weber* appeared. Instead he sold it directly to the students in his large introductory sociology courses and reserved the right to publish the text later by securing a contract with Heath. Between 1947 and 1949, however, he changed his plans and decided to write his own sociology text, delegating to Martindale the task of canceling their contract. In his capacity as advisory editor, he would then propose that Heath offer Martindale a new contract for a casebook. Martindale's book would either complement his text, serve as a companion volume, or perhaps become volume 2 to his first volume. Gerth interpreted this change of course as an attempt by Becker to retain Martindale as his "sleeping partner" and ghostwriter. Shocked by such an arrangement, he advised Martindale to insist on an unconditional release from Heath before proceeding further. Martindale followed this advice, asking Walden for a release on the grounds that Becker no longer wanted him as a coauthor. Becker, unpleasantly surprised by this request, was reluctant to agree unless he could bind Martindale to the casebook or at least to a promise to wait two years after the publication of his own text before bringing out a competing work. Martindale refused to meet Becker's conditions and withdrew his volume of the Becker-Martindale project from consideration by Heath in order to publish elsewhere.

Thus Becker, who had arranged a tidy scheme for himself, seemed to be left with nothing. There would be no casebook, since Martindale refused to do it, and no textbook either, since Martindale had decided to go into business under his own name without Becker's patronage. Perhaps even worse, he faced the prospect of losing three books he had acquired for Heath: the original Becker-Martindale text, which no longer interested him; the new Becker text with Martindale's companion volume, on which Martindale refused to cooperate; and *Character and Social Structure,* for which Gerth had requested a release. Gerth believed that Becker's competence as an editor was now in doubt: "The trouble for B. is that he has to ask for a double release at about the same time, and that in turn may give Heath the idea that HB is not a good man to win and hold younger authors." The delays over the cancellation of the partners' contract, he explained to Mills, were due in part to these unanticipated collapsing agreements and their consequences for Becker's editorship at Heath. He nevertheless believed that Walden would issue a release shortly and asked Mills to be patient. His solution was to avoid "a bad and awkward situation" by delaying for a week his own signature on the Harcourt Brace contract.[33]

Mills's response to Gerth's analysis of these complexities and his plea for more time was to disregard the Becker problem. The situation called for immediate action, not caution. They had nothing to gain by further delays. Did they have anything to lose? Mills could not overlook the most obvious objection to his position: the Harcourt Brace contract was not "as legal as" it should have been because the Heath matter remained unresolved. The existence of the two contracts would become a problem only if it was revealed, however. Assuming that the partners adhered to Mills's rule of confidentiality, that could happen only if Becker refused to cooperate. Mills did not pause to consider the consequences that would follow if Becker proved recalcitrant. Instead he confidently asserted that publishers could not hold authors to terms with which they refused to comply. After all, he and Gerth could send Becker a shabby manuscript and refuse to rework it. For Mills the issue of what should be done was not a question of principle governing the relations between authors, editors, and publishers but a matter of tactics and expediency. Because he believed they had nothing to lose by accepting the Harcourt Brace offer, he pressed Gerth to sign the new contract.

Mills also suggested a change in the division of labor that had prevailed thus far: it had been Gerth's job to cancel the agreement with Heath and Mills's responsibility to find a new publisher. Because Gerth had not done his part, Mills's new contract with its $3,000 advance was in jeopardy. To achieve a swift resolution of the Heath problem, Mills proposed to ignore Becker and request a release directly from the responsible person at Heath. Although he persisted in claiming that cancellation of the Heath contract posed no risks, Gerth's position at Madison would be compromised if Becker, whom Mills intended to disregard entirely, was dissatisfied with the manner in which the contract was broken. This consideration entered Mills's calculations only in the importance he ascribed to secrecy. Above all, it was necessary to conceal the Heath contract from Harcourt Brace: "Under no conditions do I want them to know about any trouble with Heath. After all, they have been damn nice guys to us." [34]

In spite of his reservations, Gerth finally conceded. Without any word from Becker or a letter from Walden, he agreed to sign the contract without further delay on the condition that the proper order of their names in the agreement be restored: not "Mills and Gerth" but "Gerth and Mills." [35]

The Chicago Protocol

Gerth's insistence on the order of the authors' names in the Harcourt Brace contract marked the occasion for a long letter from Mills, still at the University of Chicago, which set out a new plan for the distribution of credit for *Character and Social Structure*. This was the time, he suggested, to settle the issue of precedence Gerth had reopened. Reiterating his belief in complete honesty and candor as the principle that should govern their relationship and the concomitant need for clear understandings, he argued that an agreement would formalize the terms of their further collaboration and forestall the destructive quarrels that had erupted during the Weber project. These were, of course, the views he had impressed on Gerth some three years before, with a conspicuous lack of success. To avoid the impression that he intended to bargain, Mills formulated three rules for determining priority in their work on *Character and Social Structure*. Then he used these rules to develop a plan for a division of labor and a distribution of credit. His strategy for managing the partnership had not changed since the Cleveland protocol. Like the earlier proposal, the Chicago protocol stated rules on priority and applied them to arrive at a solution to the problem of precedence.

Consistency

Mills's first rule required both partners to respect any agreement they eventually reached. Once they arrived at a consensus on credit, neither would air his complaints about the results to third parties. As Mills made clear, this principle was intended to rule out a repetition of the letters that had been sent to Columbia. There would be no further allegations that he had tricked Gerth into an unreasonable and inequitable arrangement. Because he believed that his job at Columbia was at risk, he could not tolerate additional charges of underhanded and unprofessional conduct. If Gerth could be persuaded to respect an agreement, then the cause of at least some of his troubles at Columbia—circulation of malicious gossip at Madison— would be eliminated. Mills regarded this principle as an unconditional requirement for further collaboration. If Gerth refused to make a decision on precedence and abide by it, the partnership should be dissolved. After all, they now had two contracts. Should Gerth prefer to work alone, he could publish his version of *Character and Social Structure* with Heath, and Mills would take his version to Harcourt Brace.[36]

Equivalent Status

As Mills observed, there are several modes of intellectual collaboration. In some joint projects one collaborator qualifies as the senior author, often because he has done more research and achieved a more substantial reputation. Such a project is generally the first major piece of research for the junior partner, who works at the behest and under the supervision of the senior author. In such a case precedence follows from achieved and established status. Mills argued that his work with Gerth on *Character and Social Structure* did not fall under this type of collaboration. "Now I take it this is not the case between us, for we are of quite similar status, and ours is a mutual collaboration: that means that either one of us could obviously do a good character and social structure alone; we team up on the mutual assumption that together we can turn out a better job than either of us could do alone."[37] Because neither partner was the apprentice, disciple, or subordinate of the other, Mills inferred that either was capable of writing *Character and Social Structure*. Collaboration was dictated by their complementary strengths and skills: they could produce a better joint work than either could write independently.

These assertions presupposed remarkable self-confidence on Mills's part. He had been the graduate student, inferior to Gerth in his scholarly skills and the depth and breadth of his learning. In many respects he was Gerth's principal disciple, the student who had been most successful in applying what he had learned from Gerth in his own work. Earlier he had claimed that he owed all he knew about Max Weber to Gerth. The conceptual and theoretical framework of *Character and Social Structure* was based on Gerth's reading of Weber. Did this mean that Mills's contribution to the book was also owed to Gerth? To justify his claim to equal status, it was necessary for Mills to detach the criterion for the assignment of credit from the question of the theoretical and scholarly provenance of the book. He did this by shifting the issue of credit from a question about intellectual originality to a question about investment. In framing the problem of precedence, Mills used the model of commerce. The Gerth-Mills collaboration was a business arrangement in which both authors brought certain assets to the partnership, with the expectation that they would receive a greater return than either could achieve by investing his resources in another enterprise. If their undertaking was successful, how should credit be divided? Mills's commercial model provided the answer. The amount of credit due to each should be a function of the assets he invested. In Mills's calculus the party who invested more should receive a larger share of the results. But what sorts of assets defined investment?

The chief asset Gerth brought to the enterprise was intellectual capital. *Character and Social Structure* is grounded in the anthropological problematic he found in Weber's sociology: the theme of the institutional conditions for the formation of specific types of human beings. On the Weberian premises Gerth employed, the conditions for the production and selection of types of persons are situated in institutional orders. In *Economy and Society* Weber linked specific types of persons to the social and cultural forces that shape them and analyzed these links by tracing their histories in the major world civilizations. In *Character and Social Structure* the concept of character structure replaces Weber's concept of *Menschentypus,* a type of person or human being. The analyses of politics, economics, religion, the military, kinship, class, status, power, and occupations in *Character and Social Structure* follow the corresponding analyses in *Economy and Society.* The logic of *Character and Social Structure* also reproduces the strategy Weber employed in *Economy and Society.* General definitions of social categories are followed by the construction of typologies that elaborate some of their historically important possibilities, which are then illustrated by instances of these possibilities realized in a wide range of societies and periods. From its beginnings in 1941 to the final draft in 1952, *Character and Social Structure* was conceived and written within this Weberian framework. Mills possessed no comparable intellectual assets. If intellectual capital was the investment that decided precedence, the result would be obvious: he would be identified as the junior author and Gerth's apprentice.[38]

To support a claim to equal credit, it was essential for Mills to define assets in terms that diminished the significance of intellectual capital and stressed a type of contribution on the basis of which he could compete successfully with Gerth. In what domain were Mills's assets superior to Gerth's? What did he possess that Gerth lacked? Publications. Gerth may have brought more intellectual capital to the project, but Mills brought more social capital, understood as intellectual status defined by various indices tied to publication: for example, number of publications, prestige of the publisher, and reputation of the academic appointment achieved as a result of publication.

In the eight years since *Character and Social Structure* had been proposed to Heath, Gerth's independent publications amounted to three short essays, a single book review, and a bibliography on Max Weber prepared in collaboration with his wife. During the same period Mills published eighteen essays, seven substantial review articles, twenty-seven book reviews, and an indeterminate number of unsigned reviews written for the *American Journal of Sociology* in the early 1940s. *The New Men of Power* was published by Harcourt Brace and became the basis of his connection with Reid. His essays appeared in academic journals such as the *American Sociological Review,* the *American Journal of Sociology,* and the *Public Opinion Quarterly,* as well as more widely read political magazines such as *The New Republic, Partisan Review, politics, Labor and Nation,* and *Commentary.* Finally, while Gerth remained an associate professor at Madison with a minor reputation, Mills had moved from the University of Maryland to the Bureau of Applied Social Research at Columbia and on to the Columbia faculty. In 1945 he held a Guggenheim Fellowship, the most prestigious research grant then available to academic intellectuals. In 1949, when he and Gerth were considering the problem of precedence, he held a visiting appointment at the University of Chicago.

If the test of assets depended on who had amassed more social capital, Gerth was bound to lose. Therefore, it is hardly surprising that Mills emphasized "status," the social rather than the intellectual capital the partners had invested in *Character and Social Structure*. By employing the principle of equivalent status, Mills was able to redefine the problem of precedence. The important question was not who brought more ideas to the joint venture but who delivered more prestige. The first criterion favored Gerth's claim to priority; the second, Mills's. This principle also gave Mills a moral and rhetorical advantage. By asserting only that he and Gerth occupied an equivalent status, even though Gerth could not match his publication record, connections, and institutional affiliations, Mills could represent himself as modest, generous, even magnanimous, an appearance that would contrast markedly with Gerth's earlier outbursts of rage.

Performance

If Mills could convince Gerth to accept the principle of equivalent status, he would have grounds for claiming equal credit for *Character and Social Structure*. This claim would be persuasive only if he could show that his work on the project was commensurate with Gerth's. The final premise of the Chicago protocol provides the basis on which Mills made this case: precedence should be determined by the contributions of the two authors in drafting and editing the manuscript. In applying this principle, Mills suggested they review the chapter outlines for the book and divide responsibilities for first drafts and revisions. He reminded Gerth that they had performed this exercise on an earlier occasion, arriving at the conclusion that Mills had drafted more than 300 pages and Gerth had done nothing. In fact, this was not a conclusion reached jointly by Gerth and Mills but a position Mills took in the Cleveland protocol, the agreement Gerth had rejected.

Mills's principle of performance and his claim that he had already finished his share of the first draft seemed to require that Gerth submit his 300 pages to qualify for equal credit. But what if Gerth's record in writing first drafts did not improve and he failed to meet his quota of chapters? In that case Mills would face the choice of abandoning the project or completing the first draft himself. Because he believed he would lose his job at Columbia if *Character and Social Structure* was not published, Mills rejected the first alternative. As he understood the assessment of his work that prevailed at Columbia, *The New Men of Power* was regarded as an exercise in advocacy rather than a contribution to science or scholarship. *White Collar*, when it appeared, would be seen in the same way. On this view, Mills was a political writer who took stands, not a sociologist who analyzed data and developed theories to explain facts. He could not keep his job unless he persuaded his senior colleagues that he had made a significant contribution to academic sociology. If he failed, Mills concluded, referring to himself in the subroyal third person, "He is going to be out on his academic ass from writing political books like New Men and White Collar." [39]

Thus Mills seemed to face a dilemma. Because he needed a book that would certify his credentials as a sociologist, he could not afford to withdraw from *Character and Social Structure*. In the light of Gerth's past performance, however, Mills had no reason to believe that his partner would complete his share of the first draft. This meant that he would be obliged to do what Gerth had left undone. On the principle of performance, it would follow that his claim to credit would override Gerth's. Mills took this view himself, at least provisionally. If he assumed the burden of writing the first draft, he claimed, then "credit stuff would in my mind be pretty vague." Regardless of how this vagueness was resolved, he added: "I would not honestly feel ok about assuming a simply and unexplained Gerth and Mills volume. Would you?" [40] Mills was treading on dangerous ground, and as soon as he had raised this issue, he realized he had made a false move. Gerth would not tolerate any proposal that seemed to place him in a subordinate position that implied junior authorship. In view of the stormy history of the Weber project and Gerth's refusal to accept the Cleveland protocol, it was necessary to erase any suggestion that "Mills and Gerth" were the authors of *Character and Social Structure*. What could Mills do? He could not risk self-destruction of the book, and Gerth would not accept an arrangement that gave him precedence.

Mills solved these problems by proposing a division of labor for all subsequent work on *Character and Social Structure*. Although it represented a significant retreat from the principles set out in the Cleveland protocol, his plan seemed to ensure that the book would be completed on a reasonable schedule without losing Gerth's cooperation and goodwill. Mills increased his first-draft responsibilities from the 50 percent of the Cleveland protocol to 100 percent. He would write the entire first draft based on materials in "his own files" and any material Gerth might send him. Gerth's job was to rework this first draft, after which Mills would edit Gerth's revisions. In the summer of 1950 the partners would work together and agree on a final text. The book would be credited to "Gerth and Mills," and the preface would include a statement that the order of their names was purely alphabetical. Both authors would be held "jointly responsible for the book as a whole and for each of its parts." [41]

Did Mills's plan conform to his principle of performance? This question raises several possibilities. In his effort to persuade Gerth to sign the Harcourt Brace contract, did Mills's ability to execute his plan break down? This would have been quite uncharacteristic. Or did he think that the "common drafts" together with Gerth's revisions and other work on the first draft would balance his own contributions? In that case, the requirement of the performance principle would be satisfied. Did the crisis over precedence in the Weber project, its bitter consequences, and Gerth's three-year resistance to the Cleveland protocol convince him of Gerth's deep reluctance to grant him equal credit for *Character and Social Structure?* In that case he might have been willing to sacrifice the principle of performance and contribute more than an equal share of the drafting and editing.

Regardless of Mills's final judgment on the Chicago protocol, his ultimate priority was clear. He needed to devise a formula for the attribution of credit that Gerth would not reject, in spite of his doubts about Mills's integrity and motives. Mills was not concerned about the precise formulation of authorial responsibilities as long as it clearly stated that both partners could claim equal credit for the book as a whole and each of its chapters: "I do not care about the exact wording as long as the idea of senior and junior authorship is clearly excluded." [42]

Stratagems and Fictions: The Cancellation of the Heath Contract

After three years of proposals and persuasion, Mills finally succeeded in framing an offer Gerth found acceptable: on May 2, 1949, Gerth agreed to the Chicago protocol and signed the Harcourt Brace agreement, even though the book remained under contract to Heath. The work on *Character and Social Structure* would continue according to Mills's plan, and the authors' names would appear in alphabetical order. Immediately after Gerth accepted this solution to the precedence problem, Mills transmitted it to Reid. Remembering Gerth's fury over the reversal of their names in the promotion of the Weber book, he specifically instructed Reid to make sure that Gerth's name was listed first in any publicity. [43]

Mills, who now had everything he had asked for, began to arrange an escape from the Heath contract. Earlier he had claimed that a properly framed letter to the appropriate person at Heath would effect a quick release. In fact, his efforts to nullify what he had once called a "tentative contract" dragged on for more than nine months. For Mills it was a seemingly interminable struggle in which Heath responded to his petitions with frustrating counterproposals or long silences that exhausted his patience. This was a problem the partners had not anticipated. Dissolving a contract with a publisher that refused to be abandoned proved to be hard work as well as a nerve-wracking experience fraught with dangers. After all, much was at stake. In contracting with two publishers for the same book, they had violated a basic canon of publishing ethics. Their conduct also threatened to compromise Merton, who had recommended *Character and Social Structure* to Harcourt Brace, and Becker, who already had his own problems with Heath. The ethical complexities of the contractual problem were compounded by the dual roles of Becker and Merton, who were editorial advisers employed by publishers as well as colleagues of Gerth and Mills. If the two contracts were discovered, the authors, in the absence of a plausible explanation, would be unmasked as opportunists who had betrayed the trust of their colleagues to gain an illegitimate advantage. Because Becker and Merton had vouched for the professional integrity of the partners, their judgment and editorial competence could also be placed in doubt. In the spring of 1949 Gerth and Mills had good reasons to be worried.

On the same day he received Gerth's endorsement of the Chicago protocol, Mills, who had no contacts at Heath, wrote a "Dear Sir" letter intended to effect a release. The contract, he argued, was eight years old and in arrears. The authors had received no advance, and the "ties and interests" that had originally prompted them to select Heath as their publisher no longer obtained. Moreover, they were unable to fulfill its terms; Mills pleaded the burden of his current empirical research and his work on *White Collar.* Finally, he noted that in the intervening years, he had received four-figure advances for two books with other publishers, implying that the contract of 1941 no longer met the requirements of his enhanced academic reputation and commercial value. Since no manuscript had been submitted and the contract was "formally dead," why not clear the record with a statement that all parties had agreed to terminate the contract? This same suggestion, Mills recalled, had been made by Becker, Heath's own academic editor.[44]

Mills would wait more than three weeks for a response to this appeal. In the meantime, he received an uncharacteristically long communication from Gerth: Becker now knew about the Harcourt Brace contract. As soon as Reid had received the signed contracts, Harcourt Brace published an announcement of their "forthcoming text" by Gerth and Mills.

Why, Gerth asked plaintively, did their new publisher have to inform the entire sociological profession immediately after the fact? He claimed that Becker was furious—threatening, bullying, and generally berating him for his duplicitous conduct. Since the chair of his department was taking advice from senior colleagues on merit pay increases, this revelation occurred at an especially inopportune time. Becker, of course, would report the deception Gerth had practiced on Heath, Harcourt Brace, Becker himself, and the sociological community at large. As a result Gerth could expect a lecture from McCormick, who would tell him that he was "a rat or a sucker" and in any case not meritorious.[45]

Gerth, however, expressed no remorse. Because of flawed plans and unforeseen contingencies, the divorce from Heath would be more painful than he and Mills had expected. Resigned but also defiant, cognizant of the damage they had done but basically optimistic about the ultimate outcome, he was mildly amused by the uncomfortable position in which all the parties had been placed. In his view, the current embarrassment over the contract for *Character and Social Structure* was due not to the partners' decision to sign with Harcourt Brace while they were still bound to Heath but to Becker's failure to cancel the Heath agreement. If Becker had acted on the promise he made in December 1948 and requested a release, no contractual problems would have arisen. Because of his tenuous position at Heath, which had been caused by the withdrawal of the textbooks he had planned with Martindale, he delayed this request until the end of March, creating difficulties for everyone involved.

In response to Becker's complaints, Gerth devised a spurious explanation for the decision to sign with Harcourt Brace. He summarized his discussion with Becker in a report to Mills: "I simply told Howard that I took that letter [Becker's March 1949 letter to Heath recommending cancellation of the contract] to mean that in principle Heath was for the release and that formal details were simply something for him and Heath to settle. Hence in substance I felt 'free.' "[46] After Becker had written his letter, the authors concluded that they were free to dispose of *Character and Social Structure* as they wished, or so Gerth claimed to believe. Further action on the cancellation was an internal matter at Heath and of no concern to Gerth and Mills. This fiction represented an attempt to cover one duplicitous act by another. Although Gerth admitted to Becker that he found the situation awkward—he characterized the two contracts and the haste of Harcourt Brace in advertising the book as a "mishap"—he accepted no responsibility for it. Even as he attempted to deceive Becker concerning the circumstances under which he had signed the Harcourt Brace contract, he insisted on his innocence.

Gerth also advised Mills not to expect an early settlement of the Heath problem. The institutional contexts in which the key actors were placed and the cluster of individual, professional, and corporate interests at play did not favor a quick and painless resolution. Moreover, the damage caused by a cancellation would not be limited to Becker but would also jeopardize the position of John Walden, the editor to whom Gerth and Mills were appealing for a release that was not in his interest. Would the partners suffer irreparably from this incident? Gerth observed that their conduct was "not quite 'above board' " and would contribute nothing to their reputations, either in academia or in publishing circles. At least at this stage in their problems with Heath, however, he remained intransigent: "To hell [with them]," he concluded. "Are we serfs?" [47]

In Mills's judgment, the early announcement of the publication of *Character and Social Structure,* although embarrassing in its timing, indicated that Harcourt Brace was planning an ambitious promotional campaign for the book. This made it imperative to convince Heath that the authors' refusal to honor their contract was unconditional. He was also buoyed by Gerth's defiant stance, which called for an aggressive policy in dealing with Heath. For once Mills was able to compliment Gerth on thinking in strategic terms. Because the contract with Harcourt Brace was now in the open, their earlier efforts to conceal it were beside the point. Nonetheless, what line should they take if Reid, their editor at Harcourt Brace, discovered the Heath contract? Mills proposed that they use the explanation Gerth had devised, the pretense that they had understood Becker's letter to Walden as a prima facie release. His interim plan for handling Reid was twofold: if possible, keep the Heath contract secret from him to avoid minor but worrisome difficulties with their new publisher; if this did not work, feign innocence. [48]

On May 26 Walden finally responded to Mills's May 2 request for a release. He did not issue a release, however, nor did he entertain the possibility of doing so. Although he now knew about the Harcourt Brace agreement, he did not threaten Mills, refer to legal problems the partners had created, or even mention the two contracts. Instead he reaffirmed Heath's commitment to *Character and Social Structure.* It was not in Walden's interest as an acquisitions editor to lose a book that had grown more valuable through a contract from a competitor. Becker had presumably kept him informed on the progress of the manuscript and given him the correct impression that much of the work had already been done. Walden wanted to know how much. Instead of dissolving their agreement, he asked for a meeting to discuss the book in detail when Mills returned to New York.[49]

Further discussion that might lead to a rapprochement with Heath was not a possibility Mills was willing to consider. To make clear to Walden that there were no circumstances under which he would agree to publish the book with Heath, he wrote a blunt reply. Since he would be at his camp in Ontario until October, a meeting was out of the question. Gerth and Mills had asked for a cancellation and Becker had seconded this request. That should have ended the matter. Further, Mills claimed, the partners had made no progress on the project since 1942. In view of these considerations, he found Heath's failure to cancel the contract contrary to standard practice in academic publishing. In the end he gave Walden a choice without a difference. Either he could send Mills a release, or he could refuse. In the latter case, Mills insisted, "No book bearing my name will be written on social psychology." In neither case would Heath publish *Character and Social Structure*.[50]

Copies of this uncompromising letter were sent to Gerth and Becker. As Mills remarked in an attached note to Gerth, his purpose was to force a decision.[51] He did not succeed. The partners' strategy of intransigence had no effect on Walden. Determined to retain *Character and Social Structure*, he replied to Mills at his camp in Ontario. Ignoring Mills's aggressive rhetoric, he maintained a tone of amiable reasonableness, active interest, and confident professionalism. Securing a release was a more complex matter than Mills had supposed. Because Walden had no authority to nullify a contract, Mills's request would have to be forwarded to an executive committee at Heath. The issue could not be placed on this committee's agenda, however, until Walden had a clearer explanation of Mills's desire to cancel the agreement. Mills's last letter implied that he and Gerth still intended to write the book. Walden still wanted to publish it, notwithstanding Mills's threat that he would not write the book at all if Heath held him to their agreement. In Walden's view, a discussion of mutually advantageous terms of publication would be more profitable than a consideration of cancellation.[52]

By this point Gerth was convinced that Heath would not give up the rights to *Character and Social Structure* unless Walden could be persuaded that the cost of losing the book to Harcourt Brace was tolerable. Troubled by the lack of progress in resolving the contractual problem, he sent Mills a carefully organized set of suggestions designed to end the stalemate. As a demonstration of his strategic and tactical insight and his understanding of the interests of the principal actors and the organizational constraints they faced, this document is unique in the Gerth-Mills collaboration.[53]

First, Gerth considered what should be done in the event that Harcourt Brace discovered the prior commitment he and Mills had made to Heath. The contractual situation should be explained as the result of a misunderstanding for which they could not reasonably be blamed. Gerth and Mills had been conscientious in attempting to detach themselves from Heath before signing with Harcourt Brace. Years before, Gerth had informed Walden of the contentious relationship between Becker and Mills. The animosity between the professor and his former student was beyond reconciliation and excluded the possibility of a sound working relationship between editor and author. Nor could Gerth be expected to work effectively if he was compelled to take sides between his collaborator and a senior departmental colleague. Cancellation of the contract was the only way out. Further, Becker himself had proposed this solution and submitted it to Heath at the end of March. Although Heath's response was favorable, the release was delayed. Gerth interpreted the delay as a consequence of Heath's financial obligations to Becker, possibly involving a finder's fee that he would lose if the contract were canceled. That, in any case, was Gerth's most recent elucidation of his state of mind at the time he signed the Harcourt Brace agreement. Although his interpretation turned out to be mistaken, should he be blamed for the mistake? It was simply an error on his part, the result of an honest if untimely misunderstanding. He instructed Mills that if they were called on to explain themselves to Harcourt Brace, they should take an unequivocal position: at the end of March Gerth had entertained no doubt that Heath would accept Becker's proposal.

Gerth's explanation was designed to defeat any charge of professional misconduct. Suspicions of untruthfulness were forestalled by the invention of a shapeless misunderstanding for which no one could be held responsible. His account also had the advantage of apparent guilelessness. There was no attempt to excuse or exonerate, because there was nothing that called for exoneration. By introducing the friction between Becker and Mills as the key factor in the relations between the authors and Heath, he shifted the issue from a problem about two contracts to a problem about Becker and Mills. Given this redescription, the request for a release was easily explained by reference to commonplace bickering between headstrong intellectuals, one of the more banal experiences of academic life.

As a result, his explanation carried no implication of deceit and no other suggestion that he and Mills had violated academic or publishing ethics. Because they had nothing to answer for, they could not be blamed.

In addition, Gerth attempted to understand the contractual problem from the perspective of the partners' interlocutors, working on the assumption that he and Mills would not get what they wanted by acting on a purely opportunistic logic and neglecting the interests of their publisher. To develop a more comprehensive negotiating strategy, he analyzed three sets of interests: Heath's corporate interests, Becker's prestige interests, and Walden's professional interests. In considering how these interests were related, he explored the various motives for action they evoked and assessed the bearing of both interests and motives on the prospects for a release. His analysis stressed several points.

Contrary to Mills's assumption, the partners had no right to a release. Because the decision to grant a release was the publisher's prerogative, it was essential to retain Heath as an ally. Gerth believed that they could count on Heath's goodwill only by providing a credible explanation for the anomaly of the Harcourt Brace advertisement without admitting any duplicity. This was a formidable and delicate problem. Plausible answers to two questions were needed. How could they account for Harcourt's forthcoming publication of a book under contract to Heath, and how could they explain the existence of a complete manuscript of *Character and Social Structure* within weeks of their attempt to discourage Heath with the claim that the project was not much more than a sketch? Without acceptable answers to these questions, they could expect to make no progress with Heath. If they answered truthfully, however, and divulged the circumstances under which they signed with Harcourt Brace, Heath would have a legal weapon to use against them. In the worst case Heath might take the authors to court and seek an injunction prohibiting publication of the book with another publisher.[54]

In addition, Gerth speculated that Heath might attempt to enforce the contract by removing Becker from his editorial job. If Becker disappeared, Mills's problems with Heath would disappear as well, in which case their principal rationale for a cancellation collapsed. The designation of Becker as scapegoat also had advantages for Walden. If Becker could be blamed for the tensions between the partners and Heath, Walden might be able to escape any responsibility for mishandling the contract. Because Gerth and Mills needed Walden to make the case for a release, it was important to keep him in place and make sure of his support. Walden would give them what they wanted only if it was consistent with his interests. He would not recommend a release if he had reason to think his position would be threatened. He had acquired the rights to a book that now seemed to hold some commercial promise, but its publication by Heath was in doubt. How had this happened? Senior management at Heath would conclude that mistakes had been made in handling Gerth and Mills; otherwise they would have not have entertained offers from another publisher. Blame would be allocated for these mistakes. Because they needed Walden, they also needed to give him a means of escaping blame. Becker was that means. To protect Walden, it was necessary to make a case for blaming Becker. Therefore, it was in their interest to sacrifice Becker in order to protect Walden.

More generally, it was in their interest to avoid antagonizing Walden in any fashion, a maxim Mills had repeatedly violated. Without a change in their strategy of dealing with Walden, no release would be forthcoming. Although Gerth did not use the language of game theory, he took the view that they would not succeed by persisting in handling their relationship with Walden as a zero-sum game. To win, to get what they wanted, they needed to convince Walden that he would not lose. As Gerth observed to Mills: "We need his [Walden's] 'good will'—as we have 'no right' to shift. The release from the agreement is 'a privilege' which he has to give us. If they feel 'hurt' by us, they will surely 'hurt' us."[55]

Mills incorporated these suggestions into his next letter to Walden, which dropped the truculent tone of his earlier correspondence. Appealing to motives that an editor familiar with academic quarrels would find credible, he provided a rationale for the release that would enable Walden to escape any blame. He and Becker, Mills claimed, were barely on speaking terms; obviously they did not enjoy the rapport essential to a productive working relationship. The animosity between the two cut even deeper: he would not be comfortable publishing a book with any firm associated with Becker. Mills had already published books with two other houses where he now had friendly contacts that he wanted to maintain. Finally, he added— with less than complete candor—these were the only factors motivating his request for a release.[56]

A two-month silence, appropriate to the desultory summer conduct of business in an old New England publishing house, ensued, following which Walden responded with a variant of a move Gerth had anticipated. The putative basis of Mills's dissatisfaction with Heath was his abysmal relationship with Becker and happier associations with other publishers. The solution to his problem was obvious: the removal of Becker, which could be achieved by withdrawing *Character and Social Structure* from his series on social relations. The book would be published by Heath, but independent of Becker's editorship. The editor Mills could not tolerate would no longer be connected with his book. If his dealings with Heath had been unsatisfactory, the cause was Becker, not the firm. Thus Walden proposed not a cancellation of the contract but a dissolution of the connection between *Character and Social Structure* and Becker. This was the only condition under which a satisfactory disposition of the book was possible. Walden was sympathetic to Mills's sensitivities and flexible on points where Heath had nothing to lose, especially in the matter of Becker, whose exclusion would provide the basis for a congenial relationship between the authors and their publisher. He remained adamant on the fundamental issue, however: Heath would hold Gerth and Mills to their agreement.[57]

This new proposal left Mills depressed and confused. Walden had proven to be no less intransigent than Mills himself. As a result, Mills would be compelled to accept the meeting he had hoped to avoid. It would also be necessary to bring Harcourt Brace into the discussion, which meant that Mills would be obliged to inform Reid of the earlier contract with Heath before he discovered it independently. When Reid had been apprised of Mills's compromised ethics, Merton would also be told, and reports of Mills's affairs would circulate through the Columbia sociology department. Once again, his status at Columbia would be in question, and for the same reasons expressed in the letters from Becker and McKeel: doubts about his character and suspicions that he did not measure up to expected standards of professional ethics. As he complained to Gerth, the contractual matter would be "another club the Columbia people will beat me on the head with."[58]

Gerth, who had the advantage of consultations with Becker, was more sanguine about the ultimate resolution of the problem. His access to Becker gave him an insight into Heath's position that Mills—contemptuous of Becker, without connections at Heath, and isolated at his camp in Ontario—did not have. Becker's willingness to advise Gerth on Heath's thinking, notwithstanding his relationship with Mills, proved invaluable in finally securing a release. Because the editors at Heath knew about the Harcourt Brace contract, they did not expect Gerth and Mills to accept Walden's most recent offer and were resigned to the loss of the book. Fol-

lowing Becker's advice, Gerth instructed Mills to write yet another letter
to Walden: a polite reply graciously declining his generous offer and reiterating Mills's wish to place the book with a house where he had already
published, a preference that did not imply an averse judgment on Heath,
its reputation, or its editors.[59] Although Mills wrote the letter Gerth suggested, his draft was somewhat more inventive than the reply Gerth had
in mind. Mills referred to *Character and Social Structure* as a book he
and Gerth "might write," and he left Walden with the impression that he
would either place the book with a firm of his own choice or abandon the
project altogether.[60]

Another long silence followed, one that Mills endured with increasing
impatience. Although he claimed to need money badly, he was reluctant
to draw on his share of the Harcourt Brace advance as long as the contract with Heath was still in force; Mills was not foolish enough to take
the advice he had given Gerth some six months earlier and spend his
$1,500.[61] After more than two months had elapsed without a response from
Walden, Gerth had another conversation with Becker regarding Heath's
plans. Walden intended to arrange a meeting with Mills in New York and
agree to a release. Gerth advised Mills to suspend his correspondence with
Walden and conduct himself politely but firmly in the meeting, employing the stock of rationales, evasions, and denials they had developed and
refined over the past months of negotiations.[62] The meeting took place
early in December in Mills's office at Columbia. Although Walden promised Mills a release, by the end of the month he still had no formal noti-
fication. Mills surreptitiously taped the meeting and thus had a recording
of Walden's declaration to cancel the contract. Gerth, of course, was told
to keep this information to himself.[63]

By the beginning of February 1950, Mills, still without the release, was
"jittery as all hell": unable to fathom Heath's intentions, anxious about
Walden's next move, and unable to devise new strategies. Despite these
mounting pressures, he was intent on arranging a summer of joint work.
Nevertheless, he asked Gerth, "How can we until we hear from the bas-
tards[?] The guy sits here in my office and says yes of course and then two
months go by and nothing." His plans called for the partners to devote the
following summer to the book, but how could they be put into effect if
Heath refused to forward the promised release and it became necessary to
return the advance from Harcourt Brace? Out of spirits, Mills wondered
whether there was any point, financial or intellectual, in pressing on with

the project. How could he be expected to work "bound to Heath in this awful way"? Mills was torn: "Honest to god I've no heart for it; and yet I want very much to go ahead and do the book." [64]

Heath, fighting a war of attrition with dwindling resources, released Gerth and Mills from their contract on February 28, 1950. On March 24 they cashed their advances from Harcourt Brace. In May Mills received tenure at Columbia with a promotion to associate professor and a salary of $6,000. Harcourt Brace published *Character and Social Structure* in 1953. [65]

· 4 ·

Mills Ascending: The Young Careerist

The Main Chance

Very early on Mills concluded that the higher learning in America was an enterprise that depended on learning how to survive and thrive in a world reserved for those who were clever and aggressive in advancing their claims to credit. A work's effective presentation was no less critical to success in the competition for major rewards than was its intellectual quality. Strategies for validating claims to credit for research were as important as the research itself. Because the question of the originality of ideas might prove to be less crucial than the question of whether they could be represented as original, it was necessary to complement scholarship with salesmanship. It followed that success in academic science and scholarship depended on marketing research: analyzing the demand for intellectual goods and developing ideas for products to meet this demand.

Although Gerth was the most important asset in the early years of Mills's career, he was not the only resource. Any supplier of intellectual material or labor and anyone with power or access to power in academia might have a place in his plans. Depending on circumstances and his needs of the moment, he made use of colleagues, established academicians, authors whose books he had reviewed, editors at social science journals and academic publishing houses, New York intellectuals of the anti-Stalinist left, and students.

At the University of Texas Mills acquired skills in self-promotion at the same time that he began to develop expertise in the sociology of knowledge. Even before his baccalaureate degree, he demonstrated remarkable sophistication in making valuable contacts. His earliest method of networking was to send an essay to a well-connected sociologist and ask advice on its publication. Louis Wirth and Hans Speier both received inquiries concerning his paper "Methodological Consequences of the Sociology of Knowledge." Wirth was the author of *The Ghetto,* midwife of the English edition of Karl Mannheim's *Ideology and Utopia,* and a member of the editorial board of the *American Journal of Sociology.* As a professor for many years at the University of Chicago, he was among the most important gatekeepers in sociology during the interwar years. Speier, an original member of the University in Exile at the New School for Social Research, had come to the United States in 1933 and began writing for publication in English. In 1938, when Speier's important paper on the sociology of knowledge "The Social Determination of Ideas" appeared in *Social Research,* Mills was already citing his work.[1]

When Mills began to publish, he sent offprints of his articles to leading scholars in social theory and philosophy. During his first semester at Madison, recipients of his essay "Language, Logic, and Culture" included younger specialists in the sociology of knowledge and the philosophy of science, such as Speier, Robert K. Merton, and Ernest Nagel, and established figures, such as Alexander von Schelting, Kenneth Burke, Herbert Blumer, Talcott Parsons, Charles Morris, and Karl Mannheim. In his second year of graduate work, he added the social theorists George Lundberg and Florian Znaniecki and no less a figure than John Dewey to his list of important correspondents.[2] In initiating these contacts, Mills put his name in circulation and identified himself as a bright and up-and-coming young man in a new field. He also created opportunities for advancement, illustrated by his correspondence with Merton. Beginning in January 1940 he engaged Merton, at that time on the faculty of Tulane University, in a highly abstract discussion of the foundations and implications of the sociology of knowledge. Although this exchange of letters appeared to be purely philosophical, by November of the same year he had undertaken to enlist Merton as a referee to support the fellowship applications he intended to make to the Social Science Research Council or the Guggenheim Foundation.[3]

Early in his tenure at the University of Maryland, Mills added a third networking technique to the practices of soliciting opinions about his manuscripts and circulating copies of his publications: writing laudatory reviews of important books in leading journals and increasing his visibility by sending offprints to the authors of the books and other interested parties in a position to exercise influence on his behalf.[4] In establishing these contacts Mills's judgment was remarkably prescient. In 1942 he corresponded with Franz Neumann about his review of Neumann's book *Behemoth: The Structure and Practice of National Socialism*. Two years later Neumann assisted in promoting the Weber project to Oxford University Press by introducing Mills to H. T. Hatcher, the editor who had acquired *Behemoth* for Oxford. Mills also received favorable responses to his reviews from Merton and Robert Lynd, both of whom played important roles in bringing him to Columbia.[5]

The methods Mills used to create a network of counselors, advisers, and advocates are illustrated by his courtship of Harold Lasswell, the political scientist and theoretician of propaganda, whom he met in Washington during the early months of the U.S. engagement in World War II. Mills expected, quite correctly, that the war would open up new opportunities for intellectuals. Sociologists with his training would be needed to interpret the American role in the war, explaining and justifying the transformation of the United States from the arsenal of democracy into the leader of the crusade for freedom. The U.S. entry into the war would require a propaganda apparatus on a scale unprecedented in American history. Luminaries such as Lasswell, who were planning the strategies and techniques of Allied propaganda analysis, would have the authority to recruit other social scientists into the new wartime propaganda ministries. Influence and chances for advancement were at stake, and Mills did not want to be left out. He saw Lasswell as an important figure in the emerging political and academic alignments created by the war and the key to his access to these new opportunities. Accordingly, when he met Lasswell for a long conversation in a Washington bar at the beginning of March 1942, Mills treated the meeting as an occasion for an exercise in strategic interaction.[6]

It was important for Mills to seem impressed with Lasswell's views on the relations between propaganda analysis and social structure but not appear to be naïve. When Lasswell detailed his conception of a science of propaganda that would satisfy both instrumental criteria of technical efficiency and moral criteria of respect for human dignity, Mills wanted to subtly indicate his own understanding of what was at stake. He knew that Lasswell regarded this view of propaganda as cynical and intellectually dishonest, and he wanted Lasswell to know that he was not deceived on this point. In a carefully controlled exercise in facework, Mills attempted to communicate all this without saying anything. Listening with carefully gauged measures of rapt admiration and polite skepticism, he conducted a silent monologue on a quite different set of questions. How were academic power relations in wartime Washington shaping up? Who would have patronage to dispense, and how could he acquire a patron? How did a powerful intellectual such as Lasswell conduct himself? What devices of self-presentation did he employ to establish a sense of his own importance and originality?

Although Mills concealed his priorities and judgments, he was much less interested in Lasswell's views, which he regarded as a banal and unimaginative application of Mannheim's perspectivism, than in his Washington connections. His analysis of Lasswell as a type of intellectual was primarily motivated by a single consideration: what strategies and techniques of career management had he employed to arrive at his present eminence? While Lasswell indulged himself in a conventional display of theoretical prowess, Mills was engaged in a more complex performance involving several different objectives, all pursued simultaneously as part of the same interaction. He wanted to indicate that he was appropriately moved by the importance of Lasswell's ideas but without suggesting that his admiration was untutored or uncritical. He wanted to learn from Lasswell how a successful social scientist comported himself, and he hoped to discover how the wartime propaganda ministries in Washington would work and how he could use them for his purposes. He also wanted to take advantage of Lasswell's power and connections, which he found genuinely impressive, especially because Lasswell had no official job in Washington. Finally, he wanted to achieve all this without revealing his intentions or his real estimate of the quality of Lasswell's thinking. Lasswell could make things happen for Mills, but only if Mills succeeded in producing the appropriate impression of precociousness and protégé-like dependence.

Mills's efforts did not go unrewarded. During a subsequent meeting in the bar of the Raleigh Hotel, Lasswell referred him to several contacts and offered to arrange for research assistance to support a project Mills was planning.[7] By October 1944 Mills was a member of a private seminar Lasswell was conducting at the Library of Congress on the relevance to the social sciences of the positivist philosophy of science Rudolf Carnap and Hans Reichenbach had recently imported from Vienna. Mills and Lasswell seem to have used the seminar to score points off one another, matching methodological credentials and knowledge of the latest developments in the formal logic and systematics of social theory. Although Mills permitted Lasswell to win this contest of philosophical one-upmanship, he did not do so without demonstrating both his understanding of the way this particular academic game was played and his skills as a player, a tactic that served him well. In a postseminar conversation late one evening in another Washington bar, Lasswell suggested that Mills apply for a Guggenheim Fellowship and offered his support, noting that five of his candidates had recently been successful in the Guggenheim competition. The following year the Guggenheim Foundation awarded Mills a fellowship.[8]

In early 1942, the beginning of U.S. engagement in World War II, Mills was occupied with plans for research and publication.[9] A year later he was petitioning Lasswell and Lynd to recommend him for a special naval commission that would provide a year of study at Columbia University, residence in New York, a salary of $280 per month, and exemption from combat.[10] By early June 1943 he had received no response from the navy, and a preliminary physical examination for induction into the army had convinced him to explore other alternatives. His first choice was a position with the Office of Strategic Services (OSS) in Washington, where he hoped to be transferred in the event he was drafted, an assignment that would entail no disruption of his civilian life.[11] During the next few months his hopes for military preferment waxed and waned. In February 1944 he was confident that Franz Neumann would be able to find a place for him in the OSS. Only a month later, however, he had become much more pessimistic: the army had apparently decided that no more enlisted men would be seconded to the OSS. "See you in the army," he wrote Gerth at the beginning of March, signing himself "A Fighting Son of Freedom, U. S. Army." [12] By the spring of 1944 his efforts to secure a satisfactory wartime job were at an end. He had received a Selective Service classification of 1-A, which made him eligible for immediate induction. On May 31, 1944, however, he was surprised by the results of a preinduction physical examination: he was classified unfit for military service.

Free of his worries about the army, Mills quickly remobilized his energies and returned to the business of his career. In the same letter in which he sent Gerth the unexpected news of his emancipation from the draft, he outlined a plan designed to enable him to leave the University of Maryland, an institution he had come to despise.[13] Although he had been appointed as a tenured associate professor, he had a punishing teaching load: four courses each semester, large classes, no teaching assistants, and a full complement of summer courses. Hired at a base salary of three thousand dollars, he had received no pay increases in three years, no compensation for summer teaching or the additional courses he taught for military personnel, and no financial support for research. By the summer of 1944 he was frustrated and profoundly dissatisfied. As he wrote to Gerth: "Gerth I don't mind telling you flat out that if I don't get out of this goddamned little hole before long I'll go crazy." [14]

Mills's aim was to publish his way out of Maryland by writing books: the Weber book, *Character and Social Structure,* and his study on white-collar workers. His immediate purpose was to use the contracts for these books to secure a three-year appointment at the University of Wisconsin. In three years, he believed, he could demonstrate his indispensability to the sociology staff at Madison and become a permanent fixture. To this end he planned several moves. First he asked Gerth for a candid assessment of the weaknesses of the Madison sociology faculty so that he could write knowledgeably to Thomas McCormick, the chair of the department. In his letter to McCormick he would emphasize the decline in the University of Wisconsin's reputation as a center for advanced work in sociology and its loss of talented graduate students to Chicago and Columbia. He would also propose a solution to this problem: his own appointment, which would establish sociology at Wisconsin on a new footing. To support his central premise, the fading reputation of the graduate program in sociology at Madison, he would recruit Ben Gillingham, another Wisconsin Ph.D. and a student of Gerth, to write McCormick along the same lines and reinforce the case he intended to make. [15]

Mills's letter to McCormick began with a ritual act of deference, asking his old statistics professor to set right any mathematical mistakes he might find in a paper Mills planned to submit for publication. Then he moved to his pedagogical successes, discussing the importance of involving students in research. Listing his major publishing contracts, he stressed his decision to concentrate on book-length research projects rather than journal articles. After explaining the grounds for his dissatisfaction at Maryland, he concluded with a declaration of his availability for a job at a university with a graduate program and a budget for research, "preferably in the Midwest." [16] This letter was supported by a bibliography and a document he entitled "PUBLICATION AGENDA, as of July, 1944." The latter was a remarkably ambitious prospectus in which he envisioned the completion of four books within two years. *From Max Weber* (1946), Mills claimed, would be in print by the end of 1944, *Character and Social Structure* (1953) in 1945, *White Collar* (1951), at this point still entitled "The White Collar Man," no later than the summer of 1945, and his doctoral dissertation on American pragmatism, which was published posthumously in 1964, in 1946. [17]

Mills's efforts to escape the swamps of Maryland for the prairies of the Midwest on the strength of his publication contracts proved futile. In the East, however, his prospects improved dramatically. In October 1944 Mills received a telegram from Theodore Abel, of the Columbia University sociology department, inquiring about his availability to teach a seminar and a more general course in the summer of 1945. Asked to state his salary requirements, Mills requested $1,000, a third of his yearly salary at Maryland. Although he tried to contain his excitement, he could not suppress the hope that the summer job might lead to consideration for a permanent appointment. As he declared to Gerth: "I WANNA STAY IN NEW YORK AND GET OUT OF THIS HOLE." In the end he accepted the summer job for $800.[18] In December 1944 he interviewed for a job at Bard, a small liberal arts college in the Hudson Valley. Mills described Bard as a "swank" and "exclusively country club like place." Even in 1944 tuition and fees had reached $2,200. Although he was offered a $4,000 contract, Mills was advised by Robert Lynd to reject it. As he explained to Gerth:

> Lynd advises against it in a half-hearted way and has two good arguments: one, the library is no good for research, and two, the prestige factor is downward, or so he says. Also, the business of teaching tutorially, altho very enjoyable, and working with upper class kids pretty well selected for brains would take a gigantic amount of time away from research. I can't use the offer to boost myself here [at the University of Maryland] unless I am really serious about the job; bluffs won't work here.[19]

Finally, in early 1945, Paul Lazarsfeld, director of the Bureau of Applied Social Research at Columbia, offered Mills the position of associate director of the Office of Radio Research in the bureau, a position that led to his appointment on the Columbia faculty.[20]

The Big Shot

The initiatives Mills took in the early 1940s were important steps in the direction of becoming what he called, disparagingly but with grudging envy, a "big shot." The notion of the big shot is crucial to Mills's conception of his life and work. The Millsean big shot may be understood as an academic intellectual who exercises his skills for the purpose of self-promotion, maneuvering people, events, and decisions to ensure that arrangements turn out to his satisfaction and configuring microsocial relations as battles in the larger campaign of self-advancement. Utility in achieving the unexamined and self-evidently meritorious aim of career advancement is the big shot's only standard of value. Because everything falls under the category of use value, life is a vast repository of opportunities: advantages to be exploited and obstacles to be surmounted. Since the big shot's environment is completely plastic and manipulable, no situation is utterly resistant to his purposes. Obstacles are not in principle distinguishable from advantages. Events are always in flux, and even an apparently intractable difficulty can be overcome and turned to advantage. It follows that the world is a collection of resources that stands ready to hand, providing the materials and tools big shots need to transform their dreams into realities.

Success depends on the acquisition and management of resources. Because social relations are among the more important resources available to realize career objectives, the social life of the big shot is a project in human-resource management. Although there are irreducible contingencies that cannot be controlled, insofar as possible the big shot subjects the social world to careful planning. Under ideal conditions every social relationship establishes a contact that advances the big shot's career. The roles of other actors are defined by their expected contribution to the big shot's objectives. Because the logic of social life is strategic, social action is not grounded in moral principles or emotional bonds; it rests on calculations of the costs and benefits of investing in specific social interactions. The big shot transfers resources from unprofitable interactions and reinvests them on the basis of opportunistic considerations dictated by the imperatives of his career. Would a new relationship within the big shot's horizon of possible interactions contribute more to his objectives than an existing relationship? If so, the former should be cultivated at the expense of the latter. Has an old relationship failed to pay? If so, the big shot should withdraw the assets he has committed to that resource and invest them more profitably.

The narrow pragmatic self-interest of the big shot entails an inevitable ruthlessness, and his unconditional commitment to success reduces all other values to a purely instrumental status. Friendship, honesty, integrity, loyalty, and veracity are judged solely on the basis of their serviceability. The axiology of the big shot defines a hierarchy of values in which every person has a place. Since everyone is a means for his advancement, the positioning of all persons in his scheme of values is determined by the services he can extract from them. Persons are conceived in purely functional terms, and performance is the sole source of personal value. Some people are useful, some have potential uses, others represent obstacles or dangers, and many are simply a waste of time because of their irrelevance to the big shot's aims. Because the career is the final cause of all conduct, that for the sake of which everything exists, other persons are either instruments to be bent to the big shot's purposes, obstacles to be eliminated, or detritus to be discarded. As a social actor, the big shot attempts to position all his interlocutors to ensure their most productive use. This may require redeploying underutilized actors to extract the maximum benefits from their performance or displacing others to minimize the damage they are able to inflict.

The strategic planning and control of social affairs presupposes a corresponding mentality. The big shot must be dispassionate and clinical, otherwise his analysis of the costs and benefits entailed by alternative ways of allocating resources may be skewed by functionally irrational factors such as moral principles, emotional sensibilities, or personal proclivities. The struggle for success depends on excising from his life all human qualities that cannot be coordinated in a career plan. The big shot's conception of truth is also determined by the imperatives of planning. Because truth is defined by strategy, the criterion for truth is an ideal fit between means and ends. Strategies that work are valid, notwithstanding their other consequences. Those that fail are invalid. Since the big shot must remain flexible to take advantage of changing circumstances and needs, a position that is true today may be false tomorrow. From the big shot's standpoint, this does not nullify the concept of truth, nor does it mean that no statement can be true or that true and false statements cannot be distinguished. It means only that the criterion for truth is tied to the flexibility of sound managerial practice.

The ideal of the big shot was the fixed star by means of which the young Mills navigated the treacherous waters of academia. As early as their first joint publication, he lectured Gerth on the tactics of becoming a big shot. Gerth had failed to understand how easy it was to impress "big shots" such as James Burnham, whose book *The Managerial Revolution* they had criticized in "A Marx for the Managers." He was also mistaken in faulting Mills for overconfidence and conceit in claiming that they had already achieved this elevated status. "WE ARE BIG SHOTS," Mills insisted. "The only difference is we haven't written it down yet, don't you see?" In Mills's view, he and Gerth had become big shots by learning how to use the language of Max Weber's sociology. Mastery of Weber's theoretical apparatus enabled them to reconceptualize the basic issues of American sociology and rethink current affairs on a level that was not possible within the framework of American social science. As a result they possessed a competitive advantage in the market for intellectual goods that could not be matched by sociologists unversed in Weber's ideas. Anyone who had gained this advantage, Mills claimed, "can make it in no time."[21]

Mills regretted that he had placed "A Marx for the Managers" in *Ethics* instead of publishing it in a magazine with a larger circulation. Confirmation of their status as big shots called for more attention to packaging and distribution. Had Mills chosen a publication with a larger market, Burnham could not have avoided a response to their critique, which would have generated much more publicity for their work. As he observed to Gerth, "We have got to get a little slick, you know."[22] Being slick meant targeting several different markets of readers and "stylizing" the product to achieve a larger distribution. Becoming a "slick" writer and "stylizing" a manuscript are Millsean terms for developing a prose that impresses publishers and appeals to a large readership. To convert a manuscript into a book, it was necessary to convince a publisher that the book would sell. To produce that conviction, a slick style that would attract a substantial readership was indispensable. A larger distribution meant more publicity. If quality was conflated with quantity, intellectual substance with sales volume, and the scholarly value of a work with the size of its market, then publicity would validate the claims to credit on which their careers depended.

Mills applied these marketing concepts in his work on the Weber project. In editing Gerth's translations, his main objective was to package the manuscript for the widest possible distribution. Packaging depended primarily on simplifying the complexities of Weber's thought and language. This required breaking large blocks of text into smaller sections and labeling them with subheadings that would capture the reader's interest. It was also necessary to dismantle Weber's long sentences and rewrite them in a simpler English style. Mills's conception of editing as marketing called for polishing the translation until the style was facile and smooth. Polish, he believed, depended on the journalistic skill of writing a text that would speak to the reader, even though a few ideas might be lost in the translation from academic discourse to journalistic slickness. In 1945 he claimed that he spent roughly thirty minutes a day working on his writing to achieve this effect.[23]

Mills also attempted to gain access to the primary channels for the distribution of intellectual goods by influencing the major actors who controlled this access: editors. Even before the publication of *From Max Weber,* his confidence in his ability to sell proposals to editors was striking. At a lunch with Prentice Hall editors in June 1944, he outlined his ideas for books on white-collar workers and on social psychology. After receiving offers of advances for both projects, he shared with Gerth his observations on the mentality of the men who controlled academic publishing: with a very few exceptions, they were intellectually pretentious and insecure. Incapable of forming an independent judgment on the quality of a book proposal, they based their decisions on the opinions of referees. Because editors lacked the ability to assess the qualifications of referees, they were easily impressed by academic reputation and status. It followed that editors could be easily handled by recruiting referees with the requisite visibility and prestige.[24]

After the publication of *White Collar,* Mills was convinced that he had the credentials to bend publishers to his terms. At the end of 1951 *From Max Weber* was in its second printing and *White Collar* was selling roughly 1,000 copies a month. In Mills's view, he had succeeded because he had proven himself as an author who produced what publishers wanted: manuscripts delivered on time and books that sold well. He ascribed his ability to get what he wanted not to the intrinsic importance of his ideas or the innovative character of his work but to marketing savvy. He discovered what publishers wanted and delivered it: "I'm known as a fellow who delivers!" In explaining to Gerth why he could not consider an extended trip to Europe before *Character and Social Structure* was completed, he insisted that he could not enjoy himself until he had seen the book through the press. "That is the kind of compulsive guy I am on contracts," he claimed. When he asked Oxford University Press for a $5,000 advance for *The Power Elite,* at that time provisionally entitled "The American Elite" or "The High and the Mighty," no one flinched. To persuade him not to take the book to Alfred Knopf, Oxford was willing to pay handsomely. Mills could demand these terms only because he had made a reputation for meeting the expectations of publishers and producing marketable manuscripts. As he observed to Gerth, this was the key to success in publishing: "We've got to be 'dependable', 'reliable' and always deliver."[25]

Mills's convictions on the importance of management and marketing in the intellectual life were translated into strategies for validating claims to credit for research, a sphere in which he demonstrated remarkable skills. The exercise of these skills, especially in the acquisition of intellectual assets, was a significant contribution to the changing definition of craftsmanship in American sociology.

Mills's claim to joint credit for the Weber book was perhaps the most stunning case of his facility in assembling resources essential to academic success. His insistence that he deserved shared credit for *From Max Weber* depended on several assumptions. The editors' introduction, which covered Weber's life, political views, and thought, was based primarily on German materials: Weber's writings, a collection of his early letters edited by his wife, her biography of her husband, the secondary literature on Weber, and primary and secondary sources on German politics and intellectual history.[26] Mills's claim to credit for the introduction assumed that his German was equal to the task of reading these materials and that he had actually done so. His claim to credit for the translation rested on a more exacting premise: he could not only read Weber's German but also translate it into English. A collaborative translation did not presuppose that he had written an English draft of Weber's texts. For his work to qualify as translation, however, required at least comparing an English draft to the German original. Otherwise there would be no basis for naming him as cotranslator.

To clarify the possibilities of Mills's participation in the translation, three tasks may be distinguished. Rendering Weber directly into English qualifies as translation in the full, paradigmatic, and most restricted sense. Comparing alternative English variants of Weber's texts with the German original to select the most appropriate version or rewriting an English version so that it conforms more closely to the original qualifies as translation in a weaker and more permissive sense. Revising an English translation without considering its relation to the German does not qualify as translation in any sense. Was Mills's competence in German at least up to the requirements of translation in the more permissive sense? During the dispute over credit for the Weber book, he admitted to Hatcher that his German was not equal to the demands posed by Weber's writings, which was why he would "never have undertaken the task of translating him alone." [27] This admission seems to claim as much as it concedes: Mills had the qualifications to collaborate as a translator of Weber; he needed only the proper partner. How sophisticated was Mills's knowledge of German?

In one of the more contentious episodes of the precedence dispute, Gerth reminded Mills that he had not read Marianne's biography, her edition of Weber's letters, or the German secondary literature on Weber, materials without which the biographical section of the introduction could not have been written.[28] Most important, he had not read Weber's work in German, nor was he capable of doing so. His knowledge of Weber's life and work was indirect and derivative, based exclusively on his studies with Gerth.[29] Mills never contested these claims. On the contrary, in one of his confessional letters, he acknowledged that he owed his understanding of Weber to what he had learned from Gerth.[30] The evidence germane to Mills's participation in the Weber project supports this acknowledgment. In September 1938, at the beginning of his final year at the University of Texas, he wrote Ernest Manheim at the University of Chicago for advice on recent German work in the sociology of knowledge available in English. Although he wanted to pursue the German literature in this area beyond the English translation of Karl Mannheim's *Ideology and Utopia,* he explained that his limited ability to read German prevented him from doing so.[31]

Did Mills's competence in German improve during his studies at the University of Wisconsin? Howard Becker supervised the German language examination Mills was obliged to pass to qualify for the Ph.D. In 1958, during one of the revivals of the dispute over precedence for the Weber project, Gerth sought Becker's assistance to prevent Mills from assuming joint credit for the Weber translations. Complaining of his weariness in serving as "an accessary to lies," he asked Becker to help "stop this blunderbuss."[32] Gerth's letter, which was both inflammatory and prejudicial, hardly qualified as an invitation to offer a dispassionate judgment. In addition, Becker and Mills had been on bad terms since the time of Mills's Ph.D. candidacy, and Becker was perhaps not the most impartial judge of Mills's qualifications and conduct. This said, Becker replied not with a private opinion but with a statement he was willing to publish if Gerth's allegations could be substantiated. He maintained that to guarantee Mills's success on the German exam, he chose the least demanding text he could find. A more difficult selection, he claimed, would have taxed Mills's modest comprehension of the language, resulting in a failing grade. Becker rejected out of hand the suggestion that Mills might be capable of handling Weber's German, which posed challenges he could not possibly meet.[33]

Becker's position was confirmed by Mills himself. During the work on the Weber book, he was apprehensive about his editorial responsibilities and worried that his revisions of Gerth's translations might have distorted Weber's intentions. In his efforts to clarify Gerth's English, had he compromised the accuracy of the translations? Because Mills was not competent to answer this question, he made a point of bringing it to Gerth's attention. In particular, he asked Gerth to check the changes he had made in the section entitled "Power, Prestige, and Imperialism" from *Economy and Society* to make sure that he was not "so far off the meaning [of the

German text] as to make it impossible." Concerned about the "great blunders" Gerth would "undoubtedly find" in his revisions, he asked Gerth to examine the text carefully before working further on the drafts.[34]

Mills did not possess any German editions of Weber's writings. In preparing for Gerth's visit to Maryland in August 1944, when they worked together on the introduction, he asked Gerth to mail his own copies of Weber's books, saying, "We won't have access to them here."[35] This request is telling, for Mills was an avid collector of books he intended to use in his work. The conception of business and the manner in which businesspeople are characterized in *White Collar* were powerfully influenced by the writings of Honoré de Balzac and Thorstein Veblen. During World War II he bought all of Veblen's books and a large collection of Balzac's novels. Had he been able to read Weber and Weberiana, he surely would have acquired Weber's chief sociological works. He could not have been expected to purchase books he could not read, however, even if they were by Max Weber. When Oxford University Press was ready to copyedit the manuscript of the Weber book, the copyeditor asked Mills for publication data on the German sources of each selection in the volume. Since he had taken charge of the publication of the book, he would have supplied this information could have done so. He did not, writing instead to Gerth and asking him to collect it.[36]

Mills was in fact sharing credit for Gerth's translations before their work on the Weber book began. By 1941 Gerth had translated Georg Simmel's germinal essay on the modern city and the urban mentality, "The Metropolis and Mental Life." In 1941–42 he also compiled a manuscript entitled "The Social Psychology of the Metropolis: Appendix to the Mimeograph Translation of Georg Simmel's 'The Metropolis and Mental Life.'" The "appendix" was a compendium of ideas on the city and urbanity excerpted from the writings of several important writers of the nineteenth and early twentieth centuries, including Karl Marx, John Ruskin, Charles Horton Cooley, and Oswald Spengler. He added a few remarks on each excerpt and translated some of the German material himself, apparently using the "appendix" in his courses to place Simmel's essay in the context of modern writing on the city. There are two copies of the "appendix" in the Mills Papers. The copy in file 4B389 has a marginal note penciled in the upper right-hand corner of the first page: "1941–42 CW [C. Wright?]: Use this to write leads to Simmel." A second copy in file 4B396 is signed as follows:

C. Wright Mills
Summer, 1942
Madison, W.

File 4B396 also contains a typescript of the translation of "The Metropolis and Mental Life" with the credit line "by H. H. Gerth with the Assistance of C. Wright Mills." The words "with the Assistance of" have been marked over in blue ink. Above this phrase, the word "and" has been penned in, with the result that the revised credit line reads "by H. H. Gerth and C. Wright Mills." [37]

There is evidence that during his years at Madison, Mills was subjected to a disagreeable lesson in the acquisition of intellectual resources under the tutelage of Howard Becker. In late December 1940 Robert Schmid, a former graduate student in sociology at the University of Wisconsin who was teaching at Vanderbilt while working on his doctoral dissertation, alerted Mills to a paper Becker was scheduled to read at the Christmas meetings of the American Sociological Society in Chicago. Becker's presentation, Schmid maintained, drew heavily on an unpublished essay by Mills. Schmid found the similarities so striking that he even considered writing Becker to suggest that he include Mills as coauthor. "It's your paper," Schmid wrote Mills, so why was his contribution not acknowledged? Had Becker bought his silence? "Did he give you fifty bucks for your ideas and tell you to shut up? From here it looks like dirty work." [38]

The paper to which Schmid referred was entitled "Sociological Methods and Philosophies of Science," a critique of George Lundberg's views on the philosophy of science. In early November 1940 Mills had submitted the essay to the *American Journal of Sociology*. Although it had been accepted, Louis Wirth advised Mills against publication until he had made substantial changes. [39] Mills responded to Schmid in January, confirming his suspicions and urging him not to write Becker. "Of course you're right. Everyone knows it here and I didn't mention it to anyone. It is very obvious. He [Becker] borrowed my copy of me on lundb [George Lundberg]. I sat in the audience and heard L [Lundberg] and hb [Howard Becker] and Znan [Florian Znaniecki] and Bain [Read Bain] too congratulate each other, all of them on their papers, and it was silly and I got mad and left after a while." [40]

As Mills saw the matter, Becker had succeeded in taking possession of his work with impunity and was rewarded for doing so, presenting Mills's paper as if it were his and basking in the applause of the luminaries of pre-war American sociological theory, such as Lundberg and Znaniecki. How was this possible? Mills was a doctoral candidate. Becker was a power in his time: a senior member of the sociology staff at Madison and an important figure in the sociology profession. He was also Mills's dissertation adviser. Powerless to respond, Mills could neither prevent nor redress Becker's use of his essay, nor could he risk making the facts public.

From the standpoint of prevailing academic norms, what Schmid suspected and Mills confirmed—Becker's appropriation of Mills's manuscript—had not happened. A charge of misappropriation of intellectual resources in academic science or scholarship can be validated only if it is raised or supported by a plaintiff qualified to compete for credit. Plaintiffs who are not acknowledged as peers do not have this status. In this regard graduate students occupy an ambivalent position. Although they may undertake and publish research that meets the relevant disciplinary standards, they are not recognized as the professional equals of their professors. As a result their work may be designated as approved objects of appropriation for which no restitution or reparation can be expected. Put another way, the appropriation of student work by established academicians may be regarded as an implicit right or a mode of compensation, in exchange for which the student receives a Ph.D. and initiation into the academic community.

In fact the young Mills also used a student essay in a key chapter of *White Collar*. Conceived in his twenties and written during the 1940s, this book was his homage to the great novelists of class stratification, from Balzac to John Dos Passos. It was his attempt to "take things big" and compose a sociological counterpart of the unwritten Great American Novel, displaying on a huge canvas the major social and economic transformations that reconfigured the American middle classes after World War I and tracing the moral and psychological effects of these changes on the American character. Mills took great pains to develop a style that would create memorable images and a prose that would make the book "damn good all over." He hoped to produce a work that was "simple and clean cut in style, but with a lot of implications and subtleties woven into it." If he was successful, *White Collar* would represent both an aesthetic and a scientific achievement, "a thing of craftsmanship and art as well as science." [41]

One chapter of *White Collar* that Mills succeeded in making "damn good" was "The Great Salesroom." Interpreting American society in the twentieth century as a "time of venality," he argued that a commercial ethos had penetrated every sphere of life. Sales techniques—"the bargaining manner, the huckstering animus, the memorized theology of pep, the commercialized evaluation of personal traits"—had become the dominant style of life of the middle class.[42] The main component of this chapter is an analysis of the market position, organizational structure, and culture of Macy's department store in Manhattan. The centerpiece of this analysis is a typology of "salesgirls" that distinguishes eight types of salesgirl personalities. The chapter explores the character of saleswomen at Macy's and their occupational life chances by examining the intersection of these personality types with external market forces and the internal organizational structure and culture of the company.

Mills's typology of saleswomen was drawn from an essay by James B. Gale entitled "Types of Macy Saleswomen." Gale, a graduate student at the Baltimore campus of the University of Maryland, took a course with Mills in the autumn semester of 1942. In the courses he taught during the 1940s, first at Maryland and later at Columbia, Mills's practice was to organize student research around the themes and problems of *White Collar*. The essays submitted by students to fulfill course requirements provided data, ideas, and arguments that he used in writing the book. In the autumn of 1942 Mills referred to Gale as a former personnel director who had worked at Macy's for eight years and was gathering material on saleswomen from his files. Some two years later he described Gale as a former floor walker or supervisor of sales personnel at Macy's with ten years of experience.[43] In *White Collar* Gale's essay is identified as "a memorandum of types of salesgirls with supporting documentation." In the notes to *White Collar* Gale is acknowledged together with several research assistants and students. Mills singled out Gale's essay and claimed that his own typology was "based upon" Gale's "prolonged and intensive observations in big stores."[44] These acknowledgments make two claims: Gale developed a typology, using his fieldwork in department stores; Mills also developed a typology, using Gale's data. Thus there were two typologies, Gale's and Mills's, both of which employed Gale's data. Exactly what is the relation between "The Great Salesroom" and Gale's essay? A comparison of the typology of saleswomen in *White Collar* with the types distinguished in Gale's essay is instructive.

THE WOLF

Mills: "The Wolf prowls about and pounces upon potential customers."
Gale: "The 'wolf' prowls about the department in energetic fashion, pouncing upon potential purchasers."

THE ELBOWER

Mills: "Intensified, the wolf becomes *The Elbower,* who is bent upon monopolizing all the customers. While attending to one, she answers the questions of a second, urges a third to be patient, and beckons to a fourth from the distance. Sometimes she will literally elbow her sales colleagues out of the way. Often she is expert in distinguishing the looker or small purchaser from the big purchaser."

Gale: "While attending to one customer, she is answering the questions of another, urging a third to be patient for a few moments of waiting, and recognizing still a fourth customer a short distance away. . . . To get to these four the clerk will literally elbow her mates out of the way. . . . Her specialty consists of sizing up in one quick glance a customer's potential buying intent; the casual or small purchaser is dropped like a hot potato while the large-amount purchaser is instantly spotted and actively solicited."

THE CHARMER

Mills: "*The Charmer* focuses the customer less upon her stock of goods than upon herself. She attracts the customer with modulated voice, artful attire, and stance."

Gale: "Depending chiefly upon her natural assets, the 'charmer' endeavors to attract the customer, particularly the younger male customer, with the blandishments of modulated diction, artful hair-do and dress, and general physical appeal. She prefers this to placing emphasis specifically upon merchandise value and utility."

THE INGÉNUE

Mills: "*The Ingénue Salesgirl* is often not noticed; it is part of her manner to be self-effacing. Still ill at ease and often homesick, still confused by trying to apply just-learned rules to apparent chaos, she finds a way out by attaching herself like a child to whoever will provide support."

Gale: "Few people, as they pass through the store intent on their shopping affairs, notice the 'ingénue'. This is due in part to their own preoccupation and in part to her defense mechanism of self-effacement. Often homesick, ill at ease in the rush and roar of bargain sales and seasonal offerings, striving quickly to absorb a mass of store rules, customs, and selling techniques, she flounders about and in desperation usually attaches herself to whomever will help her."

THE COLLEGIATE

Mills: "*The Collegiate,* usually on a part-time basis from a local campus, makes up in her compulsive amateurishness for what she lacks in professional restraint. Usually she is eager to work and fresh for the job, a more self-confident type of ingénue."

Gale: "Additional color comes to many a department twice each week in the form of the 'collegiate' who brings with her to the counter the youth, vivacity, and eager exuberance of the campus. ... Replacing the calculated restraint of the professional with the impulsiveness of the amateur, she is generally liked by the customer, the other clerks, and the executives. ... Her distinguishing characteristics are her youthful color and eagerness to work."

THE DRIFTER

Mills: "*The Drifter* may be found almost anywhere in the big store except at her assigned post; she is circulating gossip, concerned less with customers and commodities than with her colleagues."

Gale: "The 'drifter' ordinarily is to be found at any point in the store except at her post of duty ... not an hour passes but she must have her morsel of gossip, or a 'gab-session' with interested groups in her own and nearby departments."

THE SOCIAL PRETENDER

Mills: "*The Social Pretender,* well known among salesgirls, attempts to create an image of herself not in line with her job, usually inventing a social and family background. She says she is selling temporarily for the experience, and soon will take up a more glittering career. This may merely amuse her older sales colleagues, but it often pleases the buyer, who may notice that the social pretender sometimes attracts wealthy customers to her counter."

Gale: "The 'pretender' in her actions, her diction, her conversation, and particularly in her anecdotes continually carries on a mild propaganda campaign in her own behalf. She seeks to create an illusion about herself, usually one of high social background and awesome family lineage. ... Practically without exception she says, in answer to the question, 'well, why are you working here?', that selling is an adventure of her own seeking, a look into the world of the working girl, merely a temporary fill-in step in her quest of a glittering career, and never in any sense a move dictated by a vulgar need for funds. She proves a source of mild amusement to her companions, and is often well liked by the buyer who tolerates her diaphanous deception because she draws to her counter or stock section the wealthier type of customer."

THE OLD-TIMER

Mills: "*The Old-Timer,* with a decade or more of experience in the store, becomes either a disgruntled rebel or a completely accommodated saleswoman. In either case, she is the backbone of the salesforce, the cornerstone around which it is built."

Gale: "The 'old-timer', who represents ten to forty years' experience in the store, falls sharply either into the embittered irreconcilable category or into one of almost complete adjustment and accommodation. She can handle any sort of selling situation. These salespersons are considered by many to be the backbone of the store's salesforce; and in most departments they form a nucleus around which a selling force is built."

The Rebel

Mills: "As a rebel, the old-timer seems to focus upon neither herself nor her merchandise, but upon the store: she is against its policies, other personnel, and often she turns her sarcasm and rancor upon the customer. Many salesgirls claim to hate the store and the customers; the rebel enjoys hating them, in fact, she lives off her hatred, although she can be quick to defend the store to a customer."

Gale: "The 'rebel' rationalizes by blaming store personalities and negatively criticizing store policies. Management and merchandising procedures, cafeteria dietetics, vacation rules, dress regulations, all are targets of her rancor. Many a customer feels the keen edge of her veiled sarcasm; many a salesclerk and executive wearies of her recurrent diatribe. Astonishingly enough, however, despite her negative viewpoints and acrimonious expression, she would never consider working elsewhere and continually springs heatedly to a defense of the store in the teeth of customer criticism."[45]

It is misleading to claim that the typology in *White Collar* is based on Gale's observations. The important relation is not the connection between Mills's typology and Gale's data but between the two typologies. The *White Collar* typology is Gale's. Mills's comments on each type of saleswoman are also drawn from Gale's paper. They repeat Gale's main points about the distinctive features of each type, often in his language. Nevertheless, none of the passages from *White Collar* reproduced above is placed in quotation marks and credited to Gale. The dependence of this section of the book on Gale's paper is credited in a general citation, with references to other assistants and students, and an acknowledgment that does not spell out the specifics of Mills's indebtedness.[46]

There are other respects in which the citation practices employed in *White Collar* present a confusing picture of Mills's intellectual debts. In citing "A Marx for the Managers" (1942), he observed that its ideas were derived from *White Collar.* By retrospectively characterizing the earlier publication with Gerth as a product of *White Collar,* he diminished Gerth's role in their joint work, strengthened his own claims for priority, and reconstructed the history of his thought as a seamless body of ideas emanating from his original conception of *White Collar.* "A Marx for the Managers" — the first product of the collaboration, in which the economic, political, and social determinants of the history of the German middle class are interpreted by employing Max Weber's untranslated sociological writings — becomes an epiphenomenon of Mills's study of the American middle class.

As a result, *White Collar* is represented as existing ab initio, fully conceived and partially written nearly ten years before it was published.[47]

Mills also cited key sources together with less important material, burying the critical sources in an indiscriminate list of more peripheral and ancillary references. In sweeping references to several sources, page numbers of the texts used are not specified, the details of obligations to each source are not spelled out, and differences in the importance of the sources listed are not indicated. For example, Gerth, whose contributions to the genesis and development of *White Collar* it would be difficult to exaggerate, is relegated to a note acknowledging the assistance of twelve other people, one of whom was Mills's typist.[48] *White Collar* was also powerfully influenced by the literature on the German middle class of the Weimar period. Originally published in German and translated into English after the intellectual emigration of the Nazi period was under way, the writings of Emil Lederer, Jakob Marschak, Hans Speier, and others argue that the proletarianization of the German bourgeoisie created a new middle class defined by its dependence on the labor market. This process transformed the old middle class ethos of individuality and autonomy into a new culture of the masses. Mills extrapolated these ideas onto the American scene. Transposing Weimar *Kulturpessimismus* and the sociology of the German new middle class of the 1920s onto the circumstances of the American middle class after World War II, he arrived at a view of American life characterized by "apprehensiveness, pessimism, tension, [and] 'spiritual disillusionment' with the social order."[49] English translations of these German sources are cited in a long note that gives no indication of the specific ideas and arguments taken from each. Their importance to the main theses of *White Collar* is also concealed by the fact that more than a dozen other publications are cited in the same note.[50]

C. Wright Mills: The Novel

Shortly after his death in March 1962, a distinctive picture of Mills appeared on the academic marketplace, one that represented him as a political idealist, an iconoclast, and a principled radical. Mills was the conscience of American social science. Unbending in his devotion to intellectual honesty, he exemplified a flinty integrity and a commitment to writing hard truths about American life that ruled out any compromise with existing institutions. An unsparing critic of corporate capitalism at midcentury, his denunciations of big business and the national security state were based on a vision of higher and more humane values. In defending this vision he stood alone, aloof from the enticements of success and impervious to the temptation to sell out. Mills became the hero who died young, waging a solitary struggle against the forces of darkness armed only with the weapons of his mind. This view was embraced by the New Left, whose enthusiasts found in Mills their prophet and muse. It has been perpetuated in the various "C. Wright Mills awards" that leading members of professional associations of social scientists confer on one another and is now enshrined as the received view of Mills, who has been canonized as a twentieth-century exemplar of the Enlightenment tradition of critical reason.[51]

It is difficult to square this portrait of Mills with the record that emerges from his collaboration with Gerth. By the mid-1940s Mills had worked out an agreeable modus vivendi with corporate capitalism and its agencies of promotion. As a director of marketing research and an advertising and public relations consultant, he became a well-paid subcontractor for the mass-culture industry. At the same time he profited from his critique of big business in *White Collar,* which sold well and was praised for its courage and integrity, and collected commissions for magazine articles published by the "culture apparatus" that he both served and derided.

Mills's career presupposed an economy that enables intellectuals to sell their skills on the labor market and bargain for the disposal of their wares on the publishing market. It was also based on an intellectual life organized socially in universities, professional associations, academic journals, and publishing houses. These economic and social arrangements are grounded in the political order of the liberal state and its commitment to the institutional underpinnings of intellectual freedom: the autonomy of universities, the academic profession, and the publishing business; the mobility of intellectual labor, which makes it possible for universities and publishers to compete for intellectual talent and goods; and the establishment of a marketplace for ideas on which intellectuals compete for buyers of their labor and its products. Insofar as any coherent political position can be ascribed to Mills, it was a politics of the status quo that favored the interests of middle-class strivers in their efforts to achieve success as defined by the dominant culture and within the framework of the existing social order. The received historiography notwithstanding, Mills was a believer in the American dream, which he pursued tirelessly and methodically.[52]

The ethos of the big shot seemed to provide Mills with a compass, a map, and an apparent destination. The destination was success, which he redefined at each step of his efforts to approximate this ideal. During World War II success meant working his way from the University of Maryland to New York, where there were celebrated colleagues, new worlds to conquer, and the unlimited prospects that stimulated him. Within three years of his move to Columbia, he was disenchanted with New York, which distracted and exhausted him. His colleagues, it turned out, were manipulative academic entrepreneurs, each with his own agenda. Even worse, no one seemed willing to acknowledge the merits of Mills's work. His response was escape. He fled the city and the urbane culture of the Ivy League intellectual for a piece of land in Rockland Country, where he built a house, farmed in a desultory fashion, and cultivated the persona of an academic beatnik. When the farm became tiresome, he sold it and escaped for a year as a Fulbright lecturer in Denmark. Finding no excitement in Scandinavia, he spent his vacations crisscrossing hundreds of miles of European landscape, speeding from one city and monument to another on his motorcycle and lecturing at various universities.[53]

In the final analysis, the life of the Millsean big shot poses a paradox. The big shot's aims are not so much difficult to attain as illusory and unattainable in principle. Every objective, once it is reached, becomes insignificant precisely by virtue of its realization. Every goal, once achieved, becomes a means for some other end. For the big shot, there is no end, only endless striving. For Mills, there was always another book to write, a bigger contract to close, a new audience to win over, and a more promising job on the horizon. When he had written the new book, gained the new position, or added another link to his network of influential contacts, the luster of the prospect was dimmed by its accomplishment. Mills mapped an endless journey. Each place was a station on the way to a more remote terminus, the charms of which disappeared once he arrived.

In his pursuit of success as an intangible goal, Mills calls to mind another child of the lower middle classes from the middle of America in the earlier years of the twentieth century. Just as Jay Gatsby was an artifact of the imagination of Jimmy Gatz, C. Wright Mills was an idea produced by Charlie Mills. Like Gatsby, Mills lived in the service of his vision of himself. Mills also believed in "the green light, the orgastic future that year by year recedes before us." Like Gatsby's vision, the future that Mills invented for himself was an impossible dream that eluded his grasp. Like Gatsby, he pressed on in spite of this impossibility, following the principle of endless striving: "Tomorrow we will run faster, stretch out our arms farther. ... And one fine morning—"[54]

Hard Times in America:
The Tribulations of Hans Gerth

Gerth on Mills

From the beginning of the collaboration, Gerth was uneasy with Mills's pursuit of the main chance and his embrace of the ethos of the big shot. In his view Mills's flash and panache indicated superficiality and carelessness, lax standards that were inconsistent with real scholarship and the exacting requirements of the life of science. Just as Mills did not develop a theory of the big shot, Gerth did not reduce his scientific ideals to an explicit statement or a credo. His position remained an unstated assumption in the collaboration and an implicit premise of his responses to Mills's publications, drafts in progress, proposals, projects, and visions.

Late in 1941 Mills sent Gerth a draft of his paper "The Professional Ideologies of Social Pathologists." After studying the manuscript, Gerth concluded that it was too weak for publication and urged him not to submit it until they had an opportunity to talk at the forthcoming American Sociological Society meetings in New York. His dissatisfaction was based on a number of considerations. Mills had posed more problems than he could responsibly handle in a single essay. His treatment of difficult issues, such as Weber's conception of the value neutrality of science, was shallow and uninformed, and his discussion of other points belabored the obvious. His remarks on theoretical and philosophical matters were confused and in some instances self-contradictory. For example, he seemed to insist on value neutrality in the social sciences and criticized social pathologists because they used concepts such as "anti-social," "normal," and "adjusted," which presuppose value judgments; on the other hand, he also seemed to take a position inconsistent with this view, arguing that social pathologists should make their political and social stands explicit. In general Gerth regarded the paper as an embarrassment. Mills's reasoning was crude, his scholarship inadequate, and the tone of the writing flippant and inappropriate in a scholarly essay.[1]

In early January 1942, less than a month after the Pearl Harbor attack, Mills sent Gerth a plan for a theoretical article on the war and its impact on American society tentatively entitled "Locating the Enemy: Problems of Intellectuals during Time of War." Mills proposed to analyze American intellectuals as members of the middle class. Due to the impact of higher taxes and price increases on relatively fixed middle-class incomes, this stratum, he thought, would bear the main burden of financing the war.[2] Gerth had several objections to Mills's prospectus, beginning with the assumption that the identity of the internal enemies of the American war effort was still an open question. Locating the enemy was not a problem. The chief domestic opponents of American military engagement had already identified themselves. They were "untrustworthy aliens, appeasers, slackers," and all opponents of the government's war policy, including labor leaders such as John L. Lewis and liberal intellectuals who had recently discovered international affairs. In transposing a question on which there was no significant doubt into a seemingly important theoretical issue, Mills had committed a fallacy of misplaced intractability. Since the identity of the enemy at home was obvious, Mills's project seemed pointless. It would produce nothing more than a banal restatement of commonplace facts drawn from the daily press.

Gerth also found Mills's conception of intellectuals insufficiently differentiated. He conflated different types of intellectual workers, such as professional thinkers, editors, popularizers, and publicists, and treated them as if they were all engaged in the same task. Moreover, he mistakenly assumed that intellectuals as a group were uniformly situated in the middle class. Gerth reminded Mills that intellectuals do not constitute a class, nor does any single class comprise all American intellectuals, who range from rentier private scholars and Ivy League professors living off private incomes to "quasi-proletarian urban school teachers."

In Gerth's view, Mills's assumption that the middle class would sacrifice most to the political economy of mobilization ignored the economic impact of the war on both business and labor. The result was a serious oversimplification of the economic sociology of the war. Some manufacturers would be deprived of access to essential raw materials; others would lose their workers to conscription and military production. Plants that could not be retooled for wartime production would be closed, their owners driven out of business. Further, it seemed that lower-class wage earners, not middle-class salaried employees, would be the major losers in the wartime economy. Because they were the largest group of consumers with the lowest earnings, increases in sales taxes would have a larger impact on their disposable income. As mobilization forced cutbacks in production for the mass retail market, consumer goods would become more scarce. The inevitable price increases would have a disproportionate effect on the working class. The assumption that the middle class would be obliged to foot the bill for the war ignored these considerations. It followed that Mills's strategy for a sociological analysis of American mobilization was useless, "meaningless to those who study the mechanics of 'defense economy.'" An investigation of the social distribution of the costs of mobilization and its bearing on American class structure was a daunting task for empirical research. Mills had not undertaken this research, nor did he have the resources to do so. Because he was in no position to do the work necessary to substantiate the large claims outlined in his prospectus, his project had no empirical significance. When his ambitious theses were measured against the methodological criteria for the investigation required to support them, his standards were found wanting. In the end Gerth urged him to expect more from himself, set higher standards, and do some serious thinking rather than follow his journalistic bent: "Let's sit down and do scholarly work rather than publishing for the day."[3]

Gerth saw the tendencies exhibited in these drafts of the early 1940s as evidence of deficits in Mills's intellectual development. The simplification of complex ideas, the search for a telling and engaging phrase, and the effort to create rhetorical effects for their own sake had led Mills to sacrifice careful analysis to literary showmanship. A facile style unrestrained by the stringent requirements of science was likely to corrupt his work, tempting him to produce intellectual goods to meet the demands of the market and conform to public tastes. Gerth counseled more disciplined writing as a way to improve the quality of his thinking. "Why be less sophisticated in writing than you are in thinking," he asked, encouraging Mills not to compromise scholarship "for the sake of a good phrase."[4]

Did Gerth subscribe to Buffon's dictum that style is the man? He seems to have believed Mills's style was an expression of the quality of his mind and an indication that his intellectual standards lacked weight and substance. As the years passed Mills's work did not give him reasons to change his mind on these matters. In *White Collar,* Mills's principal solo effort during the collaboration, Gerth found that the tendencies he regarded as objectionable in Mills's thinking had become more pronounced, forming a distinctive Millsean intellectuality: badly executed big pictures and large-scale but ill-conceived syntheses, a strained effort to achieve a sparkling and impressive prose style, indifference to conceptual clarity and logical rigor, the absence of a thorough analysis of any issue, and a lack of historiographic and scholarly discipline that resulted in oversimplifications and misjudgments.

Gerth followed the evolution of *White Collar* from its conception in the early 1940s through the decade of drafting, recasting, and revision. Generous with his comments at every stage of the work, he forwarded his ideas, suggestions, and criticisms. There is a sense in which the book formed part of his own intellectual biography, not least because it drew on Mills's work with him. The theme of Gerth's 1933 Frankfurt doctoral dissertation was early German liberalism and its beginnings in the old middle class, whose position was based on the ownership of commercial enterprises.[5] Mills's project provided Gerth with the occasion to reflect on the genesis and development of the new American middle class, whose life chances were based on the labor market for white-collar work.

Gerth's assessment of *White Collar* was equivocal. On the one hand, he was lavish in his praise, both public and private. Shortly after its publication, he congratulated Mills. "Compliments to the book once more! Will be like a 'fresh breeze' in this murky drift of trivia of 'market research' or of futility of 'specialism' and 'segmentalism.' Wished I had written it. It's altogether a book to be proud of."[6] In 1954, more than two years later, he wrote a long and heavily annotated essay in German on European and American thinking about the middle class, using Mills's book as his point of departure. This essay, apparently intended as an introduction to the German edition of *White Collar,* included several laudatory judgments celebrating Mills's achievement. *White Collar* was "the first book by an American to employ sociological means to tackle the problem of American society as a whole," a striking observation in the light of the contemporaneous publication of Talcott Parsons's book *The Social System.* Mills's work represented something "altogether new" in American sociology and was one of the most important books written by an American since the war.[7] On the other hand, Gerth's criticisms were numerous, substantial, and in the end devastating. Four of his objections may be singled out as the most

decisive: defects in concept formation and the construction of sociological typologies; weaknesses in sociological analysis; shoddy scholarship; and
intellectual exhibitionism, a pretense to sophistication in philosophy and
the history of ideas that Mills did not possess.

During Mills's work on *White Collar,* Gerth had drawn his attention to
problematic concepts that were crucial to his argument. In Mills's analysis, the increasing financial instability of American small business owners
and farmers was an essential factor in the collapse of the economic underpinnings of the old middle class. The link between the middle class and
property ownership had been broken and replaced by a new dependence
that tied the fate of this stratum to fluctuations in the labor market. To
elucidate this transformation, Mills coined the term *lumpen-bourgeoisie* to
complement the concept of a lumpen-proletariat employed by Marx and
Engels in *The Communist Manifesto.* The lumpen-bourgeoisie was located
at the "bottom of the entrepreneurial world," comprising the multitude of
tiny and insignificant farms and businesses that employed no workers beyond the labor provided by the owner's family. The economic predicament
of Mills's lumpen-bourgeoisie was determined by the deadly equation of
inadequate capitalization, a low rate of productivity, and a high rate of failure. Because of these factors, the lumpen-bourgeoisie could be crushed by
small variations in the business cycle. Because a statistically insignificant
dip in business volume could obliterate their profit margins, the mentality of the lumpen-bourgeoisie was marked by insecurity, anxiety, and
desperation. The will to power and success of an older culture of posses-
sive individualism was replaced by a new "small-scale wretchedness" and a
"fretful assertiveness," the results of an inability to control the conditions
that make the difference between minimal profitability and bankruptcy.[8]

Gerth advised Mills that he had misunderstood the German word *Lum-
pen,* which is not a synonym for victims of economic deprivation but a
pejorative term meaning roughly "riff-raff" or "scum." In the world of
The Communist Manifesto, he explained, the lumpen-proletariat was composed of pimps, prostitutes, petty criminals, and confidence men. Eco-
nomically lumpen-proletarians were parasites who performed no useful
productive functions. Politically they were dangerous elements who could
easily be hired to commit criminal acts ranging from hooliganism to terror, a point developed by Marx in his analysis of class stratification and the
bases of political power in *The 18th Brumaire of Louis Bonaparte* and later
stressed by the German sociologists who studied the recruitment tactics of
the Nazi Party. It followed that Mills was mistaken in postulating a con-

ceptual link between the lumpen-bourgeoisie and the lumpen-proletariat. The Millsean lumpen-bourgeoisie were disfranchised and impoverished small business owners. As Gerth noted, the lumpen-proletarians of Marxist theory were recruited from all strata and included "socially heterogeneous materials," the refuse that had accumulated at the bottom of the social pond. The product of the operation of a variety of processes of social disintegration, the lumpen-proletariat included not only workers who were victims of structural unemployment but also banished princes, impoverished aristocrats, and shyster lawyers, as well as tramps, vagabonds, and thieves.

Shortly after the publication of *White Collar,* Gerth registered his unhappiness that Mills had failed to take his observations on the concept of the lumpen-bourgeoisie into account during the successive revisions of the manuscript. In his view, use of this term in the book was likely to produce pernicious political consequences. Mills had not anticipated that the concept would foster an attitude of leftist *hauteur* on the part of intellectuals and labor leaders, encouraging them to view the lower middle class with contempt. Since it would drive a wedge between labor leaders and indigent small business owners and farmers, such an attitude was politically irresponsible. A genuine populism would attempt to "rally *all* threatened and downtrodden marginal strata." Intellectuals of the Left who followed Mills's unsympathetic characterization of the lower middle class would see its unfortunate members as nothing more than "poor white trash." As a result, this stratum would be driven further to the right and into the camp of religious reactionaries and anti-Semites. Gerth worried that marginal small business owners, "politically homeless" and rebuffed and despised by intellectuals such as Mills, would be easily mobilized by right-wing political movements, just as the "little men" of the Weimar Republic had been recruited en masse by the Nazi Party.[9]

In the light of his critique of the concept of the lumpen-bourgeoisie, it is hardly surprising that Gerth rejected the analysis Mills constructed on its basis. In grounding his investigation of the lower middle class on an ideological Marxian concept that he had misunderstood, Mills failed to grasp the factors responsible for the impoverishment of this group and obscured the true sources of its instability and marginality. According to Gerth, the critical feature of this stratum was its dependence on large corporations. Small business owners and farmers continued to believe in the illusions of free enterprise, entrepreneurship, and economic independence even as their autonomy collapsed. Destitute farmers lost their land and ended up as the petty "bondsmen" of giant energy companies. As managers of local gasoline stations and coal and oil distribution outlets, they were contractually obligated to retail the products of the companies that funded their operations. Putatively independent but heavily mortgaged saloonkeepers were in the same situation, tapping the beer of the breweries that financed them. Barkeepers, gasoline station operators, automobile dealers, and many other smaller retailers faced the same predicament.

> One could go through quite a range of such diversified and indebted "middle class" fractions tied to monopolistic corporations, whether it be beer breweries, oil producers, launderette owners, car-dealers, and what not. Statistically they all look alike as "independent" little businesses. Substantially, economically, however, they represent veritable armies of little bondsmen paying off their mortgages, working day and night to "get out from under," being controlled and tied to some long distance corporate organization.[10]

In Gerth's view, Mills had no grasp of the macrohistorical factors responsible for the powerlessness of white-collar workers. The loss of middle-class autonomy as an important constituent of the alienation of labor in modern capitalist societies was a prominent theme of Weber's writings, which stressed the mechanisms by which workers in bureaucracies lose control over the instruments essential to their work: the means for production, destruction, administration, management, and research. The increasing dependency of the new middle class was the result of a disjunction between the performance of work and the control of resources. As mastery of the apparatus indispensable to white-collar work became concentrated at the top of large and powerful bureaucracies, the workers employed in these organizations were reduced to functionaries whose fate varied with the vicissitudes of technological change and the labor market. *White Collar* merely appropriated the jargon of Weberian sociology, employing Weber's concepts and rhetoric without understanding the real import of his ideas or the logic of his arguments. Ignoring the larger institutional history that produced the white-collar worker, Mills composed instead a Dos Passos–like phenomenology of various middle-class organizational milieus and their economic and social settings, such as the "Great Salesroom" of Macy's department store. He also missed the societal implications of the transition from the old to the new middle class: the division of the home from the workshop and the office; the differentiation between loci of production and consumption, which led to a sharp distinction between work life and private life; and the emergence of mass leisure typified by the middle-class housewife, whose devotion to play and self-representation created an important market for novels, public lectures, and later the cinema.[11]

Gerth believed that Mills had also failed to consider how the progressive differentiation of functions in white-collar work produced novel opportunities for advancement as well as new invidious distinctions of status. In a sketch of the professionalization of white-collar work and the rationalization of managerial careers following World War II, Gerth indicated how a sociology of business education might explore this new division of white-collar labor. At the top of a corporation, managerial skills are relatively unimportant as long as the chief executive officer has access to a cadre of trained and disciplined middle managers capable of executing policy. The higher up in the hierarchy of organizational power and privilege a position is located, the more incompetent its occupant can afford to be. As a result, nothing is likely to change if "the top executive absents himself for a couple of months and waters his feet in Miami Beach." Middle management will carry on in his absence.[12] In the United States it is the function of schools of business administration to produce this cadre of middle managers and certify the qualifications of its members. It would be risky for corporations to recruit candidates for managerial positions directly from liberal arts colleges, where faculties unsympathetic to commerce produce dangerous ideas and educate students in a tradition of critical rationality. Large businesses require conformity to organizational cultures designed to produce loyalty, stability, and profitability. Their chief recruitment center is the business school, detached from university faculties of liberal arts and sciences and committed to pedagogies geared to corporate interests. As a key institution for channeling aspiring candidates into the new spectrum of white-collar jobs, the business school opens up many opportunities for corporate influence on business education, especially in funding academic programs and faculty appointments that meet the needs of their sponsors. Because of the ties between business schools and their benefactors, big business can expect that business school graduates will demonstrate the balance of technical expertise and moral flexibility critical to the management of the post-war corporation.

Business schools also teach corporate etiquette to managerial trainees uninitiated in the skills of self-promotion and impression management. As academies designed to train prospective managers in the higher sophistry of negotiation, conflict resolution, and public relations, schools of business are "vocational schools for aspiring second lieutenants down to the training of foremen in Emily Post ways of benevolently handling their men and women." [13] In Gerth's view, an adequate analysis of white-collar work would explore the division of labor produced by the proliferation of new careers in management, linking this development to the status aspirations of the middle class and their struggle to "make it," if not to the top then at least to a position of security and respectability.

This is not an exhaustive survey of Gerth's critique of the analytical weaknesses of *White Collar*. Mills had nothing to say about the various dimensions of what Gerth, in the parlance of the time, called "the Negro question," especially the migration of southern blacks into northern labor and housing markets and the whole range of issues bearing on black assimilation into the new middle class. He also ignored the importance of religion in the formation and reconfiguration of the middle classes. In *White Collar* Puritanism is said to "mirror" the impersonal fate of human beings dominated by the forces of the market, a view that reproduces the economic determinism of Marx and Engels. Mills seemed unaware of the religious bases of middle-class individualism and the underpinnings of its ethic of hard work and self-discipline in Protestant moral theology. Nor did he consider the role of clergymen as "unpaid salesmen" promoting middle-class morality. *White Collar* was silent on the major shifts in the relations between religion and the American middle classes during the first half of the twentieth century, failing to note the passing of the Protestant establishment's political ascendancy, the decline of rural Protestantism as a political force, and the rise of political Catholicism.[14]

Gerth also took Mills to task for careless scholarship. The discussion of the political consciousness of the new middle class in *White Collar* distinguished two models of political consciousness: liberalism and Marxism. Mills based the political psychology of both models on classical utilitarianism. In his understanding of Marx, class consciousness is not the objectification of a Hegelian spirit as it acquires self-knowledge but the operation of a Benthamite calculus that weighs advantages and disadvantages on a scale of self-interest. Class struggles and the processes by which classes become aware of their objective and immanent possibilities are rational calculations of competing interests on the part of opposing classes. Gerth contended that Mills's derivation of Marx's analysis of class consciousness from utilitarian psychology was a serious blunder.[15] In Gerth's view, Mills misunderstood Marx's concept of alienation and, more generally, misinterpreted the relationship between utilitarianism and Marx's theory of ideology.

On Mills's reading of Marx, the unhappy or alienated consciousness of Marx's early work is an experience in which pain outweighs pleasure. This is not the meaning of Marxian alienation, however, which is an ontological condition, not a phenomenological one. In the utilitarian tradition that traces its genesis to Bentham, happiness and unhappiness are sensations. Marxian anthropology rejects the utilitarian conception of happiness as pleasure and unhappiness as pain. For Marx, happiness and unhappiness are conditions of human existence or modes of human being. Unhappiness is not pain but a loss of humanity. In the final analysis, to be unhappy is to be dehumanized and objectified, reduced to the status of a commodity. Happiness is not pleasure but a concomitant of freedom, a condition for the full development of human potentialities and powers.

According to Marx, the utilitarianism of Bentham's *Introduction to the Principles of Morals and Legislation* is not a general science of psychology, ethics, and jurisprudence but a class ideology. In a memorable epigram in *Capital*, Marx celebrates Bentham as the genius of bourgeois stupidity: "the arch-Philistine, Jeremy Bentham, that insipid, pedantic, leather-tongued oracle of the ordinary bourgeois intelligence of the 19th century."[16] The history of utilitarianism is a reflection of the evolution of the bourgeoisie. Early utilitarian theory functioned as a critique of the obstacles that inhibited the rise of this class. The subsequent economic ascendancy of the bourgeoisie transformed utilitarianism into a philosophical apologetics, a justification for the prevailing state of affairs and a presumptive proof that the social order of Victorian capitalism had achieved an ideal state of equity and beneficence. In sum, Mills's discussion of models of political consciousness represented a failure to understand the two most influential political traditions of modernity.

Finally, Gerth was repelled by the exhibitionism and self-indulgence of *White Collar*. Mills had revealed himself as an intellectual philistine, shockingly ignorant of the history of ideas and insensitive to its subtleties. In his notes on the book, Gerth recalled a conversation in which Mills confessed his inability to understand the importance of Jakob Burckhardt's work: "You know Gerth I don't think he is so great, I can't see that [you can] get anything out of it."[17] Gerth seems to have believed that Mills was intent on achieving recognition as an important thinker, at ease in the world of high culture, serious writers, and big ideas. He regarded Mills's quotations from Kafka, however, and his references to Kierkegaard, Marx, and Henry James as nothing more than textual decoration. By reflecting the "glamour" and "sheen" of the great Western intellectual tradition, Mills demonstrated that he was au courant. Intellectual vanity led him to embellish his book with the names of fashionable authors. Understanding them was another matter. For Mills, the "young man in a hurry," life was "too short for that."[18]

When Gerth declared that he wished he had written *White Collar,* did this mean he regretted he had not written the same book Mills had written? Or did it mean something rather different, that he regretted he had not written his own sociology of the white-collar world, an observation that is less a compliment to Mills than an expression of his sense of failure because he had not undertaken an independent investigation of the major transformations in the history of the middle class, an analysis that would have complemented Weber's inquiry into the origins of the distinctive middle-class ethos? Regardless of how this remark was originally intended, Gerth's many criticisms of the book, their intensity and detailed elaboration, and the sheaves of comments he prepared on how it should have been written suggest that his declaration, like so much in the Gerth-Mills relationship, was painfully ambivalent. Gerth seems to have regarded Mills as his apprentice, the disciple who would defend his conception of social science and carry on his teaching. Although he was inevitably forced to conclude that Mills was not an ideal candidate for this mission, his reservations about the quality of Mills's work were confined to manuscripts and correspondence. From Gerth's standpoint, public criticism of Mills would constitute self-criticism. In his opinion, any publication on the theme "Gerth contra Mills" would raise questions about the ideas of the apprentice and, ultimately, the master who was their source.

Gerth's Dilemma

Even before the Weber project, Gerth had begun to suspect that Mills was more interested in pursuing status and fame than in contributing to social science. In that case, why was he willing to embark on the collaboration? If he later became convinced that Mills was deceitful and predatory, why did he persevere in the face of incidents that he interpreted as repeated acts of betrayal and humiliation? On the one hand, Gerth regarded Mills as the epitome of the vulgar American academic careerist, selling his intellectual wares even as he sold himself. On the other hand, he found Mills attractive, admirable, and, in the long run, indispensable. Gerth needed Mills. But why?

From the beginning of his sociological studies at Heidelberg and his participation in Karl Mannheim's Weber seminar, Gerth took the daunting path of Weberian historical sociology. He was not merely a translator, commentator, and proponent of Weber's ideas in the United States at a time when most of his work was unavailable in English. He also attempted to follow the research program Weber pursued in *Economy and Society* and his comparative studies in the sociology of religion. Gerth understood this program as comprising three interlocking projects: a typological analysis that produced a taxonomy of actors, actions, social relationships, and organizations; a structural analysis that demonstrated how these types were situated and linked in the institutional orders of society; and a historical analysis that explained social changes as a consequence of the intersection and interplay of these institutional orders.[19]

Gerth's contributions to Weberian sociology were limited to sketches and outlines. He never performed a full-scale investigation of any sociological issue, beginning with a construction of types and proceeding to a structural and historical analysis. Nor did he carry out a sustained piece of research within one of these three analytical areas, the closest he came being an uncompleted community study.[20] Gerth seemed unable to produce a finished piece of work. Instead of executing a single three-part analysis, or at least one of its three components, he explored many typologies, often brilliantly and with remarkable flashes of insight, illustrating each typology with examples drawn from his extensive reading in the history of world civilizations, and then moving to another typology to perform the same exercise. To picture Gerth at work, it is necessary to envision a mind racing from one set of interlinked issues to another, charting some of the more interesting logical possibilities, providing illustrative details, and speeding on to other issues without pausing for breath. The results are impressive, at times exciting and even stunning. Not surprisingly, they are also fragmentary and inconclusive. Gerth wrote proposals that suggested lines of inquiry and provided leads and references for investigating a bewildering variety of problems. He always grounded these suggestions in a historical context, both to sharpen their focus and to highlight their value for understanding the contemporary world. Nonetheless, he never succeeded in defining research problems or projects for the investigation of specific issues. Like Weber, Gerth constructed frameworks for a vast ensemble of investigations. Unlike Weber, he worked out the details of none.

In attempting to advance Weber's research program, Gerth faced a serious problem he was never able to resolve. Weber's doctrine of history's irreducibility to conceptual schemes, his thesis that "the irrational reality of life and the content of its *possible* meanings are inexhaustible," entails the necessity of a typological method for sociology.[21] Only selected aspects of historical reality qualify as possible problems for sociological interpretation and explanation. They are distinguished from the cognitively indifferent manifold of history by means of typological concepts: Weber's ideal types, which identify the features of reality that are worth knowing because they fall under some cognitive interest. If there is a *hiatus irrationalis* between concepts and reality and if every typology is the product of a conceptual apparatus that is imposed on reality to make it comprehensible, how is it possible to decide the validity of any given ideal typical construction? In *Economy and Society* Weber develops a taxonomy of cities based on economic criteria, a classification, he claims, that results in three types: consumer cities, producer cities, and merchant cities.[22] If every city is infinitely complex, why select economic criteria as the basis for a taxonomy of cities? Why not kinship, politics, or religion? In what sense, if any, does Weber's economic taxonomy have a privileged status? Moreover, how can it be established that precisely these three types, and not others, are entailed by an economic principle of classification? Finally, how is it possible to determine whether any given city conforms to one type more closely than to another?

Without a principle for deciding their validity, it seems that ideal types are inherently arbitrary. No typology is more or less valid than any other. In that case, choices between alternative ideal typical constructions of the same phenomenon cannot be made on the grounds of validity, and a sociology based on ideal types can make no claim to validity. Without a principle of typological validity, the project of constructing ideal types for any given phenomenon has no limits. The formation of a typology becomes an infinitely complex project that reproduces the irrationality of reality as the irrationality of ideal types. Gerth grasped the epistemological embarrassment of Weber's typological strategy quite early in the collaboration. Writing to Mills in the autumn of 1941 on the problem of developing a conceptual framework for *Character and Social Structure,* he elucidated the difficulty posed by any attempt to complement a general theory of social structure with a special theory of social settings or spaces. Such a project, he explained, would generate an endless typology of spaces. It would be possible to distinguish political spaces, such as the Roman forum, the assembly hall, and the village green; religious spaces, such as the cathedral, the Puritan meeting house, and the confessional booth; and economic spaces, such as fairs, exhibitions, stock exchanges, warehouses, waterfronts, railway stations, workshops, and plants. There are, of course, many other types of space as well, but just how many is not clear, nor is it clear why one category of space rather than another should be selected for the typology. "In short," he concluded, "one could casuistically go [on] ad infinitum."[23]

Unable to devise a coherent logical solution to this difficulty, he proposed to handle it in a pragmatic fashion. Social spaces could be categorized by tying them to the personnel who occupy them and the roles performed within their confines. The castle and the chateau could be considered in a discussion of the aristocracy; the parlor room in the context of bourgeois intimacy; markets, workshops, and other economic settings in an account of economic roles; and military spaces such as camps, barracks, and drill grounds in an analysis of military roles.[24] Gerth's maneuver, however, does not solve the problem of a typology of social spaces. It merely transposes this issue into a parallel unresolved problem of devising typologies for the actors or roles that are situated in various spaces. The general question of typological validity remains.

Although Gerth's discussion of the problem posed by a typology of social spaces shows that he understood the fundamental difficulty posed by Weber's theory of ideal types, he was unable to profit from this insight. Gerth possessed a vast reservoir of historical knowledge that he could evoke as needed for illustrative purposes, enabling him to link typologies to specific cases that exhibited their logic. Nonetheless, he did not tie the construction of typologies to specific research questions. As a result, his thinking provided no basis for a pragmatic closure of any typological analysis. Instead he indulged in the production and internal elaboration of typologies. As these taxonomies became more recondite and refined, it was sometimes a challenge for Gerth to follow the systematics of his own constructions and maintain control over their logic. In a taxonomy of leaders and leadership, for example, he distinguished two types: traditional and charismatic. Under the former he included patriarchical heads of families and households, patriarchical warlords, and gerontocracies. Under patriarchical warlords he listed the following subtypes: charismatic warlords, magicians, kings, and religious leaders. In addition, he introduced another typology called "Leaders of Voluntary Associations: cults, cliques, schools, and currents" that is developed independently of the taxonomy of leadership.

This second typology poses a number of problems. The leadership of voluntary associations is a subtype of leadership generally. It is not independent of Gerth's classification of leadership types but falls under this classification, along with traditional and charismatic leadership. The category of leaders of voluntary associations is confusing in other respects as well. Under this heading Gerth collected every sort of leader and mode of leadership that does not fit easily under traditionalism and charisma: leaders of political and social movements, trend and fashion leaders, and leaders of intellectual and artistic coteries and cults. These subtypes are distinguished not by types of leadership but by types of movements: status-group movements, class movements, political movements, and movements in commerce, style, and fashion. Because Gerth conflated types of leaders with types of social and cultural movements, his classification shifts from a typology of leadership to a typology of movements and movementlike developments.

In addition to these confusions, which compromise the coherence of the taxonomy, another confusion stems from the way Gerth subsumed charismatic business leaders under the category of leaders of voluntary organizations, even though they seem to belong under the heading of charismatic leaders. Under the category of leaders of voluntary organizations, Gerth included imperialist leaders such as Cecil Rhodes, Winston Churchill, and T. E. Lawrence. Leaving aside the consideration that Lawrence seems to belong under Gerth's subtype of charismatic warlords, the commercial empires of the nineteenth century can hardly be understood as voluntary associations. Marxism is listed both as a status-group movement, along with the Stefan George circle and the Wagner cult, and as a class movement, together with trade unionism and anarchism. Middle-class movements are given an independent heading, even though they belong as a subheading under class movements. The same holds for movements in fashion, which belong under status-group movements. Finally, Gerth's conception of status is so comprehensive that its value is questionable. It embraces race (the abolitionist movement), religion (Zionism), and gender (the suffrage movement), as well as politics (Marxism), ethics (the temperance movement), art (surrealism), and science (Darwinism and psychoanalysis). Gerth did not attempt to clear up these difficulties, nor did he undertake a structural or historical investigation of any of these types and subtypes of leadership.[25]

Once in the grip of a typology's logic, Gerth found it difficult to escape. As he built type on type and subtype within subtype, the exploration of the subtypes of one taxonomy suggested a new typology, the categories of which led to yet another classification, as the shift from a typology of leaders to a typology of movements indicates. Because there is no principle that determines when a set of ideal types is complete, there are no limits on the multiplication of typologies. In practice Gerth's typologies were limited by his schedule, his creative powers, or his interest in the exercise. He did not finish a typology by completing it—this was impossible. The end point was decided by the exhaustion of his time, energy, or current supply of ideas. In his manuscripts there is no indication of where this form of intellectual play would lead or what results it might produce.

As an accomplished pianist and a musicologist and historian of music, it occurred to Gerth that the language of musicology could be used to analyze the significance of numbers in the constitution of small groups. Moreover, he performed this analysis creatively, using the vocabulary of chamber music to sketch a typology of small groups based on the criterion of size: the duo and the trio; the quartet, which might be formed by two duos; the quintet, which could be formed by a duo and a trio, or by two duos and a solo role, as in a piano quintet; and the sextet, which opens up several possibilities—a double trio, a triple duo, or a core quartet with two ancillary members who acquire a joint identity only by virtue of their affiliation with the core. The sextet and the octet can also be subdivided into various configurations. These considerations led to a typology of power alignments in small groups based on the chamber music metaphor. The members of a duo may have the same role, playing in unison; one member may follow the other with a separate but equal contribution offset in some way, as in imitative music; or one role may be subordinated to the other, as in accompanied solos. Gerth took up this typology only to abandon it, pursuing instead the idea that small group size might be correlated with erotic possibilities as well as sex and age differences. In the erotic case, a trio might be composed of a man and two women, for example, a husband and his wife and mistress; or by a woman and two men, for example, a wife and her husband with the addition of her lover. He left these possibilities unexplored to consider, with equal brevity, how small group size could be linked to the *Gemeinschaft/Gesellschaft* distinction, the differentiation and segmentation of roles in large organizations, the conditions for the formation of friendship, the prerequisites of group solidarity, and the ties between solidarity and the circumstances under which group members escape or transcend their roles. All this territory is covered in a mere three pages of a nine-page letter to Mills, in which Gerth engaged in an untrammeled flight of taxonomic fantasy, introducing further typologies of dance forms, play groups, and political alliances.[26]

In April 1952 Gerth wrote Mills with some enthusiasm for his musicological typology of small groups. In the early 1950s what he termed "the 'small group racket'" was an influential trend in sociology and an important component of standard texts in social psychology. He suggested that *Character and Social Structure* might include a section on small groups based on this typology, or at least he and Mills could write an article on the area. "I think it would pretty well allow us to pick up anything they [the small-group analysts] have done and actually 'expand' what typological schemata are available, and at the same time put us in the position of not 'inventing' anything but merely telling them what the 'small play group' vocabulary (in music) has long developed and what the sociologists have not 'discovered' thus far."[27] After Mills made no response to this proposal, Gerth's enthusiasm waned. "Never mind the small group stuff," he wrote a week later. "Throw it away if you don't see any use for it," as if to say that he had sketched the typology only because he found the possibility intriguing.[28]

If, as Gertrude Stein instructed Ernest Hemingway, remarks do not constitute literature, neither do they qualify as science or scholarship. To borrow a favorite Gerthian metaphor, his thinking took the form of etudes: exercises and studies for future works that remained unwritten and, for the most part, unplanned. Although his taxonomic performances provide a fascinating picture of a powerful sociological intelligence at work, he did not move beyond these exercises to undertake concrete theoretical or historical investigations. Instead his thinking remained suspended in the rarified space of abstract types illustrated by interesting but ultimately inconsequential historical cases. Following Weber's research program, he employed the ideal typical methodology with abandon. Unable to surmount the epistemological difficulties created by the theory of ideal types, he constructed hundreds of typologies that led only to the construction of additional possibilities. Paralyzed by his understanding of Weber's assumptions, he proved incapable of framing the research problems on which the advance of Weberian sociology depended. As a result, his attempt to follow in Weber's path led to an impasse.

Confronted with this dilemma, what did Gerth need? Above all, he needed an editor who understood his ideas well enough to enhance their strengths and diminish or conceal their weaknesses, someone who could impose order on his encyclopedic but shapeless erudition and discipline the free play of his imagination. The solution to Gerth's problem was Mills, every professor's dream and an ideal research assistant as well. As Gerth observed some ten years after Mills's death, he was "very eager to learn, and it was rather wonderful to see with what alacrity he 'lapped it all up.'"[29] Mills had the background and intelligence required to understand

Gerth's lectures and monologues, and he was quick to grasp their importance. With his impressive powers of discrimination, he apprehended the
key points buried in Gerth's digressions and placed the crucial ideas in relief from more secondary or incidental themes Gerth had pursued at length
and analyzed for their own sake. He also knew what to do with Gerth's
lecture notes and drafts, recasting them in a hard-boiled and distinctively
American prose that stripped away pretense, hypocrisy, and cant to expose the underlying and, more often than not, morally deflating truths
of social life. Mills organized Gerth's notes into coherent texts designed
for publication, simplifying the complexity of his typologies and on occasion reducing them to sloganlike headings and subheadings for chapters
of books or sections of essays. His commitment to publication ensured
that Gerth's dilemma would not be an obstacle to the completion of any
project in which he participated. In the construction of typologies, what
mattered was simplicity, plausibility, and above all intellectual dazzle, not
some ultimate theoretical consistency, lapses from which could be concealed by means a variety of literary devices.

Comparison of Gerth's notes and drafts for *Character and Social Structure* with the published text demonstrates that this book was Mills's major
achievement as the editor and expositor of Gerth's thought.[30] The book
develops historical models of character structure and a theory of the institutional formation and selection of types of actors. Employing Weber's
conception of institutional orders, Gerth and Mills examine political, military, economic, kinship, and religious institutions in a variety of historical
periods and with reference to the themes of social control, stratification,
power, and status. They construct models for investigating the unity of
social structures and modes of institutional integration. Finally, they address large questions of social change, collective behavior, and the sociology of leadership by tracing the course and fate of the "master trends" of
modernity: bureaucratization, the decline of liberalism, and the coordina-
tion of political, economic, and military institutions. The book ends with
a breathtaking global tour of the prospects for communism and capitalism
in the late twentieth century.

Because Gerth needed a savvy guide to the new world of American academia, where ideas were commodities and careers depended on effective
self-promotion, he also relied on Mills's skills as an academic career manager. The intellectual life may be understood in both philosophical and
sociological terms. Philosophically it is a realm of thought governed by
the logic of conceptual schemes and arguments, a sphere in which ideas

struggle for ascendancy. Sociologically it is a realm of power governed by the logic of career formation, a sphere in which partisans, patrons, and promoters of ideas compete for assets, influence, and position. Gerth was at home in the world of ideas but not in the world of careers. An intellectual at ease in the milieu of leisurely discussions and long debates, he was a devotee of cultivated conversations and learned monologues that might go on for hours and lead nowhere.[31] He never became comfortable in the American university, which he regarded as morally compromised and dominated by charlatans, con artists, and "inside operators." Although he had an impressive theoretical grasp of American middle-class life and its socioeconomic underpinnings, he was conspicuously deficient in the practical methods necessary for success in this sphere. In particular, he lacked the presentational skills needed to merchandise his work and promote himself as an valuable asset and showed no interest in acquiring these techniques. He took no pleasure in the enterprises of self-advancement: the streamlining of character to meet the demands of the academic marketplace, the strategy and tactics of networking, and the cultivation of a stable of prestigious referees. He was incapable of currying the favor of colleagues or department chairs and did not know how to ask for an increase in salary, nor did he have the ability or the disposition to impress editors at lunch, pitch a book on the basis of a few large, possibly promising, but inchoate ideas, or match wits in negotiations over jobs and contracts. On critical occasions when he acted independently, attempting to put to use what he had learned about American universities and academic publishing, he did not have reason to be pleased with the results. As the controversy over the credit for *From Max Weber* demonstrated, when under stress Gerth was capable of misperceptions of persons and their intentions, serious errors of judgment, and badly calculated tactics.

In the American university of his time, Gerth cut a somewhat pathetic figure: intellectually arrogant but also irresolute and lacking self-confidence, acutely conscious of his status as an emissary of the higher culture of *Alt-Europa* to vulgar Americans and at the same time envious of those who had mastered the requirements for success in American academic life. A child of the German lower middle classes, he aspired to the style of life of an older German aristocracy for whom having and being took precedence over doing. Who you were was detached from what you had achieved, and status was independent of performance. His sole claim to such a position was his marriage to Hedwig Ide von Reventlow, the "countess" to whose background and connections he sometimes alluded when he felt his own honor or dignity was in doubt. The analyst and interpreter of institutional orders and cultural spheres did not seem to grasp an elementary truth of his life in the United States during the 1940s: being an assistant professor at a state university, the husband of a disinherited daughter of a family of German aristocrats, and an intellectual refugee who combined the class pretensions of the German imperial aristocracy with the cultural aspirations of the Weimar *Bildungsbürgertum* signified nothing.

Gerth's deficits in career management and his reluctance to take the steps needed to correct them left him without the interpersonal dexterity needed in the American university. It was Mills who served as his personal agent, envoy, and broker, providing advice and dealing on his behalf in promoting projects, negotiating agreements, and closing contracts. In spite of the bitter dispute over credit for the Weber book and his resistance to Mills's division of labor and credit for *Character and Social Structure,* Gerth continued to depend on Mills's counsel, editorial competence, and even his willingness to collaborate on further publications. In time, however, the moral costs that the collaboration imposed on Gerth and the compromises he made to use Mills as the solution to his dilemma became intolerable.[32]

The End: Revenge without Redemption

In 1958, twelve years after publication of the Weber book, Mills was a full professor at Columbia and a celebrated author and social critic. As Mills moved from one success to another, Gerth remained in Madison, struggling financially and living out the fate Mills had predicted for him in 1945: that of a scholar working in relative obscurity, appreciated only by a small circle of cognoscenti. In the autumn of 1958 Simon and Schuster published *The Causes of World War Three,* Mills's blistering attack on American foreign policy and national security strategy. Like much of his writing during the final years of his life, this book was a secular homily. Employing the rhetoric of pious outrage, Mills cast himself in the role of the wrathful prophet engaged in a struggle against the principalities and powers of this world. Gerth's interest was not aroused by the book itself. Oddly enough, his attention was caught by the dust jacket, which referred to the author as "the translator and editor (with H. H. Gerth) of *From Max Weber,* a selection of essays by the great German sociologist." This seemingly innocuous publisher's blurb moved Gerth to unleash a furious tirade against Mills. In a batch of letters, all composed in a white heat of anger on November 15 and 16, he attempted to enlist the combined forces of Simon and Schuster, Oxford University Press, and colleagues of both Mills and himself in a campaign to redress the distribution of credit for *From Max Weber.*

Gerth began with two drafts of a letter to Simon and Schuster, both dated November 15: a rough draft with several insertions in his handwriting and a second more polished version on the letterhead of the Department of Sociology and Anthropology at the University of Wisconsin. In the rough draft he asked Simon and Schuster's editors whether Mills had written the dust jacket copy and, if so, whether they were prepared to accept responsibility for the claims it made. He was incensed because the dust jacket named Mills as the editor and translator of *From Max Weber,* relegating him to what he regarded as a subordinate role. In Gerth's view, the language of the dust jacket implied that he was nothing more than Mills's "informant" or "understudy." Perhaps Mills had convinced himself that he actually had translated and edited Weber, "with a little help from H. H. Gerth." In Gerth's view, this was a fraud perpetrated on the public, and he wanted to correct it.[33]

When the Weber book was published, Gerth explained, Mills's competence in German did not extend beyond the language requirement for Ph.D. candidates at Madison. Moreover, he doubted whether Mills ever made stronger claims on his own behalf. To show that Mills's own representation of his participation was quite modest, Gerth reinterpreted the preface of the book, in effect rewriting it to support this position. Mills assumed no responsibility for choosing the selections. His job was only to correct Gerth's work, eliminating "occasional 'split infinitives'" and comparable shortcomings. If an editor makes choices of inclusion and exclusion, Mills did not claim that he edited *From Max Weber.* And if translation requires the transposition of a text from one language into another, he did not claim that responsibility either. Citing the preface, Gerth argued that Mills took credit only for the "formulation and editorial arrangement of the English text."[34]

The preface does not support Gerth's reading. Mills did not disavow credit for either editorial selection or translation, nor did he limit his contribution to the correction of minor stylistic lapses. The preface states: "Responsibility for the selections and reliability of the German meanings is primarily assumed by H. H. Gerth; responsibility for the formulation and editorial arrangement of the English text is primarily assumed by C. Wright Mills."[35] In his quotation of this sentence for the editors at Simon and Schuster, Gerth deleted the qualifier "primarily." "All he [Mills] claimed (p. vii of the Preface) was 'responsibility for the formulation and editorial arrangement of the English text,' i.e. never for any 'translation' of a single Weber piece, but simply for improving my English by touching my translation up here and there."[36] Moreover, both Gerth and Mills shared full responsibility for the work as a whole. This was the distribution of credit on which Mills insisted, even to the point of threatening to abandon the project and abort its publication if Gerth refused to agree: "The book as a whole represents our mutual work and we are jointly responsible for such deficiencies as it may contain."[37] In his letter to Simon and Schuster, Gerth also omitted this critical last sentence of the preface, which was decisive in resolving the question of precedence. If Mills was responsible for all the deficiencies in the book, he was responsible for deficiencies in editing and translating. That meant that the preface credited him with performing these functions, which was precisely his intention in insisting on this language.

In the more restrained letterhead draft, Gerth shifted from the claims Mills made about his responsibilities for *From Max Weber* to the facts germane to these claims. The theme of the rough draft, that Gerth was lodging a protest to protect the public from a fraudulent representation, was dropped. In this version Gerth was engaged in an attempt to protect himself against Mills. His American experience had taught him that the ethics governing the relations between doctoral students and their professors in German universities did not apply in the United States. The American professor was not a *Doktorvater* to whom the student owes obligations of gratitude and loyalty but rather a source of ideas and expertise that the student feels free to exploit without authorization or even acknowledgment. Gerth had learned that American students would "walk all over you unless you speak up." Since he had been "taken for a ride" by Mills, he proposed to set the record straight. Mills, Gerth claimed, could not read Weber's German, and his only knowledge of Weber's work was gleaned from the mimeographs Gerth distributed to his classes. He corrected Gerth's English and edited his translations to prepare a text for publication. Then he sold the manuscript to Oxford. Although Gerth appreciated this exercise of entrepreneurial initiative, he regretted that Mills, who was now famous and no longer dependent on self-promotion by falsification, did not grant him the credit that was rightfully his.[38]

On November 15 Gerth also wrote two letters to Mills: a perfunctory and obviously perturbed request for clarification concerning the dust jacket[39] and the draft of a long confession, a stunning and in many respects painful document of self-revelation.[40] In the confession he recounted his years in the United States, telling a story of disillusion and humiliation that was epitomized in his relationship with Mills. Gerth was the immigrant in "this country of 'the competitive man,' " a failure and a loser because of his commitment to principles. Mills was the aggressive exponent of the new middle-class virtues of opportunism and compromise who had succeeded because he was not restrained by principles that checked his ruthlessness. Although Gerth protested that he did not begrudge Mills the fruits of his success, his protestations were laced with sarcasm at Mills's expense. Asking Mills to read his letter to Simon and Schuster, Gerth suggested that he "reflect a bit about it and—famous man that you have become—realize that I don't think that I can take it indefinitely 'to be walked all over.' "

> Now, I am not eager to compete with you and do not begrudge your publishing and publicity success. On the contrary! I wish you good luck all along, and all the way. But I hate to be "walked all over" indefinitely, and for no good reason.
>
> I think I did you a good turn and service when helping you to meet Logan Wilson years ago and helping you to get the Maryland job, and I say this not to "exact" anything from you. Only I wish you to realize that I am not your "understudy," nor your "informant" nor your footstool or stooge. How else can I defend myself against your—shall we say slight insensitivity—than by pointing it out at least to your publisher and drawing his attention to fair and unfair advertising techniques or lack of standards. I don't expect any sense of honor anyway from anybody in this country. But that latest little way of yours to "cut corners" is slightly "gross," the more so as you could have known my sentiment toward your ways in this respect. I shall be glad to choose some public medium, if you prefer that, when "it happens" again— without, of course, any bad intention or doing of yours. I know, you managed once Mr. Oxford and directed him to act on your behalf by your lack of discretion (showing a friendly though strong letter of mine addressed to you and nobody else without bothering to ask me), and I know one has to be careful when writing to you as you know how to "operate" if you wish to. Hence this quite modest way of mine of just asking you not to do it again. It is so superfluous, Mills, you are quite famous and you don't need to engage or indulge in what, with Simmel, one might call "negative" competition.[41]

Gerth was torn between conflicting views on the position he should take. Although he had challenged Mills's veracity, he assured Mills of his abiding friendship ("in spite of all"). Apologizing for reviving the stale controversy over precedence, further discussion of which would only prove futile, he did not hesitate to excavate the painful minutiae of the dispute, dredging up incidents that, in his view, demonstrated Mills's acts of deceit and betrayal. Gerth did not pretend that he could compete with Mills, who knew how to "operate" so well. He threatened Mills in his own "modest way," however, noting that he was not prepared to tolerate another attack on his reputation. Concluding with the observation that although he hoped to hear from Mills, he also had to consider that time, especially Mills's time, was money: "Don't bother to write a letter—that is 'corny' anyway—just 'drop me a line' or 'write me a memo.'"[42]

On November 16 Gerth wrote Oxford University Press, asking its editors to interpret the final paragraph of the preface to the Weber book, the point at which responsibilities and credit are allocated. This letter constitutes a petition from an author to unnamed editors, for what purpose he did not indicate, seeking their help in deciphering a text he had written some twelve years earlier. It also includes cryptic biographical remarks and truncated observations on issues that seemed to have a private meaning for Gerth but are barely intelligible to anyone unfamiliar with his history: his experience as a journalist in Berlin in the 1930s writing under Nazi censorship regulations, his status as a German refugee during the war, and Mills's Texas background. After noting that he had been "taken for a ride" by his "old friend and student," he wrote: "I dimly remember I tried to get him not to walk all over me at the time and naturally, as a naive 'greenhorn' and 'fingerprinted enemy alien under town arrest,' which I was 'for the duration' in gratitude for what I had done in UP [United Press] Berlin and Chicago Daily News Bureau Berlin 1936–38, I was in no position 'to ride and shoot.'"[43]

On November 16 he also wrote a more pointed appeal to Howard Becker, claiming that the credit line on the Simon and Schuster dust jacket was "a lie" and seeking his help to "stop" Mills.[44] On the same day he wrote Robert K. Merton, asking for enlightenment on the meaning of the dust jacket as well as the final paragraph of the preface to the Weber book and repeating his estimate of Mills's role in the project, which he again maintained was confined to correcting a rare split infinitive and "possibly here and there a touching up of stylistic shortcomings."[45] The letter to Merton, with its interweaving of self-knowledge and self-deception, sociological insight and lapses in judgment, self-deprecatory irony and self-pity, represents Gerth at his most puzzling. Even his efforts to damage Mills are tempered by a grudging admiration for his abilities. Gerth was again the "fingerprinted 'enemy alien under town arrest for the duration,'" powerless to assert his rights when Mills took advantage of him and compelled to give in to the "operator," the "whipper snapper," the "promising young man on the make," the academic cowboy and "talented young man who has what it takes in this world of ours (as described by Mills) 'to go to town' and 'ride and shoot.'" Gerth now realized how thoroughly he had been exploited by Mills, for whom he was nothing more than "culture fertilizer," intellectual manure that Mills had plowed into his own work. By this point he had been trodden on so long that he was "almost a habitue of the horizontal." Yet his tolerance for the horizontal life was not unlimited. "Now I don't like to be treated as an 'informant' or 'dirty little German refugee' or some such exploitable creature in the eyes of my betters and other 'operators' indefinitely. Life is not long enough for that." [46]

What did Gerth's revival of the precedence dispute achieve? The responses to his letters suggest several answers to this question, none of them consistent with his objectives. Most obviously, he had committed an embarrassing blunder. The Simon and Schuster dust jacket, he learned, was a standard promotional device. Publishers' blurbs are not scholarly references but thumbnail sketches of the main accomplishments of an author. As the director of advertising and publicity at Oxford University Press explained, if the roles of Gerth and Mills had been reversed and Oxford had published a book by Gerth, the dust jacket would very probably have named him as the translator and editor (with C. Wright Mills) of *From Max Weber*. Such a designation would have no implications for the relative weight of the contributions of either author.[47] In using the dust jacket as an opportunity finally to assert himself and redress an old injustice, Gerth demonstrated a lack of savoir faire, reading a conventional publishing practice as a dark maneuver by Mills to advance himself at the expense of his mentor and collaborator.

Gerth was determined to convince the world that Mills's role in the Weber project was limited to the secretarial and the promotional, but he failed to see that the book itself conclusively refuted this position. The title page names Mills as editor and translator along with Gerth, and the preface makes both jointly responsible for the book as a whole. By agreeing to Mills's conditions, Gerth certified his status as editor and translator, justifying any claim to credit he might make for performing these tasks. In his letter to Merton Gerth appealed to the preface as the basis for his question concerning what might be done about the Simon and Schuster dust jacket. Merton's answer to this question was nothing at all. Gerth had declared in print that the essays were jointly translated and edited. Mills and his publishers were free to use the published record for their own purposes. On what grounds could Gerth now reverse what he had conceded in print and taken no occasion to deny for some twelve years?[48] This was also the import of the muted and dismayed response to Gerth by Patricke Johns Heine, a contemporary of Mills at Madison who had also worked on Gerth's translations. Since Gerth knew Mills's character well enough, she replied, what was the cause for surprise? Heine was especially troubled that he had interpreted a notice on a dust jacket as a violation of intellectual ethics. What did he propose to do? Compel Mills to withdraw the dust jacket from circulation? Institute a lawsuit? Reinforcing Merton's point, she reminded Gerth that regardless of his current view, nothing could change the fact that the book credits Mills as coauthor and joint editor and translator. Advising her former professor to take an extra deep breath, she suggested that there were considerations in his life that should take precedence over the lost battles with Mills.[49]

Mills also urged Gerth not to confuse an insignificant incident with a question of principle. Following his usual practice in arguments with Gerth, he carefully enumerated the points he wanted to make, in this case four. First, he chided Gerth for quibbling over the dust jacket instead of commenting on the book. Gerth seemed to think imaginary slights to his dignity were more important than the possibility of nuclear war, hardly the mark of a serious thinker. Mills thus deftly reinterpreted the incident, which now was not about the dust jacket but about Gerth's intemperate response. It followed that any potential blame was deflected onto Gerth. It was Gerth who had behaved badly, and if anyone had been injured, it was Mills. In any case, Mills claimed, he had no hand in writing the text of the dust jacket, nor had he even seen it until the publisher sent him copies of the book. Second, Simon and Schuster's blurb writers had committed no offense against Gerth's reputation. Once again tripping over his suspicions, Gerth had confused a standard publicity device with a scholarly citation. Third, the matter was of no conceivable consequence for either Gerth's reputation or his own. Mills found it troubling, but also wearisome, that Gerth could lose his bearings over an utter triviality. Finally, the book had been published. What did Gerth expect? Did he want to dictate the precise language to be used in all references to *From Max Weber* that might appear in Mills's subsequent works? In that case, he should do so. Or would he prefer that Mills delete the Weber book from future references to his publications? If so, Mills would agree to this stricture as well. On matters of precedence, Mills claimed indifference.[50]

Mills cut the ground from beneath Gerth's complaint by representing the dust jacket incident as too contemptible to warrant notice. As a result,

Gerth would feel contemptible as well. On a number of occasions, Mills had been subjected to schoolmasterly cautions from Gerth concerning his moral and intellectual standards. Now he returned the favor. Presumptive slights to his dignity and petty worries over priority did not trouble Mills. Unlike Gerth, his status had been established by independent publications and no longer depended on the credit he could extract from a twelve-year-old anthology of translations.

Gerth remained unchastened by Mills's reply and unconvinced by his observation that the dust jacket was a triviality unworthy of notice. In a strained comparison he linked his current miseries and his situation at Madison to the circumstances of impoverished German academicians who had survived World War II.

> Pardon me if I feel you are not "the translator of the great German sociologist Max Weber," which, of course, is old stuff and not worth the hubbub some little German refugees want to make of it in all their concern with trivia, when in 17 years they managed to come up at long last to the full professorship, $2000 below the statistical average of an associate professor at the University of Wisconsin and about $1000 above the salary of an instructor before the Ph.D. You will understand that the hungry have only trivial interests which are of no possible interest to the better fed. I have seen German professors in 1947 fighting over the privilege of emptying the ashtrays of the conquerors in Berlin in order to get the cigarette and cigar stubs. Also trivia. You will pardon me possibly for not yet being so well assimilated and still having sufficient kinship to such people.[51]

Blinded by resentment, Gerth did not see that his earlier concessions made the failure of this latest attempt at restitution inevitable. It is striking that the student of Karl Mannheim did not grasp the fundamental difference between the truths of history and the truths of marketing. He failed to understand that in every institutional sphere, a consensus on what qualifies as the facts of a case is determined by interpretations that succeed in gaining currency and legitimacy. By agreeing to the title page and the preface of the Weber book, Gerth had confirmed the legitimacy of the view he so passionately contested. Regardless of how the book was actually written, Mills's claim to credit had been authenticated. In the process of authentication Gerth's agreement was the indispensable and binding factor.

On March 20, 1962, Mills died, perhaps not at the height of his powers but certainly at the peak of his fame thus far. A memorial was held on April 16 at Columbia, and Gerth, who was asked to speak, flew to New York for the occasion. He was not impressed by Columbia's homage to

Mills, which he characterized as a shabby and hypocritical performance. "Mr. Robert King Merton 'was out of town' and prevented from being there. Mr. Lazarsfeld was indisposed. The absence of his colleagues was somewhat 'dysfunctional' to the *image of the Columbia faculty* in the eyes of an outsider like myself, who did not mind to fly in from 1000 miles distance and be back to teach my classes on time." [52] A number of speakers seemed eager to "parcel out Mills' prestige among themselves by crying 'Charlie and I.' " [53] Gerth delivered a measured address, in the main a decorous appreciation of Mills's life and work appropriate to the occasion.[54] Celebrating Mills's passion for ideas by comparing him to Saint-Simon, the intellectual adventurer of the Napoleonic era, he praised Mills as the first homegrown sociologist to tackle the big questions concerning the genesis and destiny of the American experience and the distinctiveness of the American identity. In this respect Mills was the legitimate heir of Tocqueville, James Bryce, and Brooks Adams, the tradition of distinguished writers who interpreted American society for a world public. Nevertheless, he also indulged in a few observations on Mills the phrase maker, intellectual entrepreneur, and man in a hurry who repaired Gerth's clumsy English and sold his translations. Although Gerth noted that Mills was an enthusiastic student of Marx and Weber, he did not fail to add that the man who called himself the translator and editor of Max Weber's work could not read German and was not interested in learning it.

In the peroration of his address, Gerth declared that with Mills's death, he had lost his "alter ego." This judgment was wrong on two counts. First, Mills was not Gerth's alter ego or soul mate. He represented a type of intellectuality that Gerth regarded as alien to his view of the life of the mind and a threat to the tradition of social science in which he worked. Second, there is a sense in which Gerth did not lose Mills at all. The precedence dispute continued after his death, pursued by Gerth with the ghost of Mills and the guardians of his legacy. Gerth's private estimate of Mills departed markedly from the pieties of his eulogy. Within weeks of the Columbia memorial, he returned to the troubled chronicle of their collaboration, now debating with an adversary who was no longer able to respond. Gerth's entries in this final chapter of the partnership were an attempt to put his stamp on the first draft of the history of the collaboration by writing it himself, without the interventions of his late editor. In telling his story Gerth stressed his importance as the source of the intellectual capital on which the collaboration was based, diminishing Mills's contribution by casting doubt on his scholarly credentials, competence, and ethics. In looking back over his long sojourn in the United States, he also used his reflections on the collaboration as an opportunity to exact some measure of revenge not only against Mills but on higher learning in America and the character of American life generally.

Gerth's initial efforts in this direction were addressed to Mills's widow and third wife, Yaroslava. Four days after his speech at Columbia, he wrote Yaroslava, criticizing Mills's later works as exercises in political pamphleteering. *The Causes of World War Three,* he said, was an apology for Stalinist terror and the American appeasement of Soviet expansion in Europe. The book exhibited a signal lack of compassion for the victims of Soviet communism: the martyrs of the East German rebellion of 1953 and the Hungarian uprising of 1956, the more than three million Eastern European refugees displaced by the Red Army, and the two million Berliners incarcerated in the "West Berlin Ghetto." In the light of these considerations, it was difficult for Gerth to take seriously the received conception of Mills as a humanist and advocate of human rights. Mills's indifference to the truly defeated suggested that the political persona he had cultivated as the voice of the oppressed and disfranchised was something of a fraud. Gerth judged his book on Cuba to be nothing more than a "sentimental journey," proof that fame had corrupted his intellectual standards. Mills had become "too successful to sit down and think twice." His final book, *The Marxists,* was compromised by the same weakness. Although Gerth had sent Mills several pages of comments explaining the shortcomings of the manuscript, he ignored them. In the end, Gerth asserted, the partners drifted apart because Mills preferred short-term success to serious intellectual work. As a result, he no longer found Gerth useful.[55]

In the summer of 1962 Irving Louis Horowitz published his memorial essay on Mills in the *American Journal of Sociology.* Horowitz, whom Gerth twitted as Mills's posthumous legate, had already begun to promote Mills's work and reputation. His panegyric on the death of an intellectual hero stressed the importance of "Mills's already masterful introduction to *From Max Weber*" but ignored *Character and Social Structure.* At the same time Don Martindale informed Gerth of the gossip that Horowitz intended to exclude him from a festschrift he was planing in honor of Mills.[56] Following Horowitz's article and Martindale's report, Gerth intensified his efforts to defend his reputation at the expense of Mills, writing both Peter Blau, editor of the *American Journal of Sociology,* and William Sewell, the chair of his department at Madison.

In his letter to Blau, Gerth registered a protest against publication of the

Horowitz article. The editorial board of the *American Journal of Sociology* included Shils, who was acquainted with the history of the Weber book and, Gerth insisted, knew that Mills did not read Weber in the original, could not have collaborated on the translation, and in fact "never translated a single sentence of Max Weber." Gerth claimed that he had dictated the introductory essay to Mills in the late summer of 1945, during his visit at Mills's home in Maryland. Mills's sole contribution to the essay was to do the typing and, Gerth added, to "put the dot on my 'I's.'" Although Mills may have learned Weber by reading his translations, however, Gerth found that Mills had taught him an important lesson too: "Salesmanship in this country counts for as much as authorship." Mills's true forebears were not the great figures of the French Enlightenment, such as Diderot, Voltaire, and the other "highsounding European names" with which Horowitz embellished his article, but the jobbers, operators, and racketeers who thrive on the underside of American commerce.[57]

In writing Sewell, Gerth damned Horowitz as the author of a deliberately fraudulent and slanderous account of the collaboration. He also speculated that he had been victimized by a clique intent on degrading him to the status of Mills's "editorial assistant." By means of innuendo and defamation as well as a "silence campaign" against *Character and Social Structure,* this clique had undertaken to "get" Gerth and deprive him of the credit he deserved. To counter its machinations, he repeated the main themes of his version of the Weber project.

> I, not Mills, then a graduate student of our department, who through my help received from Logan Wilson an associate professorship in Maryland before his Ph.D., translated and introduced the essays *From Max Weber.* Mills sold them (mimeographs accumulated over the war years) without my knowledge to Oxford University Press and exploited my status as a fingerprinted enemy alien under town arrest to drive a tough bargain with me. When I tried to at least gain the right to sign the introductory essay alone, Mills succeeded to have Mr. Vaudrin of Oxford Press write to Mr. McCormick, who then obliged and put me in my place.[58]

These fulminations led nowhere. Gerth's purpose was to protect his reputation, secure his priority for *From Max Weber* and *Character and Social Structure,* and regain the recognition for his senior status in the collaboration, which he believed Mills had successfully appropriated. His method was to tell the story of their partnership so that the manner of the telling would expose Mills's pretensions. As Mills moved from academic success to fame, Gerth saw himself as unappreciated, exploited, and underpaid. His sensitivity to his rights in matters of intellectual priority kept the fires of resentment burning for more than a quarter of a century. As he finally admitted, his tolerance for the role of the dirty little German immigrant, reduced to life in a permanently horizontal position by being trodden on by Mills, was exhausted. In his more earthy metaphor, he could not accept as his intellectual legacy the prize of qualifying as the best fertilizer for Mills's writings. In the end his efforts to diminish Mills proved futile, gaining him nothing and leaving untouched the picture of Mills as the secular prophet of postwar American sociology.

❖ ❖ ❖

Epilogue

In the first few pages of "Science as a Vocation," Weber surveys both the "external" institutional conditions indispensable to science as a career and the "inward" moral and spiritual conditions essential to science as a calling. Institutionally science operates as a social selection mechanism, placing certain candidates in career paths and eliminating others. Ethically it is a set of values commitment to which differentiates candidates who have a genuine vocation from those who, as Weber claims, "should do something else."[1] The lecture is silent on the relations between the institution and its ethos. Conflict between the criteria for recruiting candidates into scientific positions and the criteria that define science as a calling is not a possibility Weber considers. Do the accommodations required by a scientific career compromise the imperatives entailed by the values of science? Are there circumstances under which success as a scientist depends on violating the ethics of science? Because Weber regarded science as an autonomous sphere of culture governed by its own immanent logic and a distinctive and internally consistent conception of rationality, these questions do not arise in his analysis of science.

The ideal values of science appear to be translated without remainder, distortion, or loss of meaning into the professional life of the scientist, a view that brings Weber, the arch anti-Hegelian, uncomfortably close to one of the chief doctrines of Hegel's metaphysics: the rationality of reality. Although Weber observes that deliberations over appointments to academic positions are "seldom agreeable," he goes so far as to claim that "in the numerous cases known to me there was, without exception, the good will to allow purely objective reasons to be decisive." [2] Science as an ideal, it seems, is embodied in the most mundane realities of the academic job market. Conceptually, however, axiological and institutional premises are independent. It follows that "Science as a Vocation" leaves open the question of an ultimate and irreducible scientific irrationality: an incompatibility between the ethics and the pragmatics of science. The collaboration between Gerth and Mills exhibits several facets of this incompatibility. On what premises were tensions between the ethics and pragmatics of the collaboration grounded? This question is tied to the more general issues in the sociology of intellectual life posed by the collaboration: the role of secrecy, deception, and information management in the production of academic reputation; conflicting conceptions of the life of the mind that were sharpened by the disagreements the collaboration produced; the interplay of differences in knowledge and power in the collaboration and their role in determining the career chances of the collaborators; and competition for credit and the adjudication of competing claims to priority.

Ideals and Illusions

Early in the collaboration Mills proposed two rules, one covering the relations between the partners and the other governing their dealings with third parties. A principle of friendship required that internal disputes be settled by frank and unsparing dialogue. Maintaining a relationship based on trust would require a full airing of differences, especially on fundamental issues. A principle of secrecy defined the products of the collaboration as proprietary documents to be held in confidence. To protect their work in progress from theft or fraudulent use, no manuscripts would be circulated or otherwise divulged.[3]

Mills's first principle failed, largely because he misunderstood its moral logic. He regarded the principle of friendship as a means of establishing the collaboration on a foundation of trust. Belief in the veracity and good faith of dialogue partners is a premise of dialogue, however, not a consequence. Trust is a presupposition of candor, not its result. Mills could expect Gerth to be forthright and open only if Gerth trusted him, which he did not. On the crucial issue in the collaboration, the question of priority and precedence, Gerth believed that Mills had traduced and manipulated him. Mills knew this, which led him to mistrust Gerth. The moral history of the collaboration is a chronicle of increasingly corrosive distrust. When the names of the authors were inadvertently reversed in a notice of the forthcoming publication of *From Max Weber,* Gerth accused Mills of treachery and threatened to expose him as a fraud. Mills responded in kind, turning to their editor at Oxford, whom he used to disarm and humiliate Gerth. Even though Gerth apologized, Mills had doubts about the authenticity of his remorse and suspected him of complicity when letters originating from the University of Wisconsin and designed to damage his reputation arrived at Columbia. In 1946, when Mills framed the Cleveland protocol as a basis for sharing responsibility and credit for *Character and Social Structure,* Gerth refused to accept his terms or even discuss them, preferring evasion, obfuscation, and confusion to negotiation with a collaborator in whom he had no confidence. Each of these incidents diminished the possibility that subsequent differences could be resolved on the basis of Mills's principle of friendship.

The principle of secrecy succeeded all too well, however, enmeshing Gerth and Mills in a network of collegial and commercial relations dominated by prevarication, suspicion, and deceit. Shils suspected that Gerth had appropriated his translation of Weber's "Class, Status, Party." Gerth and Mills mistrusted Shils, fearing he might charge them with plagiarism or perhaps forestall publication of *From Max Weber* to gain priority for his Weber edition. Gerth deceived Shils concerning his possession of Shils's Weber translations, which he claimed he had never seen. He also deceived Mannheim by suggesting that if Shils had offered to cooperate in a joint Weber edition, he would have accepted. Mills deceived Shils on a number of counts, denying knowledge of his translations and misleading him about the publication of "Class, Status, Party" and the history of the Oxford contract for *From Max Weber.* Mills mistrusted his editor at Oxford, suspecting that Hatcher might be in league with Kegan Paul to prevent publication of *From Max Weber* in order to distribute the Shils edition in the United States without competition. Gerth and Mills deceived James Reid at Harcourt Brace, leading him to believe he had purchased sole rights to *Character and Social Structure.* They also deceived John Walden and Heath, who held a contract that gave them exclusive rights to the project. When the Harcourt Brace contract could no longer be concealed, Gerth deceived Becker concerning his reasons for signing it. Mills deceived Walden concerning the lack of progress on *Character and Social Structure* to extract himself from a contract he no longer found advantageous. Even when Walden agreed to a release at a meeting in Mills's office, Mills secretly taped their conversation. More generally, Gerth and Mills deceived everyone who believed that they would place the requirements of formal commitments and contracts above the shifting contingencies of career opportunities.

As the foregoing chapters demonstrate, these incidents were not ancillary or tangential features of the collaboration. On the contrary, the partnership functioned as a social mechanism for breaking down trust and engendering deceit. Gerth and Mills mistrusted one another and at the same time deceived and mistrusted their colleagues and editors, some of whom learned to mistrust them as well. All these machinations were evoked, enacted, or imagined below the surface of official ethical rules governing conduct in academia and academic publishing, revealing the underside of official appearances.

Information Management, Mistrust, and Deceit

Mills seemed to see his career as a drama in which he was not only the starring actor but also the writer and director. As director he concealed his script from the other players until he was ready to place them on the stage. As playwright he employed an implicit theory of action based on the premise that every player had an undeclared agenda. This premise included Mills himself, whose secret tactic was to play other actors off one another, diminishing the power of each and making it possible to impose terms that would maximize his advantages. The relationship between actors' avowals and their behavior was opaque. Expressions of intent were always suspect, generally nothing more than a front for unspoken motives and concealed objectives. Mills's social world was a Goffmanesque theater of feints, subterfuges, fictions, and artifices. He could understand the conduct of his interlocutors only by ascribing to them a hidden rationale, even if he had no evidence of its existence and was forced to speculate on what it might be.

Mills's decision to sign *Character and Social Structure* with Harcourt Brace while he was still under contract to Heath was based on this conception of action as subversion. This decision implicated Mills, and then Gerth as well, in an unexpectedly complicated project of deceit. Deceivers mask or misrepresent their intentions in order to mislead third parties, typically by giving them putatively good reasons to believe what is not true. The discovery of deceit casts doubt on the truthfulness of deceivers, their commitment to saying what they believe. Perhaps more basically, it calls into question their trustworthiness: their commitment to performing what they promise and demonstrating a general consistency between seeming and being, saying and doing, and avowing and acting. It follows that deceit poses risks that increase as the conditions for the control of information and misinformation become more complex.[4]

Mills's reading of the problems posed by the two contracts for *Character and Social Structure* assumed that he could maintain control over a complex aggregate of information, all the pieces of which were known only to him. This assumption presupposed that the success he had enjoyed in restricting access to knowledge of the two contracts would continue: he would be able to manage the flow of information, releasing to all parties only those bits that served his interests. In Mills's view, it was critical to conceal the earlier contract with Heath from Harcourt Brace and equally important to conceal from Heath the new agreement with Harcourt Brace. If Reid discovered that the partners had a commitment to Heath, he might withdraw his offer. It was also necessary to conceal the Harcourt Brace contract from Becker, who was in a position to damage both Gerth and Mills by informing the two publishers as well as the sociologists at Wisconsin and Columbia. Because of the number of potentially insecure repositories of information, the difficulty of preventing leaks, the intricacies of the information networks, and the possibilities of exchange among editors, editorial advisers, and colleagues at Heath, Harcourt Brace, Columbia, and Wisconsin, Mills's task of information management was truly daunting. Moreover, even if his luck held, other actors might enter one of the networks and upset his calculations.

Intellectual Rationalization and Ethical Irrationality

In the collaboration Mills demonstrated a mastery of that mode of flexibility and impersonal detachment that Karl Mannheim called self-rationalization: the dispassionate examination of the inner resources necessary to achieve objectives. Mills dichotomized his identity into subject and object, the observer and the observed, analyst and analysand. Notwithstanding the emotional energy and professional self-interest he had invested in the collaboration, he was able to disengage his analytical faculties from his passions, making a clear distinction between his longer-term interests and his feelings of the moment. The result was a facility for conceptualizing personal problems as material for microsocial experiments, enabling him to calculate the costs and benefits of the options at his disposal. Gerth, on the other hand, generally found it difficult to detach judgment from emotion and analysis from passion. In the precedence dispute he was paralyzed by doubt and insecurity or driven to paroxysms of anger, depending on the circumstances that obtained. In the former case he despised himself because of his weaknesses; in the latter he was forced to debase himself with humiliating apologies.

Mills insisted on formal understandings, unambiguous commitments, and explicit agreements. As he saw it, clarity was not only possible but also desirable. A precise definition of terms and conditions would establish the basis for a consensus on fundamentals and avert potential problems. Gerth favored a more indirect and informal approach. Certain matters, he felt, perhaps even the most important, cannot be stated explicitly. As the unexpressed premises on which agreements are based, they are not possible objects of agreement. Every formal understanding presupposes a background of tacit assumptions; thus not all understandings can be formalized. Moreover, precision changes the import and practical significance of agreements, sometimes in unanticipated directions. A clarification of positions not only articulates differences but also forms them. The reduction of ambiguity, vagueness, and uncertainty in a relationship generates difficulties that would not otherwise arise. Seen from Gerth's standpoint, Mills's translation of informal arrangements into formal protocols was self-defeating, creating the conflicts it was intended to avoid. By exposing sources of disagreement and opposition that would remain invisible, it encouraged deceit and suspicion instead of solidifying the basis of trust. Gerth found it wiser to delay choices, resist definitions, and refuse to make commitments, preferring to leave matters where they were, even if it was not clear exactly where that was or what the matters were.

"Science as a Vocation"

In their deliberations over the contract for *Character and Social Structure* in the spring of 1949, Gerth and Mills had two primary concerns: nullifying the Heath agreement and reaching the most advantageous arrangement with Harcourt Brace. Reflections on the moral implications of practicing information management on colleagues and associates were conspicuously absent from their exchanges, and they raised no questions and engaged in no discussions on the ethics of concealment and deceit. In the end Mills succeeded in convincing Gerth to treat a contract as a shifting process of negotiation rather than a promissory statement of joint intentions and

terms. Given this conception of contracts, violations of the trust of publishers and betrayals of the confidence of editor-colleagues had a purely
instrumental significance. A promise was a tactic, to be kept or broken
depending on its serviceability in realizing the ultimate objective of publication, which was beyond good and evil and not subject to moral scrutiny.

Problems quite different from moral questions were thus paramount in
the partners' thinking about their contractual predicament. Mills needed
the advance from Harcourt Brace. The bloom was off his relationship
with Paul Lazarsfeld at the Bureau of Applied Social Research. Dissatisfied at Columbia, he was exploring the possibility of other appointments
at the University of Illinois, the University of Chicago, and the University
of Wisconsin. The prospects were bleak, however, forcing him to stay at
Columbia and make up the difference between his academic salary and the
demands of his domestic economy. With nothing from Heath and a $1,500
advance from Harcourt Brace—more than 25 percent of his Columbia
salary—the choice was clear. As for Gerth, he needed the book to advance
himself at Madison. After devoting much of his career to the writings
of Max Weber, he had little to show for his labors. *Character and Social
Structure,* which employed the Weberian approach to social psychology on
which he had worked for more than a decade, was an attempt to establish
his reputation and win him the recognition he regarded as commensurate with his efforts. Because he did not believe he could write the book
alone, he needed Mills, whom he followed to Harcourt Brace. In the final
analysis, the partners' deliberations on their contractual difficulties were
governed by the imperatives of their careers.

Competition for Credit in the Academic Career

Mills regarded academic life as an implacable struggle for survival, a contest in an arena where the risks were great and the unexpected might appear
at any turn. Working in American universities, he and Gerth faced a market governed by the pitiless god of competition. Those who possessed the
qualifications needed to meet the dictates of this god would be rewarded;
those who did not would fail. Although academic intellectuals may live for
the ideals of science, understood in the broad sense of science and scholarship, they must also live off science as an institution in which practitioners
are recruited, selected, winnowed, and placed in career paths. Because science is a career, success and failure and the procedures for their determination are essential to the life of the scientist. Success in science is achieved by

making claims to credit and validating them according to established criteria. Credit claims are validated by demonstrating priority in the performance of research. In science a claim to credit is a claim of precedence. The motivations, calculations, and emotions at play in the collaboration cannot be understood without appreciating the role of priority claims for research.

Precedence of discovery or performance is institutionally determined by priority of publication: who publishes first, whose name appears on the title page of an article or a book, in what order, and with what qualifications and restrictions. Although precedence may be irrelevant to the value of the research and its use by other practitioners, it is decisive in the allocation of credit.[5] Because the number of problems that are recognized as key issues in a scientific discipline is smaller than the number of researchers at work on these problems, competition for the validation of credit claims is inevitable. This means that a successful scientific career may not depend primarily on who actually performs the research. In principle, research and the validation of credit claims for research are independent activities. There is no essential connection between the ability to do scientific work and the qualifications required to validate claims to credit for such work. Scientists who perform first-class research may fail miserably in the enterprise of producing, managing, and marketing representations of research that certify claims to priority in the scientific community, and scientists with a talent for promoting credit claims may not be especially gifted researchers. It follows that scientists may do work for which they receive little or no credit, just as they may be credited for work to which they have contributed little or nothing.

Unless claims to credit are validated, the path to a scientific career is blocked. The perquisites that mark success in science also provide the resources that make a career even more successful. Tenured professors in universities have a stable supply of students who can be used as research assistants, and, under certain conditions, drafted to do work for which their professors claim credit. Established academicians are able to exercise institutional power in science through positions on editorial boards, committees of professional associations, research councils, and foundations. Membership in the visible and invisible colleges that pass judgment on claims to credit improves the chances of members to acquire the resources needed to validate their own credit claims. These memberships have numerous advantages, including access to the citation strategies employed by footnoting and reviewing networks in disciplinary cliques.[6] In academic science it would be difficult to exaggerate the importance of this premise of the maxim that Robert K. Merton has christened "the Matthew Principle": to those who have shall be given. The assets produced by successful claims to credit reproduce scientific success by creating opportunities to validate further claims. All these opportunities are foreclosed unless initial credit claims can be validated.

For a social theorist the most impressive credit claim was and remains a book judged to be a significant contribution to a key area of research. Contracts for books are critical because they are the first step in validating such a claim. If a scholarly book is understood as a venture in which the scholar invests intellectual capital to gain credit that can be exchanged for institutional rewards, a source of intellectual capital is essential to academic success. In the collaboration Gerth's function was to supply intellectual capital, the ideas, arguments, and scholarship on which Mills's first two book contracts were based. Mills performed other functions. He managed Gerth's intellectual labor, organizing his work, setting deadlines, motivating him to adhere to production timetables, and generally keeping him on his mettle. He also packaged Gerth's work, editing and "stylizing" it to conform to the demands of the market and promoting it by handling the partners' relations with publishers. Finally, his most challenging task was to control the collaboration so that he would be able to receive equal credit for the results, an impressive achievement in view of the strength of Gerth's claims to precedence for both books.[7]

Although some scientists may have compelling motives to claim credit for work they have not done, all scientists have powerful reasons to protect themselves from charges that they have made illegitimate credit claims. Scientific fraud, making a false claim to the work of another, represents an attempt to steal credit. Just as scientific success is not possible without validating claims to credit, it also depends on invalidating claims of fraudulence. Whereas proven claims to credit are essential to scientific success, a certified claim of theft is the mark of failure. A charge of fraudulence, or even a plausible suspicion of misappropriated credit, may be sufficient to terminate a budding career in which significant claims to credit have not yet been validated. It follows that scientific success is possible only by forestalling fraudulence charges or escaping, neutralizing, or negating such accusations once they are made. In view of these considerations, it is not surprising that Gerth and Mills acted quickly to dispose of Shils's initiative before doubts could be raised about the originality of their translations. Mills correctly interpreted Shils's suspicions as fraught with danger. The potential threat was not confined to embarrassment or even damaged reputations. Had Shils's implicit charge been more fully elaborated and widely circulated, it could have placed the veracity of the partners in question and seriously compromised their ability to validate future claims to credit. In short, the Shils affair represented a crisis that, handled ineptly, could have blocked Gerth's tenure at Madison and Mills's efforts to leave the University of Maryland.

The relationship between claims to credit and claims of fraud entails that success in science depends on two independent factors: competitiveness, which is required to validate claims to credit, and honesty, or at least a sustained production of its appearance, which is necessary to invalidate claims of fraud. To succeed, scientists must compete for priority, but not so ruthlessly that they appear to violate canons of scientific ethics. They must also be, or perhaps seem to be, truthful, but not to a fault; otherwise they will not survive the struggle for scientific rewards. In sum, success in science is determined by a selection mechanism that operates according to two principles: opportunism and truthfulness. Neither can be employed systematically and without qualification, and each limits the efficacy of the other. The path to a successful scientific career is traced by the fine line between overweening ambition that inspires doubts about honesty and a diffidence or restraint that disqualifies its possessor from participation in the contest for priority.

◆ ◆ ◆

Notes

We have used two principal collections of unpublished sources: the Nobuko Gerth Collection (NGC), which includes the correspondence and literary remains of Hans Gerth in the possession of Nobuko Gerth, and the Mills Papers (MP), which is archival material in the C. Wright Mills Papers, housed at the University of Texas at Austin. Undated documents are designated *n.d.* In some cases a document can be dated by its contents or a comparison with other documents. In other cases only approximate datings are possible. Our inferential datings are in brackets. Misspellings, orthographic and typographical errors, and grammatical mistakes have been routinely corrected. Abbreviations have been retained; when the referent of an abbreviation is unclear, it is identified in brackets. Drafts or copies of letters from Gerth in NGC and corresponding drafts or copies of letters from Mills in MP are identified as drafts.

Introduction

1. Mills's diploma from Dallas Technical High School in 1934 identifies him as Charles Mills. By 1939 he had become "C. Wright Mills," as on his University of Texas degree. On Mills's years at the University of Texas, see his letters to his parents in MP, 4B453. Beginning in 1937 they are generally typed on the letterhead of the sociology department.

2. C. Wright Mills, "Language, Logic, and Culture," *American Sociological Review* 4 (1939): 670–80; and "Methodological Consequences of the Sociology of Knowledge," *American Journal of Sociology* 46 (1940): 316–30.

3. MP, 4B453, Mills to Mother and Father, draft, April 3, 1939.

4. Don Martindale, *The Monologue: Hans Gerth (1908–1978): A Memoir* (Ghazia-bad, India: Intercontinental, 1982), 2. Mills's first reference to Gerth in correspon-dence was a letter to his parents written during Gerth's first semester at Madison and remarking that he occasionally spent evenings with the new refugee professor and his wife (MP, 4B353, draft, n.d. [autumn 1940]).

5. By his midsixties, some thirty-five years after his immigration to the United States, Gerth's memory of his departure from Germany was wavering. Sometimes he placed it in 1937; on other occasions, in 1938. On July 27, 1937, Mannheim wrote Walter Adams of the Academic Assistance Council of the Royal Society, recommending Gerth for funds to support a brief stay in England, following which he would immigrate to the United States. To secure authorization from the American consulate in London for Gerth's admission to the United States, Mann-heim wrote Louis Wirth at the University of Chicago, his principal American contact and sponsor, on November 4, 1937, asking him to arrange *"immediately for an official personal invitation"* for Gerth to speak at the Christmas meetings of the American Sociological Society in Atlantic City (emphasis in original). In December 1937 Gerth attended the American Sociological Society meetings in Atlantic City, speaking in a session on the sociology of knowledge organized by Talcott Parsons. With Mannheim's imprimatur, he responded to a critique of *Ide-ology and Utopia,* by Hans Speier. See Mannheim's letters to Adams and Wirth in Éva Gábor, ed., *Mannheim Károly: Levelezése 1911–1946* (Budapest: MTA Lukács Archívum, 1996), 126, 128. See also David Kettler and Volker Meja, " 'That typi-cally German kind of sociology that verges towards philosophy': The Dispute about *Ideology and Utopia* in the United States," *Sociological Theory* 12 (1994): 279–303. The contributions to this session by Gerth and Speier were finally pub-lished in 1985: Hans Speier, "Review of Karl Mannheim's *Ideology and Utopia,*" *State, Culture, and Society* 1 (1985): 183–97; Hans Gerth, "Speier's Critique of Karl Mannheim," *State, Culture, and Society* 1 (1985): 198–207. In the winter and spring of 1938, Gerth worked at Harvard as Carl Friedrich's assistant and conducted a seminar for a group of Harvard sociology instructors who were preparing for their Ph.D. language examination in German, using as his text Weber's essay "The Meaning of 'Ethical Neutrality' in Sociology and Economics" (NGC, Gerth to Hans Speier, draft, May 31, 1938; NGC, Gerth to Richard Gillam, draft, Octo-ber 9, 1973; NGC, Gerth to Richard Gillam, draft, January 1, 1974).

6. " 'As in the Book of Fairy Tales: All Alone . . .': A Conversation with Hans Gerth," in *Politics, Character, and Culture: Perspectives from Hans Gerth,* ed. Joseph Bensman, Arthur J. Vidich, and Nobuko Gerth (Westport, Conn.: Greenwood, 1982), 22. This is a translation by Jeffrey Herf of " 'Wie im Märchenbuch: ganz allein . . .' Gespräch mit Hans Gerth," in *Die Zerstörung einer Zukunft: Gespräche mit emigrierten Sozialwissenschaftlern,* ed. Matthias Greffrath (Hamburg: Ro-wohlt, 1979), 59–95. As early as October 6, 1933, Mannheim had applied to the Academic Assistance Council of the Royal Society for funds to arrange a position

for Gerth at the London School of Economics, where Mannheim had been appointed to a lectureship in sociology only a few months earlier. Gerth, Mannheim wrote, was "the most gifted of all my former students" and had "the first claim among the rising generation of German sociologists to study in England." Mannheim renewed his support with another letter to the council on December 19, 1934, describing Gerth's doctoral dissertation on the origins of German liberalism as the best work on the history of the intelligentsia. See Gábor, ed., *Mannheim Károly,* 68–69, 87.

7. NGC, Gerth to Hans Speier, draft, May 31, 1938.

8. NGC, Hans Speier to Gerth, June 5, 1938. For a bibliography of Gerth's work as a journalist in 1934–37, see Bensman, Vidich, and Gerth, eds., *Politics, Character, and Culture: Perspectives from Hans Gerth,* 279–88.

9. NGC, Gerth to Hans Speier, draft, May 31, 1938. See also George Orwell, *Inside the Whale and Other Essays* (Hammondsworth: Penguin, 1962). On Gerth and the *Berliner Tageblatt,* see Margret Boveri, *Wir Lügen Alle: Eine Hauptstadt Zeitung unter Hitler* (Freiburg im Breisgau: Walter-Verlag, 1965). Boveri was a journalist on the editorial staff of the *Berliner Tageblatt* from 1934 to the beginning of 1937 and a colleague of Gerth. The *Berliner Tageblatt* was one of the more important liberal newspapers of the Weimar period, featuring contributions by leading writers of the time, such as Alfred Döblin, Lion Feuchtwanger, Hermann Hesse, Heinrich Mann, Thomas Mann, and Stefan Zweig. Boveri provides an account, amusing and at the same time terrifying, of the adjustments, compromises, and surrenders the paper made in a futile attempt to maintain its autonomy during the first five years of Nazi rule, as the new government gradually tightened its control over the press. Gerth's work at the *Berliner Tageblatt* falls in the domain of heterodox writing published under the restrictions of censorship and official intolerance of deviation from the truths of state propaganda. For a preliminary discussion of this genre, see Leo Strauss, *Persecution and the Art of Writing* (Glencoe, Ill.: Free Press, 1952). See also Anabel Paterson, *Censorship and Interpretation* (Madison: University of Wisconsin Press, 1984), and *Fables of Power: Aesopian Writing and Political History* (Durham, N.C.: Duke University Press, 1991). For an extreme case, the composition of Osip Mandelstam's ode to Stalin, see Clarence Brown, "Into the Heart of Darkness: Mandelstam's Ode to Stalin," *Slavic Review* 26 (1967): 583–604; and J. M. Coetzee, "Osip Mandelstam and the Stalin Ode," *Giving Offense: Essays on Censorship* (Chicago: University of Chicago Press, 1996), 104–16.

10. Agnes Erdelyi, *Max Weber in Amerika* (Vienna: Passagen Verlag, 1992), 100–101; Max Weber, *General Economic History,* trans. F. H. Knight (London: Allen and Unwin, 1927); Max Weber, *The Protestant Ethic and the Spirit of Capitalism,* trans. Talcott Parsons (London: Allen and Unwin, 1930). Early sales of the English-language translation of *The Protestant Ethic* were not impressive: barely 1,000 copies by the end of 1933. Writing in July 1934 to Weber's German publisher, the managing director of Allen and Unwin noted the modest demand for the

book and voiced his doubt that sales would ever reach 2,500 copies. See Guenther Roth, "Max Weber at Home and in Japan: On the Troubled Genesis and Successful Reception of His Work," *International Journal of Politics, Culture, and Society* 12 (Spring 1999): 515–25.

11. Talcott Parsons, *The Structure of Social Action,* 2 vols. (New York: McGraw-Hill, 1937).

Chapter 1: "Translated and Edited by Hans H. Gerth and C. Wright Mills"

1. "'As in the Book of Fairy Tales: All Alone . . .': A Conversation with Hans Gerth," in *Politics, Character, and Culture: Perspectives from Hans Gerth,* ed. Joseph Bensman, Arthur J. Vidich, and Nobuko Gerth (Westport, Conn.: Greenwood, 1982), 37.

2. MP, 4B369, Mills to Cleanth Brooks, draft, June 27, 1941; MP, 4B369, Cleanth Brooks to Mills, July 25, 1941; MP, 4B369, William Jay Gold [managing editor of *The Virginia Quarterly*] to Mills, August 25, 1941; MP, 4B369, Mills to Charner Perry, draft, September 11, 1941; MP, 4B369, Mills to Gerth, draft, October 11, 1941. "A Marx for the Managers" was published in *Ethics* 52 (1942): 200–215.

3. NGC, Mills to Gerth, February 6, 1942.

4. NGC, Mills to Gerth, March 2, 1942. For Macdonald's review of *The Managerial Revolution,* see "The Burnhamian Revolution," *Partisan Review* 9 (Jan.–Feb., 1942): 76–77, 80, 84. On Macdonald and *politics,* see Stephen J. Whitfield, *A Critical American: The Politics of Dwight Macdonald* (Hamden, Conn.: Archon, 1984); and Gregory D. Sumner, *Dwight Macdonald and the politics Circle* (Ithaca, N.Y.: Cornell University Press, 1996).

5. NGC, Mills to Gerth, n.d. [between October 16, 1943, and December 7, 1943].

6. C. Wright Mills, "The Powerless People: The Role of the Intellectual in Society," *politics* 1 (April 1944): 68–72.

7. NGC, Mills to Gerth, June 1, 1944. The last sentence of this quotation is a handwritten addition by Mills to the typescript of his letter.

8. NGC, Mills to Gerth, June 1, 1944.

9. Ibid.

10. NGC, Mills to Gerth, n.d. [June or July 1944].

11. NGC, Mills to Gerth, June 1, 1944.

12. NGC, Mills to Gerth, "Tuesday Nite," n.d. [June or July 1944].

13. Ibid.

14. NGC, Mills to Gerth, n.d. [June or July 1944].

15. Ibid.; NGC, Mills to Gerth, "Thursday," n.d. [June or July 1944].

16. NGC, Mills to Gerth, n.d. [June or July 1944].

17. NGC, Mills to Gerth, n.d. [July 1944].

18. NGC, Mills to Gerth, "Saturday 5 p.m. office," n.d. [August 1944].

19. NGC, Mills to Gerth, October 10, 1944; NGC, H. T. Hatcher to Mills, October 11, 1944.

20. In the summer of 1944 Daniel Bell wrote Mills from the offices of *The New Leader* in New York with a troubling piece of gossip. In the autumn, Bell had been told, Talcott Parsons and Howard Becker would publish in England a translation of *Economy and Society* and possibly one or two of his other works as well (NGC, Daniel Bell to Mills, n.d. [July 1944]). This rumor proved to be false, or at least premature, and mistaken as to details. After the war Parsons published a translation of parts of *Economy and Society* in collaboration with A. M. Henderson; see Max Weber, *The Theory of Social and Economic Organization,* trans. Talcott Parsons and A. M. Henderson (New York: Oxford University Press, 1947). Nevertheless, the rumor gave Gerth and Mills notice that other English editions of Weber might be under way.

21. NGC, Edward A. Shils to Nobuko Gerth, June 6, 1987. On November 4, 1937, while Gerth was still in England, Mannheim wrote Wirth, praising Gerth's research skills and his competence in the sociology of culture and the new field of the sociology of knowledge and suggesting that Wirth consider Gerth for a position as a research assistant at Chicago. Should such a position not be available, he asked Wirth to make appropriate introductions for Gerth at the Atlantic City conference of the American Sociological Society. Mannheim was interested not only in advancing the career of his protégé but also in placing Gerth in America as his personal emissary. Gerth would defend *Ideology and Utopia* against its German critics in the United States, such as Hans Speier and Alexander von Schelting, canvass the opinions of Mannheim's work held by leading American sociologists and give him confidential assessments of his American reputation, and evaluate his prospects for a professorship at an American university. Mannheim was weighing the relative advantages of continuing his work in England or relocating in America. Once Gerth was on the scene in the United States, he could help Mannheim make this judgment. See Éva Gábor, ed., *Mannheim Károly: Levelezése 1911–1946* (Budapest: MTA Lukács Archívum, 1996), 132–33, 137.

22. NGC, Shils to Gerth, "1938" [summer, before August 15].

23. H. H. Gerth, "The Nazi Party: Its Leadership and Composition," *American Journal of Sociology* 45 (1940): 517–41. In Shils's letter to Nobuko Gerth, written nearly fifty years after the summer of 1938, he offered a considerably revised version of the publication of Gerth's first American article. In his reconstruction Gerth showed Shils a confusing set of notes on the social composition of the Nazi Party, a manuscript that was not only unpublishable but without structure, argument, analysis, or even a significant body of data. After examining these materials, Shils devised the thesis that the Nazi Party operated on both charismatic and bureaucratic principles of authority, wrote a paper supporting this thesis with Gerth's data, and had it published under Gerth's name in the *American Journal of Sociology*. Shils claimed that although Gerth asked him to include his own name

on the article, he declined on the grounds that Gerth's interests would not be served by identifying himself with a relatively unknown coauthor. In Shils's 1938 correspondence he portrayed himself as the editor of an important study that was poorly organized and badly written. In his retrospective account he became the ghostwriter of an essay credited to Gerth, whose only contribution was an insubstantial collection of data. See NGC, Edward A. Shils to Nobuko Gerth, June 6, 1987.

24. NGC, Shils to Gerth, October 28, 1944.

25. NGC, Gerth to Shils, draft, n.d. [first week of November 1944].

26. Ibid.

27. NGC, Shils to Gerth, n.d. [early November 1944].

28. NGC, Gerth to Mills, draft, n.d. [first week of November 1944]. Shils was forced into an unhappy choice: either give up his translation project altogether or reorient it to avoid overlap with the Oxford volume. The former course would entail the loss of years of effort. The latter would call for much more work. He chose the latter alternative, redefining his edition to concentrate on Weber's studies in the philosophy of the social sciences. Gerth's November 1944 list of Shils's translations includes only one of the writings he eventually published: "The Meaning of 'Ethical Neutrality' in Sociology and Economics." In reworking his edition as a collection of Weber's philosophical writings, Shils translated three new selections, each a substantial monograph, collectively amounting to some 150 pages of text. These materials imposed on the translator tasks more onerous than those presented by the sociological texts he had already completed. Shils's book was not published until 1949 and had a much more limited market than the Gerth-Mills volume. See Max Weber, *The Methodology of the Social Sciences,* trans. Edward A. Shils and Henry A. Finch (Glencoe, Ill.: Free Press, 1949).

29. NGC, Mills to Gerth, "Thursday evening," n.d. [first week of November 1944].

30. NGC, Mills to Gerth, n.d. [first week of November 1944].

31. NGC, Mills to Gerth, "Thursday evening," n.d. [first week of November 1944].

32. Ibid. See also NGC, Gerth to Shils, draft, n.d. [November 1944, written after consultation with Mills]. Gerth's response conceded nothing. After delivering the unwelcome news of substantial redundancies between the two editions, he praised Shils's proposed two-volume work but observed that he had been unable to find notice of the initial one-volume plan in the promotional material Kegan Paul had circulated on Mannheim's International Library of Sociology. Again he implied that Shils faced a problem of his own making. Because of extensive duplication in the two projects, Gerth's obligations to Mills as his coeditor, and the obligations of both to Oxford, Gerth found it unlikely that any redistribution of material among the two editions based on "bargaining" would be acceptable.

Finally, he absolved himself of responsibility for any hypothetical resolution of Shils's difficulties by noting that Mills had handled all negotiations with Oxford.

Shils continued to petition Gerth for an accommodation, proposing to delete "Politics as a Vocation" from his edition on the condition that Gerth and Mills give him "Science as a Vocation" and "Bureaucracy" in return, not a trade that would have appealed to them even had they been disposed to compromise. He also reminded Gerth more explicitly of his signal contribution to the earliest phase of Gerth's American career. The meaning of this reminder was clear. Gerth had benefited from Shils's assistance when he needed it badly, incurring a debt that had now come due. Refusal to pay would constitute unconscionable ingratitude (NGC, Shils to Gerth, January 4, 1945).

Shils was overmatched. He did not understand the game Gerth and Mills were playing against him or the strategic considerations that dictated its rules. In any case, by January 1945 there were significant changes in Gerth's priorities, as chapter 2 of this book demonstrates. His polite exchange of letters with Shils over credit for the translation of Weber's writings was replaced by a more dangerous contest with Mills over credit for the Weber book. This struggle led to a crisis in Gerth's career and finally moved him to reject unequivocally Shils's pleas for a compromise: "Without raising the question of whether your proposal actually would lead to the elimination of all overlap, and without haggling about equivalents, I cannot accept your suggestion. For various reasons, which partially emerged only recently, it is quite important for me not to forgo possible credit for work I have done" (NGC, Gerth to Shils, draft, January 15, 1945). To this pragmatic consideration he added a more strained argument: "Even in view of everlasting obligations to you, I assume you would hardly expect me to exert pressure on Mills to surrender work of his that I pay debt to you, would you? Mills, reporting on a conversation about the matter with the Oxford agent [editor], wrote 'anybody can invade a field of the mind and nobody can monopolize it'" (NGC, Gerth to Shils, draft, January 15, 1945).

Although Gerth acknowledged his debt to Shils, the means for its payment were not at his disposal. Because he did not hold exclusive rights to the disposition of the Oxford Weber book, he would not be justified in taking what belonged to Mills, who owed nothing to Shils, to repay his old friend. Thus he resolved the problem of his indebtedness on the basis of a principle of formal justice: debts can be fairly paid only with resources that belong to the debtor. Since Gerth did not believe that Mills deserved substantial credit for the Weber book, his argument was, at best, evasive. He concluded his rejection of Shils's petition with the premise that underpinned Mills's strategy: "A word of yours or of Mannheim's in time could and would have saved us this regrettable state of affairs" (NGC, Gerth to Shils, draft, January 15, 1945). In other words, Shils himself was responsible for any damage he might incur due to publication of the Oxford Weber volume.

Nevertheless, Gerth remained troubled about his conduct in the Shils affair. In a letter to Mannheim written in English shortly after publication of *From Max Weber,* he engaged in a tortured exercise of self-exculpation, representing himself as an innocent and unhappy victim of circumstances for which he was not responsible and could not have anticipated. In the early 1940s he had sent copies of his Weber translations to Mannheim, Parsons, Speier, Wirth, and others. When he and Mills signed their contract with Oxford and accepted an advance, he felt that his options had become much more limited. After Shils returned from London with the surprising news that he planned to publish a Weber edition in Mannheim's series with Kegan Paul, Gerth saw himself as a weak chess player facing a stronger one. Shils, he believed, was in a position to maneuver him out of the game altogether. Further, Shils had made the matter more difficult by his disposition to bargain rather than cooperate. "Shils has at no time proposed to join hands and bring out Weber together, which I could hardly propose. May I say, I would have felt elated and happy if Shils had been willing to cooperate that way." It is not clear what an invitation from Shils to create a tripartite editorship would have achieved, however, especially since Mills, "not feeling under any obligation toward Shils, was not even willing to consider the issue." Gerth confronted a dilemma: a choice between Shils, to whom he owed so much, and Mills, who would have become his enemy had he decided in favor of Shils. As Gerth reconstructed his predicament, his choice was dictated by the constraints of his career. In 1944–45 his job at Madison and his future in the United States were in doubt.

I could not take that course [i.e., the compromises proposed by Shils] because I was in trouble at the time. I was still an enemy alien. The Dean of the College (a mathematician) had given me a warning not to use so much "alien material" in my courses, and the Department were uncertain whether to renew my contract or rather drop me, as they were afraid of the veterans' ire against men who speak as heavy a German accent as I do. Besides, I am not a platform man who draws [illegible] crowds. Hence my job was wobbly. My wife has still some months to go before she gets her naturalization papers. We were expecting a second child. The book hence was the one thing that might have tipped the balance (manuscripts do not count). It was this pressure which prevented me from "forgetting" about the book in order to please Shils. As a matter of fact, the Department gave me notice in so many words, the only comfort being that the Chairman, Dr. McCormick said: Hans, I think the Department have made a mistake. As the war was still on, and as Wisconsin among the state universities rates tops, it would have been hard for me to find another academic job, especially as an enemy alien. I might as well have given up. And what then? I do not know which firm would have hired an enemy alien. So much in explanation of my motives for not trading chapter by chapter with Shils. (NGC, Gerth to Mannheim, draft, June 21, 1946)

An invitation to Shils to visit him in Madison and discuss the matter was spurned, and his telephone calls, letters, and messages went unanswered. Thus Gerth learned that Mills was not mistaken when he observed, in his best hard-boiled manner, that their Weber book would be published only at the cost of his friendship with Shils.

Mannheim responded to Gerth's letter, which he characterized as a "sincere human document," on July 7, 1946. Claiming that both parties had made mistakes, he offered no judgment on the merits of Gerth's position. His only complaint was against Oxford for accepting *From Max Weber* without informing him or Kegan Paul. For the future, he suggested to Gerth that Oxford assign the British rights to *From Max Weber* to Kegan Paul, in which case he might advise Shils to "write a comprehensive study of Max Weber, on which he has been working for many years" (see Gábor, ed., *Mannheim Károly,* 222–23).

33. NGC, Mills to Shils, n.d. [first week of November 1944]. This is a draft of a letter from Mills to Shils, sent to Gerth with the handwritten marginal note "*proposed draft.*"

34. Ibid.

35. NGC, Mills to Gerth, n.d. [shortly after November 18, 1944].

36. Ibid.

37. NGC, Mills to Gerth, n.d. [first week of November 1944].

38. NGC, Mills to Gerth, November 7, 1944.

39. Ibid.

40. NGC, Mills to Gerth, n.d. [ca. November 14, 1944].

41. NGC, Mills to Harry Hatcher, November 17, 1944; NGC, Mills to Gerth, November 18, 1944.

42. NGC, Mills to Gerth and HI [Hedwig Ide, Gerth's first wife], January 22, 1945. The colleague is not identified.

43. NGC, Mills to Gerth, November 20, 1944. See also NGC, Mills to Gerth, December 22, 1944. In January 1945 a notice of the forthcoming publication of Shils's edition of Weber translations appeared in the "News and Notes" section of the *American Journal of Sociology* 50 (1945): 311: "Edward A. Shils will shortly publish an English translation of the major sociological, political, and methodological writings of Max Weber under the title of 'Science, Politics, and Power' (in the 'International Library of Sociology' [London: Kegan Paul])." Although this announcement caused no consternation at Oxford, Hatcher wrote Mills urging the partners to complete the introduction in a timely fashion so that Oxford could begin production of the book. Gerth and Mills were not to worry, however. Oxford was "in the saddle as far as distributing the Mannheim series is concerned" (NGC, Mills to Gerth, February 2, 1945).

Chapter 2: The Precedence Dispute

1. NGC, Mills to Gerth, the fourth page of a four-page letter missing the first two pages, "Early thursday morning," n.d. [November 16, 1944].

2. Ibid.

3. Ibid.

4. NGC, Mills to Gerth, January 2, 1945; NGC, Mills to Gerth, "Sunday afternoon," n.d. [between January 22, 1945, and February 2, 1945]; NGC, Gerth to Mills, draft, February 3, 1945; NGC, Gerth to Mills, draft, February 4, 1945.

5. NGC, Mills to Hatcher, February 5, 1945; NGC, Mills to Gerth, February 5, 1945.

6. The correction was not made. In the first sentence of his article, Schapiro refers to "C. Wright Mills and Hans Gerth" as the authors of the prefatory note to the translation of "Class, Status, Party" and on the same page again identifies the partners as "Mills and Gerth." See Meyer Schapiro, "A Note on Max Weber's Politics," *politics* 2 (Feb. 1945): 44.

7. NGC, Mills to Gerth, February 7, 1945.

8. NGC, Mills to Gerth, Friday night, February 16, 1945.

9. NGC, Mills to Hatcher, February 16, 1945.

10. NGC, Mills to Gerth, Friday night, February 16, 1945.

11. NGC, Gerth to Hatcher, draft, February 19, 1945.

12. NGC, Gerth to Mills, draft, February 19, 1945.

13. NGC, Gerth's untitled first draft of the last paragraph of the preface to *From Max Weber,* n.d. [late February or early March 1945].

14. NGC, Mills to Gerth, "Monday afternoon 5 p m," n.d. [last week in February or first week in March 1945].

15. NGC, Hatcher to Gerth, March 5, 1945.

16. NGC, Gerth to Hatcher, draft, March 10, 1945.

17. NGC, Gerth to Mills, draft, March 10, 1945.

18. NGC, Gerth to Mills, draft, n.d. [last week in March or first week in April 1945].

19. NGC, Gerth to Mills, draft, n.d. [last week of March or first week of April, 1945]. The letters from Madison to Columbia continued. Early in November 1945 the executive head of the sociology department at Columbia informed Mills of a June letter from a professor at the University of Wisconsin accusing him of insulting and exploiting Gerth. Although he was neither asked to explain the matter nor given an opportunity to do so, he was told that the letter would be considered in the decision on his appointment.

The Nobuko Gerth Collection includes a typescript of a letter that reproduces Gerth's version of the precedence dispute. Nobuko Gerth identifies this document as a letter of October 12, 1945, to Robert K. Merton from Howard Becker; the letter advises Merton to share its contents with Robert Lynd. In the letter Gerth is represented as a shy and unworldly scholar, exclusively interested in sociological theory and the unwitting victim of his research assistant. Mills, who "knew little German and no Weber," is said to have taken advantage of Gerth's dependence on his editorial skills by selling Gerth's translations, first to Dwight Macdonald and then to Oxford, and having himself credited as cotranslator and coeditor: "Instead of the thing [*From Max Weber*] appearing as Gerth's translation with some assistance by Mills, it is Mills-Gerth now in all the catalogues, and credit is equally shared."

Mills wrote Gerth on November 21, deeply troubled about the impact of the letter on his reputation and job prospects. Although he did not believe that Gerth had written the letter or caused it to be written, he suggested that Gerth, still resentful over the precedence dispute, had regaled Mills's old enemies at Madison with stories of his opportunism and deceit. Gerth and Mills could be reasonably certain of the author of the offending letter: "We know from the scribbling he has done on ms I have sent you who he probably is" (NGC, Mills to Gerth, November 21, 1945). Mills asked Gerth to desist and demanded an explanation of his intentions. Would he continue these "behind the scenes discussions with irresponsible people," making moral charges against Mills under circumstances in which he had no opportunity to defend himself (NGC, Mills to Gerth, November 21, 1945)?

Although Gerth found it regrettable that "nasty stuff" about Mills was in circulation, "peddled by third persons and without [his] intention or . . . conscious doing," he distanced himself from the problem. If rumors about their collaboration were abroad, he argued, Mills was to blame. After all, Mills had made the dispute public by appealing to Hatcher. Repeating that he had meant what he said in his letters of apology, he gave Mills the freedom to use these letters as he saw fit, even proposing that Mills might consider publishing them. He rejected Mills's implication of chicanery on his part, however, and refused to be held accountable for his colleagues' judgments on Mills's conduct, noting that during Mills's years at Madison he had consistently spoken on Mills's behalf. In Gerth's view, the fact that they were still working together should have been sufficient to satisfy the sociologists at Columbia (NGC, Gerth to Mills, draft, n.d. [November 23 or 24, 1945]).

20. NGC, Mills to Gerth, April 9, 1945.

21. Ibid.

22. Ibid.

23. NGC, Gerth to Mills, draft, April 12, 1945.

24. Ibid.

25. Ibid. In this letter Gerth allowed his meditations on the death of FDR and its consequences to distract him from the immediate problem of defending his priority in the Weber book. Whereas Mills's epistolary style was confessional and self-absorbed, Gerth's letters to Mills tended to indulge in world-historical interpretations of large scale issues, remote from his practical concerns of the moment.

26. NGC, Gerth to Mills, draft, n.d. [last week of March or first week of April 1945].

27. NGC, Mills to Gerth, including Mills's draft of the last page of the preface to *From Max Weber,* n.d. [April 14 or 15, 1945]; NGC, Gerth to Mills, draft, April 17, 1945.

28. On June 26 Mills discussed with Gerth plans for promoting the book, observing that although Oxford hoped it would stimulate controversy, he did not share their expectations of large sales. Mills sent copies to Parsons and to colleagues at Columbia. Gerth's list of recipients has not been located. See NGC, Mills to Gerth, June 26, 1946. On the day *From Max Weber* was published, Gerth apparently wrote Mannheim in confidence, seeking his help in returning to Germany as a professor at Frankfurt. Mannheim was sympathetic: "I can quite understand that you prefer to work in Germany." To expedite Gerth's request, which we have not seen, he forwarded it to Ilse J. Ursell of the Society for the Protection of Science and Learning at Cambridge University and also offered to write the rector of the University of Frankfurt on Gerth's behalf. In his letter to Ursell Mannheim identified Gerth as his former student and one of the most gifted younger sociologists: "He seems ready to go back to Germany, first for a period of trial and then for good. I think he would be a real asset. He is not of Jewish origin but left because he found life unbearable in Nazi Germany." See Éva Gábor, ed., *Mannheim Károly: Levelezése 1911–1946* (Budapest: MTA Lukács Archívum, 1996), 222–23.

29. See Irving L. Horowitz, ed., *The New Sociology: Essays in Social Science and Social Theory in Honor of C. Wright Mills* (New York: Oxford University Press, 1964); and James Miller, *"Democracy Is in the Streets": From Port Huron to the Siege of Chicago* (New York: Simon and Schuster, 1987).

Chapter 3: Credit, Contracts, and the Ethics of Publishing

1. For Parsons's estimation of Becker, see Gary D. Jaworski, "Parsons, Simmel, and the Eclipse of Religious Values," *Simmel Newsletter* 1 (1991): 99; and his *Georg Simmel and the American Prospect* (Albany: State University of New York Press, 1997), 59.

2. NGC, CWM [C. Wright Mills], "General Memorandum for HB [Howard Becker], Gerth-Mills: SOCIOLOGICAL PSYCHOLOGY," n.d. [1941].

3. NGC, Mills to Howard Becker, draft, October 15, 1943; MP, 4B399, Mills to Gerth, draft, October 1943.

4. NGC, Mills to Gerth, n.d. [summer 1944, after June 1].

5. NGC, Mills to Gerth, July 17, 1944. Mills's response to Becker's 1940 American Sociological Society presentation is discussed in chapter 4.

6. NGC, Mills to Gerth, "Thursday," n.d. [summer 1944].

7. NGC, Mills to Gerth, March 13, 1946.

8. Ibid.

9. NGC, Mills to Gerth, March 25, 1946.

10. MP, 4B339, Gerth to Mills, May 5, 1946.

11. NGC, Mills to Gerth, May 8, 1946. Mills's plea for an endorsement of what he called "our" agreement was renewed some four months later. See NGC, Mills to Gerth, "August 46 Monday" [August 1946].

12. MP, 4B339, Gerth to Mills, August 27, 1946.

13. Ibid.

14. NGC, Mills to Gerth, August 30, 1946.

15. C. Wright Mills, with Helen Schneider, *The New Men of Power: America's Labor Leaders* (New York: Harcourt, Brace, 1948). On Mills's work at the Bureau of Applied Social Research, see NGC, Mills to Gerth, "Wed." [Thanksgiving eve, 1948]. On Gerth's revisions of the galley proofs of *The New Men of Power*, see NGC, Mills to Gerth, December 4, 1947; NGC, Mills to Gerth, February 13, 1948; NGC, Mills to Gerth, n.d. [late May or early June 1948]; NGC, Mills to Gerth, June 16, 1948. On the development of *White Collar*, see MP, 4B339, Mills to Gerth, draft, November 26, 1946; NGC, Mills to Gerth, n.d. [late May or early June 1948]; NGC, Mills to Gerth, n.d. [November 1948]; NGC, Mills to Gerth, "Wed." [Thanksgiving eve, 1948].

16. Hans H. Gerth, with Hedwig Ide Gerth, "Bibliography on Max Weber," *Social Research* 16 (1948): 70–89; Karl Mannheim, *Freedom, Power, and Democratic Planning*, ed. Hans H. Gerth and Ernest K. Bramsted (New York: Oxford University Press, 1950). On Gerth's work as editor of the Mannheim volume, see NGC, Gerth to Mills, draft, October 21, 1948. On Mills's response to Gerth's proposal of new Weber translations, see MP, 4B339, Mills to Gerth, draft, November 26, 1946.

17. NGC, Mills to Gerth, "Wednesday," n.d. [Thanksgiving eve, 1948]. This is a response to a letter from Gerth that has not been located. The context of Mills's letter makes it clear that Gerth had recently proposed the revival of *Character and Social Structure*.

18. MP, 4B339, James M. Reid to Robert K. Merton and Ernest R. Hilgard, January 13, 1949.

19. NGC, James M. Reid to Mills, January 14, 1949.

20. MP, 4B339, James M. Reid to Robert K. Merton and Ernest R. Hilgard, January 13, 1949.

21. NGC, James M. Reid to Mills, January 14, 1949; MP, 4B339, James M. Reid to Mills, February 8, 1949.

22. NGC, Mills to Gerth, "Saturday morning" [February 1949].

23. Ibid.; NGC, Mills to Jimmie [James M. Reid], February 17, 1949.

24. NGC, Mills to Jimmie [James M. Reid], February 17, 1949. Mills sent a copy of this letter to Merton.

25. NGC, Mills to Gerth, "Saturday morning" [February 1949].

26. NGC, Mills to Gerth, n.d. [late February 1949].

27. NGC, Mills to Gerth, "Thursday morning; just before leaving for New York" [shortly before March 11, 1949].

28. NGC, Mills to Gerth, n.d. [shortly before March 11, 1949].

29. NGC, Mills to Gerth, March 15, 1949.

30. NGC, Mills to James M. Reid, April 6, 1949.

31. NGC, Mills to Gerth, n.d. [April 6, 1949].

32. Ibid.

33. MP, 4B339, Gerth to Mills, April 2, 1949; MP, 4B339, Gerth to Mills, n.d. [shortly before Easter 1949, Gerth's reply to Mills's letter of April 6, 1949]. For Martindale's version of the plans for a Becker-Martindale sociology text, see Don Martindale, *The Monologue: Hans Gerth (1908–1978): A Memoir* (Ghaziabad, India: Intercontinental, 1982), 8–69, 117. According to Martindale, Becker received royalties of 2 percent for each book he signed as editor of Heath's series in social psychology. Sales of his independent text, Martindale's companion volume, and *Character and Social Structure* would have paid him author's royalties for his own book, and perhaps for Martindale's as well, and editor's royalties for all three.

34. NGC, Mills to Gerth, "Apr. '49" [late April 1949, before April 25].

35. NGC, Gerth to Mills, draft, April 25, 1949.

36. MP, 4B339, Mills to Gerth, draft, April 26, 1949.

37. Ibid.

38. On the anthropological problematic of Weber's work, see Dieter Henrich, *Die Einheit Max Webers Wissenschaftslehre* (Tübingen: Mohr, 1952); Karl Löwith, *Karl Marx and Max Weber,* trans. Tom Bottomore and William Outwaite (New York: Routledge, 1973); and Wilhelm Hennis, *Max Weber: Essays in Reconstruction,* trans. Keith Tribe (London: Allen and Unwin, 1988). On the links between *Character and Social Structure* and *Economy and Society,* compare the following: for politics, Hans H. Gerth and C. Wright Mills, *Character and Social Structure: The Psychology of Social Institutions* (New York: Harcourt Brace, 1953), 192–213, and Max Weber, *Economy and Society,* ed. Guenther Roth and Claus Wittich (Berkeley: University of California Press, 1978), 941–55; for economics, *Character and Social Structure,* 213–23, and *Economy and Society,* 63–211, 311–55; for the military, *Character and Social Structure,* 223–29, and *Economy and Society,* 905–8, 917–18, 1050–55; for religion, *Character and Social Structure,* 230–45, and *Economy and Society,* 399–634; for kinship, *Character and Social Structure,* 245–50, and *Economy and Society,* 356–69; for occupations, *Character and Social Structure,* 308–10, and *Economy and Society,* 140–44, 306, 483; for class, status, and power, *Character and Social Structure,* 310–30, and *Economy and Society,* 302–10, 941–55. Just as Weber drew illustrations of his typologies from the *Kaiserreich* and World War I, so Gerth used the totalitarian regimes of the 1930s and World War II as sources for the illustrations of typologies in *Character and Social Structure.* In many cases Gerth simply reproduced Weber's illustrations. See *Character and Social Structure,* 104–5, 172, 188–90, 197, 360–63, 366–71. Throughout the book Gerth followed Weber's emphasis in *Economy and Society* on warmaking, mobilization of resources

for war, and changes in military organization, discipline, and practice as agents of major historical changes.

The concept of intellectual capital employed in the foregoing is not derived from the work of Pierre Bourdieu, nor should it be conflated with the various modes of academic capital he distinguishes: for example, symbolic, educational, social, cultural, economic, and inherited capital; capital of academic power; scientific power; economic power; political power; scientific prestige; and intellectual renown. By classifying so many aspects of academic life under this single heading, Bourdieu elevates capital to the status of a master concept for interpreting all aspects of academic life. See Pierre Bourdieu, *Homo Academicus,* trans. Peter Collier (Stanford, Calif.: Stanford University Press, 1988), a stimulating work that should perhaps have been entitled *Homo Academicus Gallicus.* On the examination and critique of Bourdieu's concept of capital, see Craig Calhoun, Edward LiPuma, and Moishe Postone, eds., *Bourdieu: Critical Perspectives* (Chicago: University of Chicago Press, 1993). The pretensions of our concept are much more modest. Intellectual capital is one of the resources needed to validate claims to credit for research: the ideas, theories, and scholarship on which these claims are grounded.

39. MP, 4B339, Mills to Gerth, draft, April 26, 1949.

40. Ibid.

41. Ibid.

42. Ibid.

43. NGC, Dorothy Mott [secretary to James M. Reid] to Gerth, May 2, 1949; NGC, Mills to Gerth, May 2, 1949; NGC, Mills to James M. Reid, n.d. [May 2, 1949].

44. NGC, Mills to Text Book Editor, D. C. Heath and Company, May 2, 1949.

45. MP, 4B339, Gerth to Mills, May 7, 1949.

46. Ibid. In a May 31, 1949, memorandum to Gerth, Becker reported that he had recommended to Walden the unconditional cancellation of the contract for *Character and Social Structure.* Having done so, he refused to be a party to further negotiations. As the editor of the series for which this book was intended, Becker had supposed he was negotiating on behalf of the authors. Now he realized that Mills had been dealing directly with Heath. Becker wondered whether Gerth was aware of this and whom he had authorized to negotiate for him. Because Gerth had failed to assert himself on this matter and had done nothing to protect Becker from being blindsided by Mills, Becker divested himself of any responsibility for what might happen next. If Mills mishandled matters, Becker claimed, Gerth would be answerable for the consequences, adding the ominous warning that if he continued to allow Mills to manage his affairs, he might face serious legal problems. As Becker diagnosed the situation, Mills was embarrassing him and manipulating Gerth to further his career. He did not consider the possibility that Gerth and Mills were collaborating not only on *Character and Social*

Structure but also on a plan to use him as a lever to extract themselves from their agreement with Heath. NGC, Howard Becker to Gerth, May 31, 1949.

47. MP, 4B339, Gerth to Mills, May 7, 1949.

48. NGC, Mills to Gerth, May 12, 1949.

49. NGC, John Walden to Mills, May 26, 1949.

50. NGC, Mills to John Walden, June 1, 1949.

51. NGC, Mills to Gerth, June 1, 1949.

52. NGC, John Walden to Mills, June 3, 1949, with copies to Howard Becker and Gerth.

53. MP, 4B339, Gerth to Mills, June 6, 1949.

54. Ibid.

55. Ibid.

56. NGC, Mills to Gerth, with a draft of Mills's letter to John Walden, n.d. [early June 1949].

57. NGC, John Walden to Mills, with a copy to Gerth, August 18, 1949.

58. NGC, Mills to Gerth, "Wednesday, August 24" [1949].

59. MP, 4B339, Gerth to Mills, n.d. [last week in August 1949].

60. Coincidentally and not inappropriately, Mills observed that he had just finished reading *The Good Soldier,* Ford Maddox Ford's novel of elaborately calculated deceptions pursued in a twilight of misunderstanding (NGC, Mills to Gerth, n.d. [between August 25 and August 28, 1949]). See also MP, 4B339, Gerth to Mills, August 30, 1949; NGC, Mills to Gerth, September 3, 1949; NGC, Mills to John Walden, September 3, 1949.

61. NGC, Mills to Gerth, October 3, 1949.

62. MP, 4B339, Gerth to Mills, November 7, 1949.

63. NGC, Mills to Gerth, n.d. [late December 1949].

64. NGC, Mills to Gerth, February 7, 1950.

65. NGC, John Walden to Gerth, February 28, 1950; NGC, James M. Reid to Gerth and Mills, March 24, 1950; NGC, Mills to Gerth, "Tuesday," n.d. [May 1950].

Chapter 4: Mills Ascending

1. Late in 1938 Mills sent the manuscript of "Methodological Consequences of the Sociology of Knowledge" to Speier and inquired about the possibility of publishing the paper in *Social Research.* Speier responded with five single-spaced typed pages of suggestions for revision. See MP, 4B246, Hans Speier to Mills, January 31, 1939. Louis Wirth also sent a one-page reply concerning the same paper; see MP, 4B346, Louis Wirth to Mills, n.d. [January or February 1939].

2. MP, 4B446, Mills to Herbert Blumer, draft, October 27, 1939; MP, 4B446, Mills to Kenneth Burke, draft, October 27, 1939; MP, 4B446, Mills to Karl Mannheim, draft, October 27, 1939; MP, 4B446, Mills to Robert K. Merton, draft, October 27, 1939; MP, 4B446, Mills to Talcott Parsons, draft, October 27,

1939; MP, 4B446, Mills to Alexander von Schelting, draft, October 27, 1939; MP, 4B446, Mills to Hans Speier, draft, October 27, 1939; MP, 4B339, Hans Speier to Mills, November 1, 1939; MP, 4B339, Charles Morris to Mills, November 8, 1939; MP, 4B339, Mills to Florian Znaniecki, draft, March 25, 1940; MP, 4B339, Mills to George Lundberg, draft, August 20, 1940; MP, 4B339, George Lundberg to Mills, September 16, 1940; MP, 4B339, Mills to Herbert Blumer, draft, October 31, 1940; MP, 4B339, Mills to John Dewey, draft, December 12, 1940.

3. MP, 4B339, Robert K. Merton to Mills, January 8, 1940; MP, 4B339, Mills to Robert K. Merton, draft, January 23, 1940; MP, 4B339, Mills to Robert K. Merton, draft, November 12, 1940.

4. See the following reviews by Mills: "Review of Karl Mannheim, *Man and Society in an Age of Reconstruction*," *American Sociological Review* 5 (1940): 965–69; "Locating the Enemy: The Nazi Behemoth Dissected," *Partisan Review* 4 (Sept.–Oct. 1942): 432–47; "Review of W. Lloyd Warner and Paul S. Lunt, *The Social Life of a Modern Community*," *American Sociological Review* 7 (1942): 263–71.

5. The correspondence between Mills and Neumann, which began in May 1942, is in MP, 4B389. See also MP, 4B389, Robert Lynd to Mills, January 2, 1943; MP, 4B389, Robert K. Merton to Mills, January 29, 1943.

6. NGC, Mills to Gerth, March 2, 1942.

7. NGC, Mills to Gerth, n.d. [March 1942].

8. NGC, Mills to Gerth, October 1944. In handling Lasswell, Mills adopted a clinical attitude. From the beginning of his career, he believed that the demands of the academic life would require a studied detachment on his part. To assemble the resources indispensable for success, it was essential to be tough, aloof, and disciplined. The aspiring academician could not afford the loss of control entailed by full engagement in any relationship. Mills constructed the academic life as a social relations laboratory in which he ran experiments designed to produce useful results. Success required the experimenter to detach himself from the experiment. As a letter from the twenty-year-old Mills shows, he achieved this posture of disengagement quite early. Writing his parents from the University of Texas, he observed: "I stay on the *outside* of all groups but in touch with them all. The campus is a laboratory for sociologists" (MP, 4B353, Mills to Mother and Father, draft, October 21, 1936).

9. NGC, Mills to Gerth, n.d. [January or February 1942].

10. NGC, Mills to Gerth, March 2, 1943.

11. NGC, Mills to Gerth, June 7, 1943.

12. NGC, Mills to Gerth, March 6, 1944.

13. NGC, Mills to Gerth, June 1, 1944. In his essay on Mills's book *The Power Elite*, Richard Gillam claims that the monstrous violence and irrationality of World War II traumatized Mills, converting him into a radical political thinker. "For him the war catalyzed a sudden 'awakening' that was uniquely political and radical. Virtually alone of his generation, Mills could write that 'following [World

War II] closely and thinking about it made me a radical'" (Richard Gillam, "C. Wright Mills and the Politics of Truth: *The Power Elite* Revisited," *American Quarterly* 27 [1975]: 465–66). Gillam offers no support for the claim that Mills either followed the war closely or thought about it seriously. His only evidence for Mills's wartime radicalization is Mills's ex post facto reinterpretation of his civilian experience of the war written in the mid-1950s, when he had begun to publish political tracts that attracted a large readership. Mills's plans during the years 1942–45 point in a different direction: the war did not deflect him from his prewar pursuit of an academic career, nor did it transform him into a political radical.

14. NGC, Mills to Gerth, July 17, 1944. During Mills's years at the University of Maryland, he was preoccupied with worries about marginalization and a life of mediocrity. For Mills, this meant a lack of originality and distinction, professional invisibility due to the failure to achieve recognition, a dead-end job that emphasized teaching over research, and condemnation to routine, the existence of the academic retailer who reproduced the received wisdom of his field. Mills feared the fate of the intellectual philistine, the *Homo academicus mediocritus* that he later described in *White Collar:* "The type of man who is recruited for college teaching and shaped for this end by graduate school training is very likely to have a strong plebeian strain. His culture is typically narrow, his imagination often limited. Men can achieve position in this field although they are recruited from the lower-middle class, a milieu not remarkable for grace of mind, flexibility or breadth of culture, or scope of imagination" (C. Wright Mills, *White Collar: The American Middle Classes* [New York: Oxford University Press, 1951], 129–30).

15. NGC, Mills to Gerth, June 1, 1944; NGC, Mills to Gerth, July 14, 1944.

16. NGC, Mills to Thomas McCormick, July 15, 1944.

17. NGC, Mills, "PUBLICATION AGENDA, as of July, 1944."

18. NGC, Mills to Gerth, October 10, 1944; NGC, Mills to Gerth, n.d. [November 1944].

19. NGC, Mills to Gerth, December 22, 1944.

20. NGC, Mills to Gerth, "Sunday afternoon," n.d. [late January or early February 1945].

21. NGC, Mills to Gerth, n.d. [1942].

22. Ibid.

23. NGC, Mills to Gerth, October 5, 1945.

24. NGC, Mills to Gerth, n.d. [June 1944].

25. NGC, Mills to Gerth, January 1, 1952. Mills was also confident of his ability to get what he wanted from corporate executives. Although he claimed to despise his work as a marketing consultant, he seemed to move with ease and self-assurance in the world of corporate elites, commanding hefty fees that supplemented his academic salary and publishing contracts. In negotiating consulting agreements, he maintained that his usual practice was to charge outrageous fees, subcontract the research and much of the writing, and generally do as little work

as possible. When the project was finished, he would make a brazenly cheeky presentation to his clients, dissecting the public relations strategies of big business and exposing the cynicism of corporate managers. Mills described his consulting contracts as a way of milking big business, but not by deceiving the executives who paid him. Instead, he forthrightly declared his contempt for them and all their enterprises. In his view, this brutal candor demonstrated his honesty and established his credibility with his clients.

In March 1952 Mills recounted for Gerth a presentation he had made on a television consulting contract at the Stork Club in New York. His speech was a success. The publishing magnate William Randolph Hearst Jr. ("Bill Hearst") not only was in attendance but offered him a job: $30,000 a year with bonuses to serve as his mass-media marketing adviser, roughly five times his salary at Columbia. "Of course I laughed at him and insulted him, which was what he liked about my speech," Mills reported. Although he attempted to talk Hearst out of a tractor for his small farm in Rockland County, north of New York, the publisher was insistent. "Said he hadn't seen a real salesman around since 1925, and didn't I know that it was all horseshit except a salesman: he could write his own ticket, etc." Mills's advice to Hearst was to read *White Collar* and order a thousand copies for people in his business. "It was all a lot of fun," Mills mused, but also "somehow embarrassing because every time I see such guys perform, it's just like I say in *White Collar* although sometimes more so, like in stereotypical movies and novels" (NGC, Mills to Gerth, March 7 [1952]).

26. See the notes to the introduction of H. H. Gerth and C. Wright Mills, trans. and eds., *From Max Weber: Essays in Sociology* (New York: Oxford University Press, 1946), 445–48.

27. NGC, Mills to H. T. Hatcher, February 16, 1945.

28. NGC, Gerth to Mills, draft, February 19, 1945.

29. NGC, Gerth to Mills, draft, April 12, 1945.

30. NGC, Mills to Gerth, February 7, 1945.

31. MP, 4B339, Mills to Ernest Manheim, draft, September 4, 1938.

32. NGC, Gerth to Howard Becker, draft, n.d. [between November 15 and November 17, 1958].

33. NGC, Howard Becker to Gerth, November 18, 1958.

34. NGC, Mills to Gerth, n.d. [June or July 1944].

35. NGC, Mills to Gerth, n.d. [August 1944].

36. NGC, Mills to Gerth, May 18, 1945.

37. The appendix remains unpublished. The translation, credited to "H. H. Gerth with the Assistance of C. Wright Mills," appeared in 1950. See "The Metropolis and Mental Life," in *The Sociology of Georg Simmel,* ed. Kurt H. Wolff (Glencoe, Ill.: Free Press, 1950), 409–24.

38. MP, 4B362, Bob [Schmid] to Mills, n.d. [December 1940].

39. MP, 4B362, Mills to Herbert Blumer, draft, November 3, 1940; MP, 4B362,

Herbert Blumer to Mills, November 19, 1940; MP, 4B362, Louis Wirth to Mills, January 22, 1941. There is a heavily annotated draft of "Sociological Methods and Philosophies of Science" (11 pp.) in MP, 4B362.

40. MP, 4B362, [Mills to Robert Schmid], draft, "Monday Noon," n.d. [January 1941]. Mills asked Schmid to destroy his letter and claimed he had destroyed Schmid's. In fact, he preserved a record of this correspondence, saving Schmid's letter and a carbon of his letter to Schmid.

41. MP, 4B353, Mills to Mother and Father, draft, December 18, 1946.

42. Mills, *White Collar,* 161.

43. NGC, Mills to Gerth, n.d. [autumn 1942]; NGC, Mills to Thomas McCormick, July 15, 1944.

44. Mills, *White Collar,* 174, 356.

45. Mills, *White Collar,* 174–77; MP, 4B347, James B. Gale, "Types of Macy Saleswomen," 1–4.

46. Mills's typology departs from Gale's in three respects. The first two are insignificant. In discussing the various types of saleswomen, he does not follow the order used by Gale. In addition, he incorporates one of Gale's types, the rebel, into another, the old-timer. More important, Mills deletes all references to a type Gale calls the "social hybrid." Generally a European immigrant, her mentality, conduct, and personal fashion standards are a product of more traditional conventions governing the role and behavior of women. Because these conventions tie women to the household, the social hybrid finds it difficult to develop the techniques of self-presentation required by her job in the department store.

Mills does not mention this omission, but it seems unlikely that it was an oversight. His theory of the white-collar personality market is grounded in Weber's analysis of bureaucratization and Mannheim's concept of the rationalization of the personality, both of which he applies to the department store and the occupational life of saleswomen. The Millsean saleswoman can survive on the personality market only by streamlining her personality and developing strategies of self-formation to meet the demands of her job. Because of the social hybrid's modest skills in impression management, she cannot meet the demands of the personality market. Thus the possibility of the social hybrid is excluded from Mills's typology on theoretical grounds. See *White Collar,* 182–84.

The files on *White Collar* in the Mills Papers include many student essays on themes of the book and a few more ambitious student manuscripts as well: a 144-page monograph entitled "Study of White Collar Worker's Attitudes toward a White Collar Union," by Zena Smith (later Zena Blau), a Columbia graduate student (MP, 4B351); and a 1949 New School M.A. thesis by Mary Jayne Gold entitled "Office Life and Personal Problems of White Collar Girls," a project she began while working under Mills (MP, 4B350; MP, 4B350, Mary Jayne Gold to Mills, September 23, 1949).

47. Mills, *White Collar,* 355.

48. Ibid. The extent of Gerth's contribution to *White Collar* cannot be fully documented. In the 1970s Joseph Bensman, who had studied with Gerth in 1941–42 and 1945–47, reported to Robert Jackall that he and Gerth edited drafts of *White Collar* in Madison after the war. Mills sent drafts to Gerth, and he and Bensman worked on them weekends, returning the manuscripts with elaborate annotations and emendations (Robert Jackall, "Notes on Bensman/Mills," unpublished manuscript, 1996).

49. Mills, *White Collar,* 329. See Emil Lederer and Jakob Marschak, "The New Middle Class" (1937); Emil Lederer, "The Problem of the Modern Salaried Employee: Its Theoretical and Statistical Basis" (1937); and Hans Speier, "The Salaried Employee in Germany," vol. 1 (1939), all produced in mimeograph in the translation series "Translation into English of Foreign Social Science Monographs by U.S. Works Projects Administration." Although these works were among Mills's most important theoretical sources, it would be a mistake to read *White Collar* as if it were derived exclusively from the German literature on the crisis of the middle class. On this point see Richard Gillam, "*White Collar* from Start to Finish," *Theory and Society* 10 (1981): 1–30.

50. Mills, *White Collar,* 357–58. The manuscript of *White Collar* that Mills delivered to Oxford University Press included a substantial apparatus of notes and references, eighty-three pages of single-spaced typescript that Oxford decided not to publish. Mills regarded his voluminous notes, lengthy comments on points made in the text, statistical tables, and summaries of quantitative data as unnecessary and inappropriate for the book he had written. When Gerth suggested the inclusion of this apparatus in the German edition, Mills was not enthusiastic. Only a doctoral candidate working on the territory of the book, Mills argued, would be interested. Moreover, his manuscript of the notes was not coordinated with the printed text of *White Collar.* In view of these considerations, he did not think the results would justify the efforts required of him and the translator of the German edition (NGC, Mills to Gerth, November 29, 1953; NGC, Gerth to Dr. Niemann [an editor with Bund Verlag, publisher of the German edition of *White Collar*], draft, December 26, 1953; NGC, Mills to Gerth, January 8, 1954).

51. See, for example, Irving L. Horowitz, "The Sociological Imagination of C. Wright Mills: In Memoriam," *American Journal of Sociology* 68 (1962): 105–7; Maurice Stein and Arthur J. Vidich, eds., *Sociology on Trial* (Englewood Cliffs, N.J.: Prentice Hall, 1963); Irving L. Horowitz, ed., *The New Sociology: Essays in Social Science and Social Theory in Honor of C. Wright Mills* (New York: Oxford University Press, 1964); Joseph Bensman and Arthur J. Vidich, *The New American Society: The Revolution of the Middle Class* (Chicago: Quadrangle, 1971); Irving L. Horowitz, *C. Wright Mills: An American Utopian* (New York: Free Press, 1983); Rick Tilman, *C. Wright Mills: A Native Radical and His American Roots* (University Park: Pennsylvania State University Press, 1984); Russell Jacoby, *The Last Intellectuals: American Culture in the Age of Academe* (New York: Basic, 1987); James

Miller, *"Democracy Is in the Streets": From Port Huron to the Siege of Chicago* (New York: Simon and Schuster, 1987); Andrew Jamison and Ron Eyerman, *Seeds of the Sixties* (Berkeley: University of California Press, 1994); Steven Seidman, *Contested Knowledge: Social Theory in the Postmodern Era* (Oxford: Blackwell, 1994).

The most influential study of Mills seems to be Irving Louis Horowitz's book *C. Wright Mills: An American Utopian,* an account marred by numerous errors. For example, Mills's letters do not exhibit a disdain for professional gossip (5), nor do they conceal his personal animosities (19). His commitment to *From Max Weber* and *Character and Social Structure* was not inspired by his respect for Gerth (54). There is no evidence that he regarded his work on *Character and Social Structure* as a "repayment to Gerth" for including him as coeditor of *From Max Weber* (184–85). Since the Weber book was not under way until 1943, two years after Mills left Madison, and most of the work on *Character and Social Structure* was done in 1948–52, when he was at Columbia, it is a mistake to claim that he began these projects at Madison and cleaned them up at Maryland (57). It follows that *Character and Social Structure* cannot be accurately characterized as the "crowning achievement" of his Wisconsin years (50). Mills's letters to Gerth in the late 1940s show that *White Collar* was far from complete in early 1945 (72). This list of errors is not exhaustive.

The best scholarship on Mills to date is by Richard Gillam, who is also the most sophisticated proponent of the received view of Mills. See Richard Gillam, "C. Wright Mills: An Intellectual Biography," Ph.D. diss., Stanford University, 1972, as well as the following publications by Gillam: "C. Wright Mills and the Politics of Truth"; "Richard Hofstadter, C. Wright Mills, and the 'Critical Ideal,'" *The American Scholar* (Winter 1977–78): 69–85; "*White Collar* from Start to Finish."

For a heterodox portrait of Mills by a writer who knew him intimately for more than twenty years, see the eulogy by Harvey Swados, "C. Wright Mills: A Personal Memoir," *Dissent* 10 (1963): 35–42. The Mills of Swados's memoir is an insensitive philistine but also brooding, self-absorbed, and driven by an egomaniacal ambition.

52. See Gillam, "C. Wright Mills and the Politics of Truth"; Gillam, "Richard Hofstadter, C. Wright Mills, and the 'Critical Ideal';" and Swados, "C. Wright Mills: A Personal Memoir." The historian Richard Hofstadter, Mills's friend and colleague, first at Maryland and later at Columbia, regarded him as a pseudo-political intellectual. After reading his book *The Causes of World War III,* Hofstadter observed that in spite of its intentions and tone of exhortation, it was not about politics at all. Mills analyzed virtually no political decisions and mentioned only a few. As a result, Hofstadter found himself unimpressed by Mills's credentials as a political thinker. In his view, Mills had no political commitments and thus was not the political man he pretended to be (MP, 4B420, Richard Hofstadter to Mills, December 10, 1958).

53. On Mills's dissatisfaction with Columbia, his colleagues in the sociology

department, and life in New York, see NGC, Mills to Gerth, February 13, 1948; NGC, Mills to Gerth, "Wed," n.d. [autumn 1948]; NGC, Mills to Gerth, February 17, 1949; NGC, Mills to Gerth, August 24, 1949; NGC, Mills to Gerth, February 7, 1950; NGC, Mills to Gerth, "Tuesday," n.d. [April 1950]; NGC, Mills to Gerth, November 12, 1950; NGC, Mills to Gerth, December 18, 1950; NGC, Mills to Gerth "51" [late summer 1951]; NGC, Mills to Gerth "Wednesday in Sept., 51" [1951]; and the Lewis Coser Collection, John J. Burns Library, Boston College, Mills to Coser, n.d. [1948], and Mills to Lou and Rose [Coser], October 6, 1957. On the attractions of travel and work in Europe, see NGC, Mills to Gerth, January 11, 1952; NGC, Mills to Gerth, November 29, 1953. On his European travels, see NGC, Mills to Gerth, August 1, 1956; NGC, Mills to Gerth, October 4, 1956; NGC, Mills to Gerth, November 11, 1956; NGC, Mills to Gerth, April 8, 1957. Mills's view of his life as a continuous process of self-formation and reformation is expressed in some comments on the relationship between a new residence and a new identity. When he received a one-year appointment as a Fulbright lecturer at the University of Copenhagen, he sold his farm to build a new house on his return. Mills believed he would need a different residence because he would be a different person: "One lives on the expectation that no matter what goes on now, next year, next week, next decade, everything will be different. Not necessarily better, but surely different" (NGC, Mills to Gerth, "spring 1956").

54. F. Scott Fitzgerald, *The Great Gatsby* (New York: Cambridge University Press, 1991 [1925]), 141. Punctuation follows the original.

Chapter 5: Hard Times in America

1. MP, 4B391, Gerth to Mills, n.d. [early December 1941]; MP, 4B391, Mills to Gerth, draft, December 13, 1941.

2. NGC, n.a. [C. Wright Mills], "LOCATING THE ENEMY: PROBLEMS OF INTELLECTUALS DURING TIME OF WAR," "copy for G. [Gerth] notes done 1,3,42."

3. NGC, Gerth to Mills, draft, January 11, 1942.

4. NGC, Gerth to Mills, draft, July 22, 1943; NGC, Mills to Gerth, "Wednesday noon," n.d. [November 15, 1944], "page three" of a letter the remainder of which has not been located.

5. Hans H. Gerth, *Die sozialgeschichtliche Lage der bürgerlichen Intelligenz um die Wende des 18. Jahrhunderts: Ein Beitrag zur Soziologie des deutschen Frühliberalismus* (Berlin: VDI Verlag, 1935). After Gerth's retirement from the University of Wisconsin and his return to Germany, the dissertation was republished as *Bürgerliche Intelligenz um 1800* (Göttingen: Vandenhoeck and Ruprecht, 1976).

6. MP, B339, Gerth to Mills, "Good Friday 1951."

7. Hans Gerth, "The Development of Social Thought in the United States and Germany: Critical Observations on the Occasion of the Publication of C. Wright Mills' *White Collar*," trans. Kimberly Barton, ed. Nobuko Gerth, Harry Dahms,

and Godehard Czernick, *International Journal of Politics, Culture, and Society* 7 (1994): 525–68. When the German translation of *White Collar* appeared in 1955, Gerth's introduction was not included. Instead, a brief foreword was contributed by Heinz Maus, a German sociologist and contemporary of Gerth at Frankfurt in the early 1930s and later an editor of the famous series Soziologische Texte, comprising more than 100 books published by Luchterhand. See C. Wright Mills, *Menschen im Büro: Ein Beitrag zur Soziologie der Angestellten,* trans. Bernt Engelmann, with a foreword by Heinz Maus (Köln-Deutz: Bund Verlag, 1955). On Maus, see the folowing two articles in *Jahrbuch für Soziologiegeschichte 1994* (Opladen: Leske and Budrich, 1996): Gerd van de Moetter, "Flaschenpost einer verschollenen Kritischen Theorie: Briefwechsel zwischen Max Horkheimer und Heinz Maus, 1946–51," 227–76; and Frank Benseler, "Heinz Maus 21.3.1911–28.9.78," 277–88.

Gerth's role in the German edition of *White Collar* is not altogether clear. In October 1953 Mills expressed his delight that Gerth would contribute a foreword to the German translation (NGC, Mills to Gerth, October 13, 1953). In late 1953 Gerth was also offering advice on the notes to the translation (NGC, Mills to Gerth, November 29, 1953; NGC, Mills to Gerth, n.d. [late December 1953]; NGC, Gerth to Fr. Dr. Niemann, draft, December 26, 1953). On December 28 Gerth made the following comments concerning his foreword.

> Also, I have just finished the text for a long song on you and the intellectual situation of U.S. sociology, which I like quite a bit. I think it is a strong piece. Some will like it, some not.
>
> I put terrific bibliographical notes into it and am still at "documentation." The entire piece is 55 pp. long and "covers" practically everything. Sort of "my account of" kind of stocktaking what these twelve years have really been about. (NGC, Gerth to Mills, draft, December 28, 1953)

8. C. Wright Mills, *White Collar: The American Middle Classes* (New York: Oxford University Press, 1951), 33.

9. MP, B339, Gerth to Mills, "Good Friday 1951." Gerth maintained that Mills had no compassion for the less fortunate members of the middle class and took pleasure in demeaning "impotent underdogs," such as "powerless new middle class men" and "the suffering yet status-ridden salesgirl," compelled by the competitive forces of the job market to meet the requirements of "appearance values" by adopting changing styles, fads, and fashions. See NGC, Gerth to J. Errol Fletcher, draft, February 12, 1972. In late 1971 or early 1972, a J. Errol Fletcher of Windsor, Ontario, wrote Gerth, then at the University of Frankfurt, asking for information about Mills. Gerth replied at considerable length, writing mainly about himself, his background in Germany and life in the United States, his views on a variety of subjects, his relationship with Mills, and his judgment on Mills as a man and an intellectual. There are three letters to Fletcher: a ten-page letter, undated and

annotated by Nobuko Gerth "8 Feb. 72"; a three-page letter dated February 12, 1972; and a four-page letter dated February 14, 1972. It is not clear which of these letters, if any, was sent.

10. NGC, Gerth to J. Errol Fletcher, draft, February 14, 1972.

11. The foregoing discussion of Gerth's critique of *White Collar* is based on an undated typescript in NGC consisting of four brief documents: "Re C. Wright Mills (nasty complexes)" (two pages); "What of Mills?" (one page); "Mills" (five pages); and "Mills from Old to New Middle Class" (two pages). We refer to these documents collectively as "Re C. Wright Mills," n.d. [after April 1962].

12. Gerth to Joe [Bensman], n.d. [April 1951].

13. Ibid.

14. NGC, Gerth, "Re C. Wright Mills"; NGC, Gerth to J. Errol Fletcher, draft, January 12, 1972.

15. MP, B339, Gerth to Mills, "Good Friday 1951."

16. Karl Marx, *Capital: A Critique of Political Economy,* vol. 1, trans. Samuel Moore and Edward Aveling (New York: International, 1967), 609.

17. NGC, Gerth, "Re C. Wright Mills." Mills believed Gerth had misunderstood his assessment of Burckhardt. His reservations about the value of Burckhardt's work, he claimed, applied only to *The Age of Constantine,* not to *The Civilization of the Renaissance in Italy* or to his reflections on the philosophy of history published as *Force and Freedom* (NGC, Mills to Gerth, November 29, 1953).

18. NGC, Gerth, "Re C. Wright Mills."

19. Gerth never published a full-scale analysis of Weber's research program. His understanding of Weberian sociology is documented in considerable detail in the notes for his sociology lectures at the University of Wisconsin and is sketched most fully in the notes he compiled for chapters 7–12 of *Character and Social Structure,* which recapitulate Weber's main theoretical strategies. On *Character and Social Structure* as an exposition of Weberian sociology, see Joseph Bensman, "Hans Gerth's Contribution to American Sociology," in *Politics, Character, and Culture: Perspectives from Hans Gerth,* ed. Joseph Bensman, Arthur J. Vidich, and Nobuko Gerth (Westport, Conn.: Greenwood, 1982), 242–49.

20. NGC, Hans H. Gerth, "Morton," a 200-page manuscript on the dynamics of agrarian, religious, and industrial relations in a largely German area of Tazewell County, Illinois. Gerth did the research and wrote the manuscript during his brief tenure at the University of Illinois. He published one essay based on this work: Hans H. Gerth, "A Midwestern Sectarian Community," *Social Research* 11 (1944): 354–62.

21. Max Weber, " 'Objectivity' in Social Science and Social Policy," in *The Methodology of the Social Sciences,* trans. Edward A. Shils and Henry A. Finch (Glencoe, Ill.: Free Press, 1949), 111, translation altered. On the epistemological basis of Weber's theory of ideal types, see Thomas Burger, *Max Weber's Theory of Concept Formation* (Durham, N.C.: Duke University Press, 1976; 2d ed., 1987); and Guy

Oakes, *Weber and Rickert: Concept Formation in the Cultural Sciences* (Cambridge, Mass.: MIT Press, 1988).

22. Max Weber, *Economy and Society,* ed. Guenther Roth and Claus Wittich (Berkeley: University of California Press, 1978), 1212–17.

23. MP, 4B339, Gerth to Mills and Freya, October 11, 1941. "Freya" was Mills's first wife, Dorothy.

24. Ibid.

25. NGC, n.a. [Hans Gerth], "Social Psychology of Leadership," n.d.

26. MP, 4B339, Gerth to Mills, December 1, 1951. Gerth concluded this letter with criticisms of the typological analyses developed by Talcott Parsons in *The Social System,* which had been published earlier that year. See Hans H. Gerth, "On Talcott Parsons's *The Social System,*" ed. Michael W. Hughey, *International Journal of Politics, Culture, and Society* 10 (1997): 673–84.

27. MP, 4B375, Gerth to Mills, April 17 [1952].

28. MP, 4B375, Gerth to Mills, April 26, 1952.

29. NGC, Gerth to J. Errol Fletcher, draft, n.d. [ca. February 8, 1972].

30. Both the Nobuko Gerth Collection and the Mills Papers (4B415, 4B424, 4B339, 4B363, 4B375) contain a substantial body of manuscript by Gerth that was rewritten for inclusion in *Character and Social Structure.*

31. Gerth's chief mode of intellectual production was not the essay or book but the lecture, preferably delivered extemporaneously to an audience whose size was less important than its receptivity. The responses of his listeners evoked lengthy explanations, commentaries, and addenda that he could not repeat or perhaps even remember. Joseph Bensman, who studied with Gerth immediately after World War II and witnessed many of these performances in both formal and informal settings, described them as follows: "Gerth, in discussing an idea, could generate idea after idea: hypotheses, alternative approaches, suggestions for following-up ideas, illustrations, and bibliography and sources" (Bensman, "Hans Gerth's Contribution to American Sociology," 223). Just as one idea led to another, one typology suggested another in an endless monologue. Gerth's conception of pedagogy, and perhaps life itself, as an interminable lecture has been confirmed by the experience of sociologists who heard him over a period of more than fifteen years: Don Martindale (1940–41, 1946–48), Joseph Bensman (1941–42, 1945–47), Arthur Vidich (1946–48), and Stanford Lyman (1957, during Gerth's visiting professorship at Berkeley). On Gerth's disposition to view life as an endless monologue spoken by himself and his inclination to reduce all his social relations to the lecturer-audience model, Martindale commented as follows: "Gerth's lecture style was the freely-associated monologue. But his lecture style was also his life style. The monologue continued with his circle of disciples, with friends at dinner parties, with eminent strangers he met for the first time. The monologue could not be confined to the limits of the college class period, but continued on into the break, down the halls and in the office, into the coffee shop, through lunch and the afternoon,

and sometimes long into the evening" (Don Martindale, *The Monologue: Hans Gerth (1908–1978): A Memoir* [Ghaziabad, India: Intercontinental, 1982], 57–58).

32. On Gerth's unsuccessful efforts to win Mills's agreement to collaborate on other projects, which would have included a revised and enlarged edition of the Weber book as well as coauthored journal articles, see MP, 4B339, Gerth to Mills, November 22, 1946; MP, 4B339, Mills to Gerth, draft, November 26, 1946; MP, 4B375, Gerth to Mills, April 13, 1952. On his requests for career advice, see MP, 4B373, Gerth to Mills, August 2, 1953; MP, 4B373, Gerth to Mills, August 4, 1953; MP, 4B373, Mills to Gerth, draft, August 5, 1953; MP, 4B373, Mills to Gerth, draft, October 13, 1953; NGC, Mills to Gerth, November 29, 1953. On his requests for Mills's suggestions concerning publishers and contracts for his later Weber translations, see MP, 4B339, Gerth to Mills, November 22, 1946; MP, 4B339, Gerth to Mills, March 12, 1949; MP, 4B339, Mills to Gerth, draft, n.d. [between March 21 and April 1, 1949]; MP, 4B339, Gerth to Mills, April 2, 1949.

33. NGC, Gerth to Simon and Schuster, Publishers, rough draft, November 15, 1958.

34. NGC, Gerth to Simon and Schuster, Publishers, rough draft, November 15, 1958. See also Gerth and Mills, "Introduction," in H. H. Gerth and C. Wright Mills, trans. and eds., *From Max Weber: Essays in Sociology* (New York: Oxford University Press, 1946), vii.

35. Gerth and Mills, "Introduction," vii.

36. NGC, Gerth to Simon and Schuster, Publishers, rough draft, November 15, 1958.

37. Gerth and Mills, "Introduction," vii.

38. NGC, Gerth to Simon and Schuster, letterhead draft, November 15, 1958. The collaboration between Gerth and Mills was complicated by Gerth's academic background in Germany and his understanding of the traditional German professor-student relationship, which has no parallel or analogue in the American university. On acceptance in the seminar of an important professor, the German student often assumed a status of life-long and adolescent-like submission, requiring elaborate rituals of deference and an ethic of filial piety. The Olympian German professor created acolytes ex nihilo, forming them as disciples who would carry on his teachings, hence the innumerable doctrinal schools that contributed to the provincialism of German universities before World War II. As a product of this tradition, Gerth expected from Mills the obeisance that Mannheim had expected and received from him: Mills would become his protégé, mouthpiece, and cupbearer. In 1926, when Hans Speier asked Mannheim permission to join his seminar, Mannheim replied by asking which of his books the aspiring novitiate had read. Given prevailing expectations and the conception of the German university seminar as an instrument for the propagation of the professor's ideas, this question was neither inappropriate nor unconventional. See Hans Speier, "Mannheim as a Sociologist of Knowledge," trans. Robert Jackall, *International*

Journal of Politics, Culture, and Society 2 (1988): 81–94. For an extreme case of dominance and submission in the German professor-student relationship, see the account of Hannah Arendt and her teachers Martin Heidegger and Karl Jaspers in Ezbieta Ettinger, *Hannah Arendt Martin Heidegger* (New Haven, Conn.: Yale University Press, 1995). Even in his forties the German sociologist Heinz Maus continued to address his *Doktorvater* Max Horkheimer as "Dear Teacher"; see Moetter, "Flaschenpost einer verschollenen Kritischen Theorie."

39. MP, 4B420, Gerth to Mills, November 15, 1958.

40. NGC, Gerth to Mills, draft, n.d. [November 15, 1958].

41. Ibid. Gerth met Logan Wilson at Harvard in 1938, after which Wilson went to the University of Maryland. Gerth introduced Mills to Wilson, which resulted in Mills's first academic appointment.

42. Ibid.

43. NGC, Gerth to Gentlemen [Oxford University Press], draft, November 16, 1958. Gerth's memory failed him on the period he worked for United Press and the *Chicago Daily News* in Berlin, which was 1936–37.

44. NGC, Gerth to Howard [Becker], draft, n.d. [ca. November 16, 1958].

45. NGC, Gerth to Bob [Robert K. Merton], draft, November 16, 1958.

46. Ibid.

47. NGC, Fon W. Boardman to Gerth, November 20, 1958.

48. NGC, Merton to Hans [Gerth], November 30, 1958.

49. NGC, Pat [Patricke Johns Heine] to Gerth, November 20 [1958].

50. NGC, Mills to Gerth, November 20, 1958.

51. NGC, Gerth to Mills, draft, November 24, 1958.

52. NGC, Gerth to J. Errol Fletcher, draft, n.d. [ca. February 8, 1962].

53. NGC, Gerth to Yaroslava [Mills], draft, April 20, 1962; NGC, Gerth to Yaroslava [Mills], n.d. [summer 1962].

54. When Gerth attempted to publish the address with Norman Cousins at the *Saturday Review,* he encountered the extravagances of American cold war politics. Cousins rejected the piece, Gerth claimed, because he regarded Mills as a communist. See NGC, Gerth to J. Errol Fletcher, draft, February 12, 1972. There is no authoritative published version of the speech. See Hans H. Gerth, "C. Wright Mills, 1916–1962," *Studies on the Left* 2 (1962): 7–11; and Hans H. Gerth, "On C. Wright Mills," *Society* (Jan.–Feb. 1980): 71–73. The somewhat longer and more discursive 1962 text places Mills and his work in the context of the major political and economic developments of his times. The more spare and anecdotal 1980 version was copyrighted and published after Gerth's death under the curiously misleading heading "Self-Portrait."

55. NGC, Gerth to Yaroslava [Mills], draft, April 20, 1962. See C. Wright Mills, *Listen Yankee: The Revolution in Cuba* (New York: McGraw-Hill, 1960); and C. Wright Mills, *The Marxists* (New York: Dell, 1962).

56. Irving L. Horowitz, "The Sociological Imagination of C. Wright Mills: In

Memoriam," *American Journal of Sociology* 68 (1962): 105–7. The festschrift included no contribution by Gerth; see Irving Louis Horowitz, ed., *The New Sociology: Essays in Social Science and Social Theory in Honor of C. Wright Mills* (New York: Oxford University Press, 1964).

57. NGC, Gerth to Peter Blau, draft, July 31, 1962. On the allocation of credit for research as well as the division of royalties for books, Gerth later called Mills "a 'radical' democrat from out West," which was how Mills presented himself. Gerth understood Millsean populism in an ironic and pejorative sense, however: because Mills believed in leveling others down to elevate himself, his radical posture was a conceit. In matters of credit and precedence, he "held to strictly bourgeois standards of exploitation and covetousness," a disposition that Gerth regarded as typically American, especially among "status-ridden intellectuals" driven by success (NGC, Gerth to J. Errol Fletcher, draft, February 14, 1972). In the same vein, Gerth regarded the appropriation of ideas without a proper acknowledgment of intellectual debts, in his view a characteristic Millsean practice, as an expression of conventional American middle-class morality (NGC, Gerth to J. Errol Fletcher, draft, February 12, 1972).

58. NGC, Gerth to William Sewell, draft, August 10, 1962. Gerth confuses Charles Vaudrin, an editor at Oxford in the 1950s, with Harry Hatcher, the editor with whom Mills worked on the Weber book in 1944–46.

Epilogue

1. Max Weber, "Science as a Vocation," in H. H. Gerth and C. Wright Mills, trans. and eds., *From Max Weber: Essays in Sociology* (New York: Oxford University Press, 1946), 135.

2. Ibid., 133.

3. NGC, Mills to Gerth, n.d. [shortly after November 18, 1944].

4. For an analysis of various forms and conditions of deception, see J. A. Barnes, *A Pack of Lies: Towards a Sociology of Lying* (New York: Cambridge University Press, 1994). On the importance of personal trustworthiness in establishing the moral economy that underpins modern science, see Steven Shapin, *A Social History of Truth: Civility and Science in Seventeenth-Century England* (Chicago: University of Chicago Press, 1994).

5. The investigation of the institutional definition and distribution of credit in science is one of the main contributions to the sociology of science made by Robert K. Merton, his students, and his enthusiasts, now called "the Merton school." See the following: Bernard Barber, *Social Studies of Science* (New Brunswick, N.J.: Transaction, 1990); Stephen Cole, *Making Science: Between Nature and Society* (Cambridge, Mass.: Harvard University Press, 1992); Stephen Cole and Jonathan Cole, "Visibility and the Structural Bases of Awareness in Science," *American Sociological Review* 33 (1968): 387–413; Robert K. Merton, "Priorities in Scientific Discovery: A Chapter in the Sociology of Science," *American Sociologi-*

cal Review 22 (1957): 635–59; Robert K. Merton, "The Matthew Effect in Science," *Science* 159 (1968): 56–63; Robert K. Merton, *The Sociology of Science* (Chicago: University of Chicago Press, 1973); Robert K. Merton, *The Sociology of Science: An Episodic Memoir* (Carbondale: Southern Illinois University Press, 1979); Robert K. Merton, "Reference Groups, Invisible Colleges, and Deviant Behavior in Science," in *Surveying Social Life: Papers in Honor of Herbert H. Hyman,* ed. H. J. O'Gorman (Middletown, Conn.: Wesleyan University Press, 1988), 174–89; Michael Mulkay, *Science and the Sociology of Knowledge* (London: Allen and Unwin, 1979); Michael Mulkay, *Sociology of Science: A Sociological Pilgrimage* (Philadelphia: Open University Press, 1991); Norman Storer, *The Social System of Science* (New York: Holt, Rinehart, and Winston, 1966); Harriet Zuckerman, "Deviant Behavior and Social Control in Science," in *Deviance and Social Change,* ed. Edward Sagarin (Beverly Hills, Calif.: Sage, 1977), 87–138; Harriet Zuckerman, *Scientific Elites: Nobel Laureates in the United States* (New York: Free Press, 1977). On the distinction between the use of research and the distribution of credit for research, see David L. Hull, *Science as Process* (Chicago: University of Chicago Press, 1988).

6. See Bruno Latour, *Science in Action: How to Follow Scientists and Engineers through Society* (Cambridge, Mass.: Harvard University Press, 1987), 30–62; and Joseph Bensman, "The Politics and Aesthetics of Footnoting," *International Journal of Politics, Culture, and Society* 1 (1988): 443–70.

7. Mills's research files, which are the product of formidable organization and discipline, document this division of labor. He catalogued his reading into different substantive areas, preparing a separate manila folder for each. These folders, stuffed with bibliographies, note cards, offprints, and clippings, generally correspond to articles or book chapters on which he was engaged. Mills's files contain a remarkable amount of material by Gerth, including manuscripts and detailed outlines on an astonishing range of subjects: love and marriage, types of social spaces and settings, types of social time, humor, power, capitalism, religion, propaganda, social classes, the rise of the town in Western civilization, the Russian family, and the work of Marx and Weber. There is a long critique of Talcott Parsons's book *Social System* written by Gerth only months after its publication, analyses of current political and economic conditions in the United States and Europe, and extended discussions of cold war politics and economics. Finally, there are Gerth's extensive criticisms of Mills's publications and works in progress. Gerth's critique of *The Social System* is reconstructed in Hans H. Gerth, "On Talcott Parsons's *The Social System,*" ed. Michael W. Hughley, *International Journal of Politics, Culture, and Society* 10 (1997): 673–84.

Index

Guy Oakes is the Jack T. Kvernland Professor at Monmouth University and the author of *Weber and Rickert: Concept Formation in the Cultural Sciences* and *The Imaginary War: Civil Defense and American Cold War Culture.* He is also the translator of five volumes of works by the German sociologists Georg Simmel and Max Weber.

Arthur J. Vidich is a senior lecturer and emeritus professor of sociology and anthropology on the Graduate Faculty of the New School for Social Research. He is the author of *The Political Impact of Colonial Administration* and the coauthor of *Small Town in Mass Society, American Society: The Welfare State and Beyond,* and *American Sociology: Religious Rejections of the World and Their Directions.*

Typeset in 11/13 Adobe Garamond
with Garamond display
Book design by Dennis Roberts
Composed by Tseng Information Systems
Manufactured by Maple-Vail Book Manufacturing Group

University of Illinois Press
1325 South Oak Street
Champaign, IL 61820-6903
www.press.uillinois.edu